WAGNER

Prelude and Transfiguration
from
Tristan and Isolde

Authoritative Scores

Historical Background   Sketches and Drafts

Views and Comments   Analytical Essays

D0326076

NORTON CRITICAL SCORES

Richard Wagner

PRELUDE
AND
TRANSFIGURATION
from
TRISTAN AND ISOLDE

Authoritative Scores

Historical Background   Sketches and Drafts

Views and Comments   Analytical Essays

Edited by

ROBERT BAILEY

EASTMAN SCHOOL OF MUSIC

W • W • NORTON & COMPANY

New York • London

ISBN 0-393-02207-2 {CLOTH}
ISBN 0-393-95405-6 {PBK}

Published simultaneously in Canada by
Penguin Books Canada Ltd.,
2801 John Street, Markham, Ontario L3R 1B4.
PRINTED IN THE UNITED STATES OF AMERICA.

The text of this book is composed in Baskerville, with display type set in Deepdene.
Composition by PennSet, Inc. Manufacturing by The Murray Printing Company.

FIRST EDITION

Library of Congress Cataloging in Publication Data
Wagner, Richard, 1813–1883.
[Tristan and Isolde. Einleitung]
Prelude and Transfiguration.
(Norton critical scores)
Opera excerpts.
Bibliography: p.
1. Operas—Excerpts—Scores. I. Bailey, Robert, 1937–   . II. Wagner, Richard,
1813–1883. Tristan und Isolde. Liebestod. 1985. III. Title: Transfiguration.
IV. Series.
M1505.W13T83   1985   84-758104

W. W. Norton & Company, Inc., 500 Fifth Avenue, New York, NY 10110
W. W. Norton & Company Ltd, 10 Coptic Street, London WC1A 1PU

4 5 6 7 8 9 0

Contents

Preface

This volume is somewhat different from its companions among the
Norton Critical Scores. First of all, it contains an authentic score not of
an entire composition, but rather of the two well-known instrumental
excerpts from *Tristan and Isolde*. Whether, like Sir Donald Francis Tovey,
we prefer the Prelude with Wagner's special concert ending, or the
Prelude (with its operatic conclusion) coupled to the Transfiguration
(nowadays mistakenly called the *"Liebestod"*), we can at least rest assured
that Wagner himself was responsible for both possibilities. Even though
he performed the Prelude and Transfiguration with orchestra alone, I
have retained the vocal part in the latter excerpt since it is a subject for
discussion by both Tovey and Leonard Meyer.

There are many reasonably accurate scores of the Prelude and
Transfiguration, and constructing an authentic edition of those excerpts
posed few difficulties. The situation is vastly different with Wagner's
concert ending for the Prelude, however, because the only two published
scores contain numerous errors, which undoubtedly constitute the
primary obstacle to its performance. For the first time, the concert
ending appears here in a performable version that conforms to Wagner's
autograph. I have also included transcriptions of the two excerpts as
they appear in Wagner's Preliminary Draft, as well as an analytical study
of his sketches and drafts for them.

Before Wagner finished composing the opera, the Prelude had two
performances with a concert ending by Hans von Bülow, published
here for the first time in its complete form in the chapter called
"Historical Background." From that point in early 1859 to the opera's
premiere in mid-1865, *Tristan* became known through performances of
the excerpts included in this volume. I therefore decided to eschew any

attempt to deal with the whole opera and its complex history and to concentrate instead on Wagner's situation and the story of these excerpts during that six-year period. Contemporaneous reviews are incorporated in the "Historical Background" rather than put at the back of the volume, by themselves and out of context—another respect in which this edition differs from others in the series.

Probably no piece in musical history was more radically perplexing to hear or more fiendishly difficult to perform when it was new than *Tristan*, nor has any piece ever called forth a larger body of literature than the opera's Prelude—the ultimate testimony to what an imaginative and daring conception it was when Wagner created it, and to how elusive and problematic it has remained to the present day. The final portions of this volume contain a representative sampling of twentieth-century critical and analytical writings. I hope that those included under the heading "Views and Comments" will comprise a comfortable intro-duction for the reader new to Wagner and *Tristan*. Here are Tovey's plea for performance of the Prelude with Wagner's concert ending, a fine introductory program note on the Prelude by Newman, and some more advanced analytical observations and aesthetic commentaries by Sessions and Cooke.

On a still more advanced level, the next section contains specialized analyses of the Prelude and the so-called "*Tristan* chord" by twentieth-century composers and theorists. Here I had to make more decisions about what to leave out than about what to include: the volume came dangerously close to exceeding spatial limits set for the series. I hope that what remains constitutes a reasonable survey of different theoretical methods.

The complement of the Prelude with its enormous literature is the Transfiguration with relatively little. There was, of course, Lorenz, who dealt with every section of the opera, but I felt that his approach was more effectively illustrated by his chapter on the Prelude. The final section thus contains only two brief studies, by Reti and Meyer.

As far as possible, I have arranged the selections in chronological order within each section. They fall roughly into three general categories with some inevitable overlapping, particularly between the first two:

1. *Motivic* (linear approaches, including *Leitmotiv* descriptions and other types of thematic analysis): Newman's introduction, plus Hindemith, Jackson, and Cone on the Prelude; Reti and Meyer on the Transfig-uration.

2. *Harmonic*: Sessions's introductory analysis (the most familiar view), plus Cooke, Schoenberg, Kurth, Karsten, and Mitchell.
3. *Formal*: Leichtentritt and Lorenz.

In spite of their wide divergences in method and perspective, I have chosen for the most part to regard these selections as self-sufficient and self-explanatory and to let their authors speak for themselves. There are two notable exceptions, however: Lorenz, whose essay requires some understanding of Hugo Riemann's basic theoretical concepts, and Hindemith, whose analysis requires understanding of his own fundamental hypotheses. In both cases, I have supplied what I felt was necessary in my introductory notes and in occasional footnotes along the way.

I have tried to make this volume instructive and useful to people with a wide variety of musical backgrounds and experience. I hope that the "Historical Background" will provide something of interest, perhaps even some surprises, for everyone concerned with Wagner, and that his sketches and drafts will offer some food for thought to those concerned with composers' working methods. And finally, technically advanced students can tackle the analyses of the Prelude, either as material with a common focus from which to survey the history of twentieth-century theoretical applications, or as analytical stimuli to a deeper appreciation of this altogether extraordinary masterpiece.

I have acknowledged the inclusion of copyrighted materials in the notes at the bottom of each selection's first page. In addition, I should like to express my thanks to the Manuscript Division of the New York Public Library and to the Gesellschaft der Musikfreunde in Vienna for allowing me to study the Wagner autographs in their collections and for supplying reproductions of them. It is also fitting to record here my abiding debt of gratitude to the late Winifred Wagner, who gave me unrestricted access to the composer's sketches and drafts in Bayreuth.

This edition would not have been possible without the help of many friends, several of them former students—it is indeed gratifying how those categories overlap. At appropriate places, I have credited in footnotes specific points of information supplied by John Deathridge, Jenny Kallick, and Rena Mueller. Andrew Porter kindly provided his translation of the text for the Transfiguration. For translations in the "Historical Background," my colleagues Ralph Locke and H. Ross Wood made useful suggestions concerning the French, Jurgen Thym concerning the German. David Mead provided invaluable assistance with the typing of that section. Christopher Lewis, Patrick McCreless, and Deborah Stein read over most of my own contributions to this volume and were extraordinarily generous with beneficial criticism. To all these friends, and to three others—Carolyn Abbate, Marcia Lazer, and above all Joseph Clark—who remained a constant source of support in ways they probably never realized, I offer my long overdue but nonetheless heartfelt gratitude.

Finally, I want to thank David Hamilton and Claire Brook for their unfailing though heavily taxed patience, and for their continuing interest and encouragement which enabled me to complete what often seemed an awesome and insurmountable assignment.

ROBERT BAILEY
August 1984

HISTORICAL
BACKGROUND

Historical Background

The premiere of *Tristan and Isolde* in 1865 was a major turning point in Wagner's artistic career. Nearly fifteen years had elapsed since the last premiere of one of his operas—Franz Liszt's production of *Lohengrin* at Weimar in 1850. Wagner had not been able to attend those performances because of his exile in Switzerland owing to the treasonable role he had played in the Dresden uprising of 1849. During the 1850s, Wagner created many of the masterpieces of his artistic maturity—*Das Rheingold, Die Walküre,* the first two acts of *Siegfried* (Act II not yet actually realized in full score), and finally *Tristan.* By 1860, with all this music finished but not yet performed, Wagner found himself in an extraordinary position—not unfamiliar to many later composers, perhaps, but unique in musical history at that time. Circumstances had effectively isolated him from his audience, and during his long isolation, his compositional development had been so extensive that he was in danger of losing that audience altogether. At the same time, his frustrating and bitter struggle for the bare means of survival made these years the most difficult of his life, and his situation grew steadily worse and more hopeless until the King of Bavaria became his patron for life in 1864.

Meanwhile, in early 1859, before Wagner even finished the opera, the *Tristan* Prelude had two performances—which he also could not attend—and the aftermath of those performances in the German press intensified his controversial position. After he finished *Tristan* in August 1859, Wagner spent the next several years desperately trying to rectify that position by getting the new opera produced. All through the period of his work on *Tristan,* Wagner had been counting on a production in Karlsruhe. After that scheme collapsed in the autumn, he toyed with one possibility after another and engaged in negotiations, mostly of his own instigation, with several different theaters—first Paris, then Karlsruhe all over again, finally Vienna, and meanwhile also Dresden, Leipzig, and Prague. Some of these possibilities never amounted to more than wishful thinking on Wagner's part, while most of the others never got beyond preliminary discussion. Ultimately, they all came to nothing, and during the period when prospects for a production were becoming progressively more bleak, Wagner resorted to giving concerts as the only practical method for getting some of his unperformed music heard on the one hand, and of stimulating sufficient interest in his latest operas to generate a production on the other.

He included at least one selection from *Tristan* in many of these concerts, and the excerpts he chose thus led a life of their own during the years preceding the opera's premiere. Their story is the primary subject of the following pages, and it properly begins with Wagner's decision to write the opera in the first place.

Siegfried *or* Tristan?

Wagner made that crucial decision in the summer of 1857. It was a difficult and painful decision, because it meant temporarily abandoning what he regarded as a much more important project—his monumental cycle *Der Ring des Nibelungen*, to whose poem and music he had already devoted the better part of nine years. The external considerations by which Wagner rationalized setting the *Ring* aside in favor of *Tristan* are well known: no commission for the *Ring* had materialized; there seemed no immediate prospect of finding singers suitable for this kind of heroic conception, let alone any possibility of properly training new singers; Wagner had neither performed nor even published any new music for a long time. *Tristan*, designed for performance on a single evening and thus on a much smaller scale than the *Ring*, seemed likely to be more appropriate for the theaters in their current state and thus much more readily acceptable for production. Finally, if Wagner were to forge ahead with the *Ring*, he would soon have to confront the third act of *Siegfried*, with its joyous life-affirming treatment of human love, whereas his own sympathies lay much more in the direction of *Tristan*'s very different treatment of that subject.

Even though he did not speak about it to his friends, however, Wagner was also going through a compositional crisis. By the time he began working on the music for the first two acts of *Siegfried* in 1856–57, the act of composition had more and more come to require elaboration of materials he had conceived earlier—some of them as early as 1851, when he made some musical sketches for *Der junge Siegfried*.[1] Conversely, he found himself in the confusing position where many of his *new* musical inventions were simply not appropriate to those first two acts, and perhaps not even to the third. Some of these new ideas he knew to be for *Tristan*, and Wagner made the first set of *dated* sketches to survive for the later opera on December 19, 1856.[2] Other new ideas from this period finally did get used in Act III of *Siegfried*, while still others left Wagner in doubt about just where they belonged.

Toward the end of April 1857, Wagner moved into a little house called *Asyl* ("Refuge") on the grounds of the Wesendonks' estate outside Zurich. On May 21, he was able to inform Mathilde Wesendonk:[3]

> The muse is beginning to visit me: does that mean I can be certain you will visit too? The first thing I found was a melody, and I simply didn't know what to do with it until words for it suddenly came to me from the final scene of *Siegfried*. A good sign. Yesterday I also worked out the beginning of Act II—"Fafner's Repose," which gave me a humorous and genial moment.

Wagner wrote out the melody in question, with words from *Siegfried* adapted to it, in his working copy of that opera's poem:[4]

---

1. Wagner's title for the original version of *Siegfried*, conceived in 1851 before he thought of adding *Das Rheingold* and *Die Walküre* to the cycle.

2. For the Editor's presentation of these sketches, plus the others demonstrating Wagner's musical problems *vis-à-vis Siegfried* and *Tristan*, see Peter Burbridge and Richard Sutton, eds., *The Wagner Companion* (London, 1979), pp. 308–27.

3. Wolfgang Golther, ed., *Richard Wagner an Mathilde Wesendonk: Tagebuchblätter und Briefe 1853–1871*, 40th printing (Leipzig 1912), p. 20. Except where specifically indicated otherwise, all translations in this chapter are by the Editor.

4. Wagner's first sketch for this material has no text and bears the inscription, *"Im Asyl / erstes Motiv / 16 Mai."* This sheet and Wagner's copy of the poem are in the Nationalarchiv der Richard-Wagner-Stiftung, Bayreuth.

16 Mai (im Asyl)

Sang'st du mir nicht, dein Wis - sen sei das Leuch - ten der Lie - - - be zu mir?

This fragment affords a good illustration of Wagner's "confusion," since he eventually used this music not for this particular passage in *Siegfried*, but instead for the section known as Brangäne's Consolation in the first act of *Tristan*! By early summer, the crisis had intensified to the point where Wagner felt he had no choice but to give up working on the second act. On June 28, he told Liszt:[5] "I have led my *Young Siegfried* up to the point of his lovely solitude in the forest. I left him there under the linden tree and bid him farewell with heartfelt tears. He's better off there than anywhere else."

Two days later, Eduard Devrient, director of the Karlsruhe theater, arrived to be Wagner's houseguest for a few days. The two men discussed the possibility of producing *Tristan* in Karlsruhe, and that prospect remained Wagner's constant hope throughout the period when he actually wrote the opera. For the time being, however, he had still not made the final decision to shelve *Siegfried*. By July 13, he had resumed work on it, and he finished composing Act II on August 19, leaving the full score for this act to be done at some later time. Only then did he put the opera aside once and for all and shift his attention entirely to *Tristan and Isolde*.

5. Erich Kloss, ed., *Briefwechsel zwischen Wagner und Liszt*, 3rd ed. (Leipzig, 1910), Part 2, p. 171. Even though Wagner had decided in 1856 to change the title to *Siegfried*, he continued for some time to refer to the opera by its original one familiar to many of his friends from the private imprint of the cycle's poems issued in 1853.

Composition of Tristan

Wagner began an elaborate Prose Scenario for *Tristan* on August 20, and he finished the poem based on this scenario on September 18. Ideas for the drama had been in his mind for more than a year and a half, and somewhere along the way, he had made hasty pencil sketches for some of its essential details in a little pocket diary. Musical ideas for the new opera, as we have seen, had been occurring to him with some regularity, at least since the previous December.

After Wagner moved into the *Asyl*, his relationship with Mathilde Wesendonk quickly reached a level of great intensity, and both came to look upon *Tristan* as a collaboration—the symbolic "child," as it were, of their spiritual and platonic[1] union. Wagner modified several aspects of his customary working procedure in order to accommodate their "collaboration." At the very outset, he sent Mathilde his only manuscript of the poem, which she kept and from which she made the copy Wagner used for setting his text to music.

Wagner's method of composition for *Tristan* corresponds exactly to the method he had finally worked out for *Siegfried*. For each act, he first made a Preliminary Draft in pencil, which in turn served as the basis for a much more fully elaborated Developed Draft in ink. From this later draft, he constructed his definitive full score. Thus *Tristan*, like *Siegfried*, was composed one act at a time, and each act was finished in full score before Wagner began to compose the next act.

Wagner passed along his Preliminary Draft, a few sheets at a time, to Mathilde so that she could trace over with ink what he had written out in pencil. After she returned what he had sent, Wagner was able to make his Developed Draft from the document to which both he and Mathilde had set their hands. They followed this procedure for the first two acts, as their proximity to each other made the necessary exchanges quite simple. But Wagner composed the third act in Lucerne, and sending sections of the draft back and forth between Lucerne and Zurich was obviously too cumbersome, and thus Mathilde traced over

---

1. To suggest otherwise demonstrates ignorance of Wagner's letters to her and the diaries he kept for her, or constitutes a deliberate and insensitive misreading of those documents.

only the first few sheets for Act III. Once Wagner no longer had any practical need for the Preliminary Draft, he sent it back to Mathilde to keep.

The final manifestation of their collaboration was the set of five *Wesendonk-Lieder*, as they are called today. Mathilde wrote these poems in the style of Wagner's poem for *Tristan*, and Wagner set four of them to music during the period when he was working on the music for the first act of the opera. He set the fifth poem a few days before he began to compose Act II. Wagner also arranged one of them—*Träume*—for a small orchestra with solo violin, as a gift for her at Christmas 1857. He also gave her his manuscripts of all five songs,[2] retaining for himself only his pencil sketches for them. Wagner and Mathilde looked upon the songs as private documents not intended for public consumption, but about the middle of 1862, in a desperate moment, Wagner sold them to the publisher Schott, who issued them later that year as *Fünf Dilettanten-Gedichte für eine Frauenstimme*. Mathilde Wesendonk was not identified as the poet until after her death in 1902.

While still in the *Asyl*, Wagner composed Act I and made the entire Preliminary Draft for Act II. He also started in on his Developed Draft but soon broke off work, about midway through the first scene. His wife, Minna, precipitated a crisis over Wagner's relationship with Mathilde, and they decided on a temporary separation. About the middle of August, Wagner left Zurich and took up temporary residence in Venice, where he finally resumed work on his Developed Draft and completed Act II in full score. He then went to Lucerne, where he composed Act III. About a month after finishing the opera, he moved to Paris, which remained his base of operations until early 1862. The composition of *Tristan* is outlined in the Chronological Table:

Chronological Table

Dates are from the original documents, all in the Nationalarchiv der Richard-Wagner-Stiftung, Bayreuth.

Zurich

1856	Dec. 19	First dated sketches
1857	Aug. 20–Sept. 18	Prose Scenario and poem

Act I

	Oct. 1–31	Preliminary Draft	Prelude and Scenes 1–4
	Nov. 5–Dec. 1	Developed Draft	

2. These were published in facsimile in Leipzig, 1962.

	Nov. 30	*Der Engel*
	Dec. 4/5	*Träume*
	Dec. 8–31	Preliminary Draft–Scene 5
	Dec. 17	*Schmerzen*
	Dec. 18	Instrumental version of *Träume*
1858	Jan. 4–13	Developed Draft–Scene 5
	Feb. 22	*Stehe still!*
	April 3	Full Score finished
	May 1	*Im Treibhaus*

Act II

	May 4–31;	
	and June [26?]–July 1	Preliminary Draft
	July 5–[?];	Developed Draft to m. 352

Venice

| 1859 | and Oct. 15–March 9 | Developed Draft resumed and completed |
| | March 18 | Full Score finished |

Lucerne

Act III

	April 9–30	Preliminary Draft to m. 713
	May 1–8	Developed Draft begun
	May 9–16	Preliminary Draft to m. 840
	May 17–June 5	Developed Draft to m. 840
	June 19–July 16	Preliminary Draft completed
	July 19	Developed Draft completed
	August 6	Full Score finished

Paris

| 1860 | early January | Full Score published |
| | late October | Piano-vocal Score published |

Publication of Tristan

Tristan was the first of Wagner's operas to be published in *engraved* full score. In the mid-1840s, he had published the full scores of *Rienzi, The Flying Dutchman,* and *Tannhäuser,* essentially at his own expense, and the firm of Meser in Dresden printed them using the much cheaper method of autograph-lithography.[1] Breitkopf & Härtel became Wagner's publisher with *Lohengrin*, and they agreed to engrave the piano-vocal score (prepared by Theodor Uhlig) but not the full score, which they issued by the same lithographic process Meser had employed for the earlier scores.

Wagner informed Breitkopf & Härtel about *Tristan* at the beginning of September 1857,[2] before he had even finished the poem. Hermann Härtel visited Wagner later that autumn, and the final negotiations took place in January 1858, while Wagner was finishing the music for the first act. He signed the contract and returned it towards the end of February, along with the first portion of his full score for Act I.[3] He had already outlined the details for Hans von Bülow in a letter of February 10:[4]

> I just have to be glad now that Breitkopf & Härtel are willing to give me at least *something* for *Tristan*. They reduced my original request to 200 Louis d'or[5] with the single additional prospect of a modest bonus in the event of extraordinary success. That is all I can hope for now, and I am going to take it, because when all is said and done I don't think anyone will offer more, and because they have also committed themselves to engraving the full score immediately. I now intend to get the instrumentation of the first act done quickly, because I can count on advance payment when I've sent it off. Now that you see how things are going for me, I also want to tell you how things are supposed to go for you. You're to do the complete piano-vocal score and the arrangements for piano alone (2-hand and 4-hand). Breitkopf & Härtel will only go as high as 3 Thalers per printed folio (of 4 pages), as they usually pay only 2. I have accepted pending your agreement, and you, poor fellow, are now obliged to do a lot of work for me for a pittance. To get the piano-vocal score moving along as quickly as possible, you'll be getting proof-sheets of the full score plus my manuscript sent to you in installments (for you're also going to have to help me out with the proof reading).

1. A process whereby a score was copied out onto lithograph masters, so that the final product has a handwritten appearance. In the case of *Tannhäuser*, Wagner simply made the lithograph masters himself, instead of first writing out a full score on paper. Thus, the 100 copies run off from those masters constitute all that survives by way of an "autograph" for the first version of the opera.

2. Wilhelm Altmann, ed., *Richard Wagners Briefwechsel mit Breitkopf & Härtel* (Leipzig, 1911), pp. 110–11.

3. Ibid., p. 117.

4. *Richard Wagner: Briefe an Hans von Bülow* (Jena, 1916), pp. 89–90.

5. Wagner had originally asked for three times this amount! See his letter to Härtel of January 4, 1858, in *Briefwechsel mit Breitkopf*, p. 113.

Thus, *Tristan* was not only composed but also engraved one act at a time. Wagner came up with the proposal to send his full score to the firm in installments, so that the task of engraving could go forward as quickly as possible.[6] We have noted that Wagner completed each act of the opera in full score before he began composing the next act, and he posted his only copy of that full score—installment by installment—to Leipzig from wherever he happened to be. His confidence in the postal service may seem unbelievably sanguine nowadays, but in spite of the fact that one installment for Act III reached Breitkopf & Härtel in an open envelope,[7] none of his manuscript ever did go astray.

For a while, this unusual procedure worked quite regularly, and Wagner was able to read proof for the full score of Act I while he was working on Act II. Soon afterwards, however, the regularity broke down on account of Wagner's long delay in finishing Act II, which inevitably caused the firm to let their few highly qualified engravers concentrate on other projects—most notably the complete editions of Bach and Handel.[8] In their letter to Wagner of May 18, 1859,[9] they claimed that they were going ahead with *Tristan* once again and asked him to think about sending along a new installment fairly soon. By the middle of July, however, Wagner had sent the first two installments of Act III but still had not seen any proofs for Act II. Isolde's monologue at the conclusion of Act III recalls two passages from the love duet in Act II, and as Wagner got closer to that passage in his full score, he asked the firm to send him at least a copy of the appropriate section of Act II struck from the uncorrected plates.[10]

Back in mid-May, when the firm had first suggested that he could start sending more manuscript, Wagner had not even begun the full score for Act III, and he inquired about the daily or weekly rate at which the engraver could produce plates for his score, so that he in turn might calculate writing out his manuscript accordingly and send along enough to keep the engraver steadily occupied.[11] The firm's reply of June 21[12] contains the most revealing statistics we have about the

6. Ibid., p. 113.
7. Ibid., p. 166.
8. Ibid., p. 155.
9. Ibid., p. 163.
10. Ibid., p. 166. Letter of July 18, 1859.
11. Ibid., p. 163.
12. Ibid., p. 164.

engraving of full scores in the mid-nineteenth century. They informed Wagner that their three engravers could turn out 12 to 15 plates a week. The modern forty-hour work week did not yet exist, of course, and these figures indicate that it took somewhere in the neighborhood of 150 *craftsman*-hours to produce 12 to 15 plates. The full score of *Tristan* runs to 439 plates of music, so it is scarcely surprising that operatic full scores were rarely engraved just as a matter of course, for they were enormously expensive to produce and almost prohibitively expensive to buy. The sad but inevitable fact was that cheaper processes for printing music would eventually phase out engraving altogether.

Breitkopf & Härtel printed the *Tristan* poem in the latter part of 1858 and issued it as a separate publication at the very beginning of 1859. Their extraordinarily beautiful engraved full score appeared early in January 1860, under plate number 10,000—a convenient reference for dating this firm's nineteenth-century publications. With *Tristan*, the firm abandoned one of the standard features of their piano-vocal scores, because Wagner found the inclusion of a separate *printed* poem "as preface to a volume of engraved music very ugly with regard to typography."[13] The firm's confusion about Wagner's wishes in this matter was one of the causes for delay in the publication of Bülow's piano-vocal score, which finally appeared in the latter part of October.

13. Ibid., p. 201.

The First Performances of *the* Tristan *Prelude*

Bülow did agree to arrange the piano-vocal score, and forged ahead once materials began to reach him, but he refused to have anything to do with the two arrangements for piano alone. He later told Wagner[1]

1. Richard Graf Du Moulin Eckart, ed., *Hans von Bülow: Neue Briefe* (Munich, 1927), p. 437.

that he had refused to do them because it would constitute an act of "vulgar desecration" and because they could just as well be done by the craftsmen at Breitkopf & Härtel anyway. On the other hand, he argued, a well-arranged piano-vocal score could be a perfectly acceptable substitute for those who could not afford to buy a full score. His enthusiasm for *Tristan* itself knew no bounds, and on June 27, 1858, he was already giving vent to feelings he could scarcely contain in a letter to Felix Draeseke:[2]

> You should just see Wagner's *Tristan!* I have already arranged the first 40 pages of score (the amount engraved so far) for Breitkopf & Härtel, who are devouring the manuscript only in this way. In the instrumental introduction (related a bit to that of *Lohengrin*) *horribile dictu, visu, auditu*—not a single pure triad is to be found, not a single one.[3] * * *
>
> Richard is a fabulous musician. Always a new development in his works. *Tristan* is going to please you *far more* than *Lohengrin*, I'll swear to that!

In early 1859, before Wagner had even finished the second act of the opera, Bülow decided to include the Prelude on the program of what he called a *reines Zukunftsconcert*[4] ("genuine concert of the future") he was to conduct in Prague in March. He wrote to Wagner to ask about a concert ending for the excerpt, and Wagner replied on February 10:[5] "If you intend to perform the *Tristan* Prelude in Prague, I have nothing against it, but if you do, you will have to make an ending for it yourself. You cannot expect that from me."

Bülow in fact made his own ending for the piece, and beginning from Wagner's m. 100, it runs as follows:

2. Marie von Bülow, ed., *Hans von Bülow: Briefe*, Vol. 3: *1855–1864* (Leipzig, 1898), p. 179.

3. Bülow was frequently given to exaggeration!

4. *Bülow: Briefe* 3, p. 221.

5. *Wagner: Briefe an Bülow*, p. 118.

He described what he had done in his letter to Wagner of March 4:[6]

> With the ending for *Tristan* (A major), I don't think I've handled things too awkwardly for you. I retain just about everything, except that after the first G-major harmony I modulate directly a minor third lower—[Bülow then wrote out mm. 7 through 12 of the ending in a reduction to two staves]—and then gradually slower and slower reverberations of the last measure until it completely dies away (timpani roll *ppp* on E)—in the middle voices B♯ as appoggiatura to C♯, so that the harmony still seems to shift between major and minor. If you recoil, just remember that it's your own fault, since it would only have cost you a stroke of the pen to make something decent. The people of Prague are really hankering for your kindness to them, and Karlsruhe's jealousy will be balanced out in that way. * * *

Bülow's example omitted the upper three voices in the first half of m. 7, and the first seven measures of the ending as shown above are reconstructed from his description. He did in fact "retain just about everything," allowing for the transposition, including the first five notes of the "recitative" for cellos and basses which in the opera accompanies the opening of the curtain (mm. 106–8 in the Prelude). Bülow's attempt to harmonize the last three of those five notes, in particular m. 8 in the above example, is awkward at best and is undoubtedly one of the sources of Wagner's dissatisfaction with this ending. A facsimile of Bülow's full

---

6. *Bülow: Neue Briefe*, pp. 430–31.

score for the ending, beginning at m. 9, was published in 1908,[7] but since it was identified only as a "manuscript in Bülow's hand," it seems never to have been recognized for what it is. In any case, this autograph makes it possible to add the final measures (beginning at the pick-up into m. 13) and thus show the ending in its entirety. Wagner expressed his reaction to this ending in his letter to Bülow of March 8:[8]

> In the ending for the Prelude I cannot find myself, and on the whole I regret having given you my consent. While I was reading about the *Faust Overture* [Bülow had conducted this piece in a concert he gave with Liszt in Berlin on February 27], I was hoping you might have given up the idea. I've now had only annoyance because of Prague. I'm not wild about the idea of their being the first to have something from *Tristan*. There's utterly no need to give Karlsruhe any cause for jealousy. Just as, in general, I don't stand in any need whatever of making anybody jealous on my account.

But Wagner's complaint was too late—Bülow had left for Prague that very day.[9] Wagner's letter did get forwarded to Prague,[10] but probably did not reach Bülow until after the concert had taken place on March 12. The *Tristan* Prelude, according to the program,[11] was being "performed for the first time in Prague through the kindness of the composer." The concert included Wagner's own *Faust Overture*, a great favorite of Bülow, who had published an essay about the work in 1856.[12] He also conducted Berlioz's Overture to *Benvenuto Cellini* and two of Liszt's tone poems, *Festklänge* and *Mazeppa*. In a report to the *Neue Zeitschrift für Musik*,[13] Franz Gerstenkorn described the concert as consisting of "works by the three sovereigns of the present and future" and commented on the *Tristan* Prelude as follows:

> * * * In the introduction to *Tristan and Isolde*, the tone poet describes in the most vivid colors that fervent and consuming love longing from which

---

7. Heinrich Reimann, *Hans von Bülow: Sein Leben und sein Wirken*, Vol. 1 [all that was published]: *Aus Hans von Bülows Lehrzeit*, 2nd ed. (Berlin, 1908), facing p. x.

8. *Wagner: Briefe an Bülow*, p. 119. In Ernest Newman's words, Bülow's ending does not "suggest that included in the talents with which Providence had so richly endowed him was the capacity to write Wagner's music for him" (*The Wagner Operas* [New York, 1949], p. 205).

9. *Bülow: Briefe* 3, pp. 225–26.

10. *Bülow: Neue Briefe*, p. 434.

11. *Bülow: Briefe* 3, p. 218, n. 1, gives the complete program for the concert.

12. It originally appeared in the *Neue Zeitschrift für Musik* 45/6 and 7 (August 1 and 8, 1856) and is reprinted in Marie von Bülow, ed., *Hans von Bülow: Ausgewählte Schriften* (Leipzig, 1896), pp. 144–72.

13. 50/13 (March 25, 1859): 146.

all dramatic conflicts in this moving tragedy of love originate, and we perceive the unfortunate fate which gathers like a heavy dark thundercloud above the heads of the two heroes and transforms their love into sorrow. — The cultured people of Prague quickly grasped this latest work by the composer they so deeply revere and demanded a repetition of it, but that wish could not be granted because of the extreme lack of time.

The *Süddeutsche Musik-Zeitung* reported that "the success of all compositions was a brilliant one, for all numbers were overwhelmed with applause."[14]

The second performance of the *Tristan* Prelude (also with Bülow's ending) occurred while Wagner was at work on Act III of the opera, and this performance was actually far more important than the one in Prague, because it occurred in the context of the *Tonkünstler-Versammlung* (Congress of Musical Artists) held in Leipzig on June 1–4, 1859. Also dubbed *Zukunftsfest* ("Festival of the Future"), this Congress was essentially the brainchild of Liszt and Franz Brendel, who had been serving for many years as editor of the *Neue Zeitschrift für Musik*. During this Congress, in fact, Brendel pointed out in his keynote address[15] that the name *Zukunftsmusiker* ("Musicians of the Future") had given rise to vehement misunderstanding, and he proposed that the name accordingly be changed to *Neue deutsche Schule* ("New German School") or *Neudeutsche Schule* ("Modern German School").

Wagner in general had little sympathy with meetings of this kind, noting that "organizations of however many clever minds are never able to give the world a genius or a genuine work of art."[16] Evidently fully aware of these feelings, Liszt pleaded with Wagner in his letter of May 14:[17] "Don't laugh at me too much for always taking an interest in such things: they are not without influence on your royalties, and from this point of view I ask for your tolerance."

Liszt himself conducted the *Tristan* Prelude in the opening concert[18]

---

14. *Bülow: Briefe* 3, p. 218, n. 1.

15. The entire text of this address appeared in the *Neue Zeitschrift für Musik* 50/24 (June 10, 1859): 265–73.

16. Quoted in Carl Fr. Glasenapp, *Das Leben Richard Wagners*, Vol. 3, 4th ed. (Leipzig, 1905), p. 212.

17. *Briefwechsel zwischen Wagner und Liszt* 2, p. 269.

18. August Ferdinand Riccius (1819–86) conducted the orchestral works on the first half of the program, which included Mendelssohn's Overture *Calm Sea and Prosperous Voyage* and Schumann's *Manfred* Overture, as well as an aria from Berlioz's *Benvenuto Cellini*. Liszt opened the second half of the concert with the *Tristan* Prelude and also

of the Congress on June 1, but without asking Wagner's permission to include the piece on the program. This Congress may indeed have been an important festival of sorts, but as far as the actual performances were concerned, "festival conditions" of the type Wagner later envisioned for Bayreuth certainly did not prevail. Rehearsal time—for the *Tristan* Prelude, at any rate—was clearly just as minimal as it had been for Bülow's performance in Prague. As late as May 24, Bülow wrote to Liszt,[19] "The Introduction to Wagner's *Tristan* will be a most brilliant failure. Since you want me to send the score and parts, I'll do it, addressing them indirectly, however, to Weimar and not to Leipzig." Bülow explained his feelings about Leipzig in a later passage of the same letter: "As for *Tristan*, it pains me to send the parts to Leipzig. If there is a city unworthy of this piece, Leipzig is certainly it." Bülow was as good as his word, and Liszt, already in Leipzig on the 26th, had still not received the *Tristan* materials. Bülow had in fact sent them to Weimar, from which they had to be forwarded to Leipzig[20]—for a concert that took place on June 1!

Wagner was obviously none too pleased that the Prelude had been performed at all, for later in the summer Bülow apologized in a letter dated August 24:[21] "I give you my solemn word of honor that I lent out the score and parts for the *Tristan* Introduction only at Liszt's repeated and most emphatic assurance that, at his request, you would have given Brendel permission to perform it."

Richard Pohl, one of the most intrepid spokesmen for this "party" of musicians, wrote his first review of the festival for the *Neue Zeitschrift*, which printed the first installment of it in the issue of June 17. This installment did not get as far as the compositions Liszt had conducted. Wagner complained to Mathilde Wesendonk in a letter of June 21:[22]

---

conducted the duet for Senta and the Dutchman from *The Flying Dutchman* plus his own tone poem, *Tasso*.

Schumann's opera, *Genoveva*, was performed the evening before the Congress opened, and the two featured performances of the second and third evenings were Liszt's *Graner Festmesse* (conducted by Liszt) and Bach's *B minor Mass* (conducted by Carl Riedel), both in St. Thomas's Church. Riedel (1827–88), an important choral conductor, founded the chorus which bore his name (*Riedelverein*) and remained in existence until well into the 20th century. In 1868, he became president of the *Allgemeiner deutscher Musikverein* and later served as president of the Leipzig Wagner Society.

19. La Mara, ed., *Briefwechsel zwischen Franz Liszt und Hans von Bülow* (Leipzig, 1898), pp. 265–66.
20. *Bülow: Briefe* 3, p. 236.
21. *Bülow: Neue Briefe*, p. 435.
22. *Wagner an Mathilde Wesendonk*, pp. 151–52.

Nothing has happened. My discreet friends are preserving a reverential silence. Even the music journal [*Neue Zeitschrift*] is serving us the celebrated Feast of the Future[23] in snippets. Now I almost hope I receive no visitors from over there this summer. Before the completion of *Tristan*, such a noisy intrusion could scarcely do anything but disturb me. In fact, their ideas are just totally different from mine; one must admit that to oneself without any bitterness.

In the issue of June 24, Pohl reported as follows:[24]

Wagner's instrumental introduction to *Tristan and Isolde*—well known as the latest work he has created, and still in manuscript—has never before been heard publicly, except for a performance in a Prague concert under Hans von Bülow's direction in March of this year. In its opening measures this incomparable work begins with such ravishing beauty and captivates the attentive listener so completely that he is filled with amazement and admiration and struck by the elevated feeling of seeing one of the richest and sublimest blossoms of Wagner's genius open before him. The performance was excellent, the reception scarcely inferior. Every intelligent musician immediately perceived the ingenious power of the composition as well as the grandeur of its harmonic and polyphonic construction. We second the public enthusiasm for it with the fullest conviction, and we shall attempt to substantiate our view more thoroughly in our second article.

Pohl seems unaware that Wagner had not even finished composing the opera. In his second review, he discussed the *Tristan* Prelude in much the same flowery style at the conclusion of his installment for the August 5th issue:[25]

To give a rough idea of this masterpiece to those not yet familiar with it, Wagner's own creations offer the only possible points of comparison. Here the parallel with the *Lohengrin* Prelude is naturally closest, not only as regards dramatic-musical definition and external dimensions, but also the magnificient internal contrapuntal construction. To that extent, one can definitely characterize the *Tristan* introduction as the counterpart—or, even more correctly, as the poetic antithesis—of the other piece. Fundamentally different though the poetic content of the two music-dramas be, however, the musical content is equally different, as we would expect from Wagner. The character of the heroes immediately attains its most significant expression in the two introductions: on the one hand, the noble divine champion, whose immaculate image evolves out of the dazzlingly pure light radiating from the holy Grail; and on the other hand, the

---

23. *Zukunftsfest*: Wagner exploits the possible pun on the word *Fest*, which can mean a "feast" as well as a "festival."

24. *Neue Zeitschrift für Musik* 50/26 (June 24, 1859): 290.

25. Ibid., 51/6 (August 5, 1859): 48–49.

genuinely human struggling and atoning hero, who revels in the consuming passions of a forbidden love and perishes, yet who even in his moments of highest rapture is shudderingly consumed by the demonic proximity of an invisibly controlling nemesis.

In the Wagnerian drama, the instrumental introduction runs directly into the first scene of Act I, where Isolde, on board the ship which conveys her as bride to a man she does not love, hides her face in despair, and from the mast the young sailor's song seems to scoff at her:

> "Sind's deiner Seufzer Wehen,
> Die mir die Segel blähen?
> Wehe! Wehe, du Wind!
> Weh'! Ach wehe, mein Kind!"

For the concert performance, however, an ending to round off the introduction was necessary, and with the subtlest understanding and noblest reverence, Herr von Bülow (to whom the composer also entrusted the arrangement of the piano-vocal score) solved the problem so admirably that surely no one unfamiliar with the situation perceived the work of a foreign artistic hand at the conclusion of this wonderful psychological portrait. Without looking at the original score, even a connoisseur could hardly determine the spot where Bülow's work followed that of his friend and master.

Between the composition of the Prelude to *Lohengrin* and that to *Tristan and Isolde* lie ten full years of an ever deepening artistic life—the former was composed in 1847, the latter in 1857—as well as the poem and gigantic score of the *Ring*. It was surely foreseeable that this momentous period of activity could not occur in so richly developed an artistic consciousness without leaving significant traces of itself on the artist's mind. The style of the *Tristan* Prelude is even more exalted in its simple grandeur; there is such an eminent logic and continuity in its flow of thought, such a moderate yet compelling power in its intensity, that unless someone decides to tear himself away by brute force, he must submit fully to the magic with which the first measures immediately envelop his soul. But the transfer of our immortal element into that dreamlike state of other-worldly existence and perception, which we call being completely consumed by the *musical atmosphere*, is the highest task and the greatest triumph of musical art, since this power is given only to music alone.— And Wagner possesses this mysterious magic power to an almost unlimited degree.

Pohl's next installment appeared after a two-week interval and began with the following paragraph:[26]

In another respect also, Wagner's latest artistic productions surpass his earlier ones—in the method of *harmonic* treatment. Modulations, which

26. Ibid., 51/8 (August 19, 1859): 63.

already in *Lohengrin* were often of astonishing novelty, have become even bolder and freer: just take the first measures of the *Tristan* Introduction, for example. Here the stimulating and fructifying influence of Liszt's recent works is surely unmistakable. From the very first, Liszt has "dared" just as much for instrumental music in the realm of modulation as he has in the realm of form, and he has therefore also discovered more than any of his forerunners or contemporaries. There he became the "ice breaker," like Wagner for opera, and on account of it was hated by those "ice floes" who saw their inevitable ultimate destruction before their very eyes. Their hatred was directed with even greater concentration against Liszt than against his great *dioscures*, because the question of the reform of instrumental music was even more deeply ingrained and affected even more people. Ever so frequently we hear that intelligent temperaments who welcomed Wagner's operatic reform with joy and sympathy react to Liszt's instrumental reform as they would to a Book of Seven Seals. If we search for the causes, we shall almost always find that it is in part his bold treatment of *modulation*, but even more his stylistic freedom in *formal* construction that cause hesitation and give offence.

By this time, Bülow was if anything even more enthusiastic about the second act of the opera than he had been about the first, and he wrote a letter to Franz Brendel, who published its crucial passage in the correspondence column of the *Neue Zeitschrift* for September 9.[27]

Herr v. B. writes: "With the appearance of *Tristan and Isolde*, the external situation of the New German School is going to enter a completely new phase. Since the *Ring* will lie in Wagner's desk for the time being, this one-evening opera will take its place. Here is the realization of Wagner's tendencies, and in a quite unsuspected manner. No one anticipated such music from Wagner. It grows directly out of late Beethoven—no longer any analogy to Weber or Gluck. *Tristan* is to *Lohengrin* as *Fidelio* is to *Die Entführung aus dem Serail*, or as the C♯ minor Quartet is to the F major, Op. 18, No. 1. I confess I went from one delightful surprise to another. At this point, any musician not yet willing to believe in progress has no ears. Wagner hits the mark on every page through his vast purely musical knowledge. You cannot form too high a conception of this construction, this manipulation of musical detail. *Tristan* is Wagner's most powerful work as regards invention. Nothing is so exalted as this second act, for example. I have tried out fragments with various musicians, especially ones who do not belong to our party. One of them, for instance, was speechless with astonishment: 'I would never have expected anything like this from Wagner. This is by far the most beautiful thing he has written. He attains here the highest ideal imaginable at present.' After *Tristan* there will be only two parties—people who have learned something, and those who have learned nothing. Anyone this opera does not convert has no music in his body. In not all that many earlier scores is there such

27. Ibid., 51/11 (September 9, 1859): 94–95.

rich, clear, and original polyphony. You know me too well to suppose I would descend to exaggerated rapture: you are aware that to be enthusiastic my heart first asks permission from my brain's authority, and in this case my brain gave unqualified approval. *Tristan and Isolde* can hardly become popular, but any layman at all poetically gifted must be thrilled by the grandeur and power of genius revealed in this work. Apart from everything else, I assure you the opera is the zenith of musical art up to now!"

Aftermath in the Press

Wagner had moved to Paris on September 10, and it was consequently some time before he actually saw what Brendel had published. He had evidently heard about it, however, for in his letter to Mathilde Wesendonk of September 24,[1] he complained that he had still "seen nothing at all of Bülow's letter on *Tristan*." It caught up with him soon afterwards, and Wagner wrote to Bülow about it on October 7:[2]

> I have read the extract from your letter about *Tristan*. It's not going to work to your credit. I'll leave aside what you say about something beautiful and tremendous: that's your affair. But I censure as unpractical that remark concerning your doubt about the opera's possible popularity. Things like that never mean very much among ourselves, but they invariably do to outsiders who are always more or less hostile to us, and this must constantly be kept in mind when it comes to publications. Breitkopf & Härtel are already being difficult on account of this doubt articulated by a friend of mine. What is this idle question of popularity to you, me, and our few real friends anyway? Why even allude to it? There's a lot we admit among ourselves—for example, that since my acquaintance with Liszt's compositions, I've become quite a different fellow as a harmonist from what I used to be. But when friend Pohl blabs this secret before the whole world right at the beginning of a short discussion of the *Tristan* Prelude, that is simply indiscreet, to say the least—and I'm not supposed to assume he was authorized to commit such an indiscretion? Liszt, for example, can write to me—*in ink*—on the dedication page of his *Dante* Symphony that he thinks he has a lot to thank me for; I accept that as an excess of friendship. But wouldn't it be silly for me to insist that

1. *Wagner an Mathilde Wesendonk*, p. 179.
2. *Wagner: Briefe an Bülow*, pp. 125–26.

something like that actually be added to the printed dedication for the whole world to see? Such a thing would immediately arouse me to make a public protest. Herr Pohl might be recommended by both of us to exercise more discretion, for I think he is compromising Liszt, even though he may also be pleasing the Princess.

The passage from this letter about Liszt's influence on Wagner's harmony has frequently been quoted out of context to Wagner's discredit. Even Ernest Newman[3] ignores the opening section concerning Bülow's published letter. Although he takes account of Wagner's undoubtedly correct suspicion that Liszt's mistress, the Princess Sayn-Wittgenstein, had encouraged Pohl's remarks, he still accuses Wagner of being "peevish" about that matter of Liszt's influence, which, as the letter clearly shows, Wagner was perfectly willing to acknowledge within his own private circle of musical colleagues. And when we view the *entire* passage of Wagner's letter in the light of the relevant publications from the *Neue Zeitschrift*, Wagner's particular concern becomes obvious, as regards both the potential popularity of the as yet unperformed *Tristan* and the complex question of what composers can learn from each other. He was afraid that discussions of this kind could easily create a false impression, and even have deleterious side effects, when carried on *in the public press*. Liszt's handwritten dedication, incidentally, had run as follows:[4]

As Virgil guided Dante, so have you guided me through the mysterious regions of the life-imbued worlds of tone. From the depths of his heart calls to you—
  "Tu se' lo mio maestro, e il mio autore!"
and dedicates this work to you in unchangeably faithful love,
                                        Your
                                        F. Liszt

Soon after receiving his copy, Wagner had informed Liszt[5] that "we are going to keep the dedication you wrote into my copy strictly to ourselves; from me at least not a soul shall hear about it. It has made me positively red with shame, believe you me!"

  Wagner had every reason to be suspicious of the harmful side effects of being too much in view in the press, which was only too willing to exploit any potentially titillating situation with no eye to the conse-

---

3. Ernest Newman, *The Life of Richard Wagner*, Vol. 2 (New York, 1937), p. 600.
4. Translation by Newman, ibid., p. 586.
5. *Briefwechsel zwischen Wagner und Liszt* 2, p. 266.

quences. In fact, his worst fears had already been realized: the German musical journals indulged in some of their worst shenanigans over Bülow's letter. The situation became so embarrassing that Brendel felt constrained to print the following notice in the *Neue Zeitschrift* for October 21:[6]

> Several journals, including Zellner's *Blätter für Musik, Theater und bildende Kunst*, and Schlesinger's *Berliner Musik-Zeitung Echo*, have reprinted Herr H. v. Bülow's *personal letter* about Wagner's *Tristan and Isolde*, which we published in No. 11, and have accompanied it with the following comment that first appeared in Zellner's journal: "In Wagner's interest, we actively wish that these remarks adducing the sublimest claims for his opera may turn out to be true to the same extent that they publicly impede his path to just evaluation and appreciation. May Wagner, because of similar occurrences, never have cause to complain about the zeal of his friends more than about that of his adversaries." The writer of this comment (1) ignores the fact that the passage was taken from a *personal letter, as we had explicitly noted*, and he thereby completely distorts the sense and meaning of the communication; and (2) he fails to appreciate that the same was only intended as a supplement to essays we had published shortly before, *which we likewise had explicitly mentioned*, and he thereby shifts sense and meaning in the same way.[7] Omission of our explanatory introduction has thus given rise to a factual falsehood, which seems bound to arouse misunderstandings and to increase rather than lessen animosity. We therefore implore those journals to be kind enough to print a qualification explaining that the passage was taken from a *personal letter* and that, owing to this character, it should be understood quite differently from an article originally intended for the public.

Bülow had already sent his own outraged letter to Zellner on September 26, demanding that he print an explanation:[8]

> In one of the recent issues of your valued journal, which has just come to my attention, I read the reproduction of a personal letter to my friend Dr. Brendel, who was indiscreet enough to have it printed in his journal, but who nevertheless was polite enough to preface the passage with an acknowledgement of his indiscretion. The editors of Vienna's *Blätter für Musik*, on the contrary, treated my personal letter, recognizable for what it is by its rough unpolished style, as a public one and used it for a bit of friendly commentary, to which my letter was obviously not designed to be exposed. I have no choice but to tell you that I could not even be persuaded to expect this behavior from a well-bred person of tact and

---

6. *Neue Zeitschrift für Musik* 51/17 (October 21, 1859): 148.
7. Brendel is referring to the several installments of his essay *Einige Worte über Lohengrin zum besseren Verständniss desselben*, scattered in five issues of the journal from February through September.
8. *Bülow: Briefe* 3, pp. 264–65.

taste. I would rather be optimistic and deceive myself about the motives which may have persuaded the editors to reproduce it at all. However, the editors' commentary in question, particularly their variation on the well-known theme of the "zeal of friends," justifies the supposition of a personal *dolus* against Wagner's "friend." This is one of the most beloved flowers in our adversaries' anthology of sophistry, one of their arsenal's handiest weapons: *throw suspicion on the friends; if possible, make them hateful as involuntary injurors in the eyes of those for whom they fight while sacrificing all personal impulses.*

　　　I could not actually begin to imagine a plausible reason why a well-bred person should have taken that sort of stance specifically against me, when I have always spoken and written only with respect and courtesy about your operation. Accordingly, if I may appeal to the "gentleman" in the writer, I hope all the more for consideration of my urgent request that at your earliest convenience you be kind enough to supply an explanatory apology for printing a personal letter, which you omitted in the aforesaid notice. * * *

Zellner never replied, either in public or in private, and Bülow sent a copy of this letter to the *Niederrheinische Musikzeitung*, which printed it with what Bülow himself later described to Peter Cornelius[9] as a "not particularly flattering postscript": "Dr. Zellner thought it proper to take no notice of this protest. From this, it follows that I appealed to an absent or nonexistent person."[10]

　　　However "absent or nonexistent" he may have been as far as Bülow was concerned, and regardless of his evidently malicious intentions, Zellner probably had a point after all—a point which paralleled Wagner's own concern. Wagner might well fear that the "zeal" of his supposed friends could significantly undermine his own position, if only by keeping him too much at the center of some controversy, however trivial, in the German press. As far as the German musical public was concerned, Wagner was in fact in real danger of becoming merely a pawn of those well-meaning friends bent upon holding him up as a standard bearer of the New German School, even though he himself felt little if any sympathy with that "cause," as he had indicated to Mathilde Wesendonk back in June. He had now been absent from Germany for ten years, and he himself had presented none of his own new music to the public since *Tannhäuser*. In 1850 Liszt had given the premiere of *Lohengrin*, which Wagner had not been able to attend, and the public thus had

---

　　　9. In his letter of October 29, ibid., p. 275.
　　　10. Ibid., p. 266. The entire letter—with the postscript—appeared in the *Niederrheinische Musikzeitung* 7/43 (1859): 343.

only Wagner's *early* operas as a basis for understanding his later ideas, which were accessible only through a handful of easily misunderstood and therefore controversial treatises written during the first years after his flight from Dresden. Now, some nine years after the *Lohengrin* premiere, Bülow and Liszt had conducted underrehearsed performances of the *Tristan* Prelude with an ending Wagner had not even composed and did not like. By virtue of its extraordinarily new musical language, the piece was bound to baffle a public with no practical knowledge of Wagner's musical development since *Lohengrin*. In short, the "zeal of his friends" was probably doing Wagner's own cause as much harm as good, and it certainly was not improving his prospects for a premiere of *Tristan*. In the latter part of October, Eduard Devrient, the Intendant of the Karlsruhe theater, notified Wagner that the prospective production there was definitely canceled. When the news became public, the press gleefully jumped in again and exploited the situation to the hilt. The *Neue Berliner Musikzeitung*, for example, printed the following notice in their issue of December 28:[11]

> *Karlsruhe, mid-November*: The chief event in our theatrical life is the laying aside of Richard Wagner's *Tristan und Isolde* as *unproduceable*. It had to come to this: now at last the title of "music of the future," about which there has been so much fighting, is justified: the present cannot even perform this music! Ostensibly the shelving of the work was on account of our women singers; but according to trustworthy reports, the demands made on the orchestra are equally exorbitant and impossible to meet.

11. Quoted in Glasenapp, *Leben* 3, p. 225, n. 2. Translation by Newman, *Life* 2, p. 590, modified by the Editor.

Wagner's First Performances # *of the* Tristan *Prelude*

We have noted that about a month after he finished *Tristan*, having waited that long as a result of difficulties and delays in getting a passport, Wagner moved to Paris. Since he was still not able to set foot on German soil, he had decided to transfer his base of operations to Paris, and his first idea once there was to present some concerts. As he later told Mathilde Wesendonk,[1] "I had nothing in view but the possibility of a first performance of *Tristan* with German singers in Paris in May: that was the single goal toward which I was steering, on which I staked everything, and especially the frantic strain of these three concerts." In order to include the *Tristan* Prelude in those concerts, Wagner devised his own concert ending for it, the full score of which he finished on December 8. By the 15th, he had finished a neat and beautiful draft of it on two staves, essentially a fair copy of his Developed Draft, for Mathilde's birthday on the 23rd. On the reverse side of the same sheet,[2] he wrote out for her a fair copy of the program note he intended to use in the concert programs (see below, pp. 47–48). The letter he sent along with this gift includes the following passage:[3]

> You know Hans wanted to perform the prelude last winter, and asked me to make an ending for it. At that time no inspiration could have come to me: it seemed so impossible that I flatly refused. Since then, however, I have written the third act and found the complete ending for the whole thing, so while outlining the program for a Paris concert—the particular temptation to which was my wish to get a hearing of the *Tristan* Prelude— it occurred to me to foreshadow that ending as a dawning presentiment of redemption. Well, it has succeeded quite admirably, and today I am sending you this mysteriously soothing ending as the best thing I can give you for your birthday. I have written the passage out for you pretty much as I play it on the piano to myself. There are a few nasty stretches in it, and I expect you'll have to fish up some Roman Baumgartner[4] to play the thing for you, unless you would rather play it with him 4 hands, in which case you'll have to adapt the right-hand part for your two hands. Now see what you can make of this difficult gift! — Now you will understand better what I have written as an explanation of the whole prelude for my Paris audience: it stands on the other side of the calligraphic specimen. Ivy and vine you will recognize in the music, particularly when you hear an orchestra play it, where strings and winds alternate with each other.

1. *Wagner an Mathilde Wesendonk*, p. 214. Translation by William Ashton Ellis, *Richard Wagner to Mathilde Wesendonck*, New York, 1911, p. 211, modified by the Editor.

2. A facsimile of this sheet appears in both the German and English editions of the Wesendonk correspondence.

3. *Wagner an Mathilde Wesendonk*, pp. 201–2. Translation by Ellis, pp. 198–99, modified by the Editor.

4. Wilhelm Baumgartner (1820–67) was a piano teacher in Zurich and an intimate of the Wagner-Wesendonk circle. Wagner's reference to a Roman Baumgartner derives from the fact that the Wesendonks were in Rome when he addressed this letter to Mathilde.

It will turn out quite beautifully. I expect to hear it in the middle of January, when I'll listen to it for both of us.

This letter is probably responsible for the familiar description of the concert ending as simply a duplication of the conclusion of Act III, whereas it actually begins (mm. 93a–101a) with a passage from the middle of Act II. Wagner uses the first seven measures of the orchestral interlude preceding Tristan's line "O sink' hernieder" at their original pitch level and repeats the last five of those measures an octave lower. Only then does he append a transposed revision of the conclusion of Act III, beginning from m. 1681.

Bülow arrived in Paris on January 17, in part to give some piano recitals, but mostly to help Wagner out with the onerous task of copying parts (for which Wagner also employed some of the destitute German musicians in the city), and with the rehearsals, particularly the choral ones. Wagner also took this opportunity to expand the coda of his overture to *The Flying Dutchman*, a project he finished on January 19. After a certain amount of haggling for a hall, the Théâtre Italien (Salle Ventadour) was settled upon, which, as Newman has pointed out,[5] is the "old Théâtre de la Renaissance under another name." The rehearsals for the concerts were held in the Salle Herz, and the first one hit Wagner like a lightning bolt. He told Mathilde about it shortly after the first concert:[6]

Everything I have experienced is as nothing against one observation, one discovery, which I made at the first orchestral rehearsal for my concert, since it has determined the whole remainder of my life, and its consequences are going to tyrannize me from now on. I was conducting the *Tristan* Prelude for the first time; and—scales fell from my eyes with regard to the immeasurable distance I have traveled from the world during these last eight years. This little Prelude was so inscrutably *new* to the musicians that I at once had to lead my players from note to note as if we were exploring for precious stones in a mine.

Bülow, who was present, confessed to me that the performances attempted of this piece in Germany had been taken on trust and faith by the audience, but in itself it had remained entirely unintelligible. I succeeded in making this prelude intelligible to the orchestra and to the audience, yes—people assure me it produced the most profound impression. But don't ask me *how* I managed that! Enough that it now stands

---

5. Newman, *Life*, Vol. 3 (New York, 1941), p. 4.
6. *Wagner an Mathilde Wesendonk*, p. 206. Translation by Ellis, pp. 202–3, modified by the Editor.

sharply and clearly before me that I must not think of creating anything further until I've filled out the dreadful gap behind me. I *must* perform my works first. * * *

The concerts took place on January 25, February 1, and February 8.[7] Evidently following a suggestion made by Mathilde, who thought it too intimate, Wagner withheld the extended program note about the *Tristan* Prelude with concert ending he had sent to her and substituted for it a "short note about the subject" of the opera:[8]

> Now I'll tell you a little more about the concerts. The strings were splendid—32 violins, 12 violas, 12 cellos, 8 double basses: an extremely sonorous mass which would have given you great joy to hear. The rehearsals were still scarcely sufficient, and I was not yet able to extort the proper *piano*. The winds were merely partly good; none of them had any energy, the oboe in particular remained pastoral all the time and never rose to passion. The horns were miserable and cost me many a sigh: the unfortunate players excused their numerous false entrances by the terrifying effect of my signal to them. Trombones and trumpets had no brilliance. Everything was finally made up for, however, by the really great enthusiasm for me which seized the whole orchestra from first to last musician and proclaimed itself so openly throughout the performance that Berlioz is said to have been stupefied.
>
> Thus the three evenings turned out to be actual festivals, and as far as demonstrations of enthusiasm go, the Zurich festivals [Wagner's concerts of May 1853] were a mere shadow compared to them. The audience was fascinated from the outset. * * * The prelude to *Tristan* was played to my satisfaction only in the third concert: on that evening it gave me a great deal of pleasure. Even the audience seemed thoroughly stirred by it, for when an objector ventured to hiss—after the applause—such a storm broke forth, and so intense, protracted, and continually renewed, that I, poor fellow, got really embarrassed on the platform and had to ask people with gestures to stop finally, for god's sake, I was completely satisfied; but that sent the temperature up again, and the storm broke loose all over again. In short, I've never yet experienced anything like it.

As often happened at Wagner's concerts, the favorable reception by the audience was not matched by that of the press. Ernest Newman gives an effective summary:[9]

---

7. Aside from the *Tristan* Prelude and the *Flying Dutchman* Overture, the programs were made up entirely of excerpts from *Tannhäuser* and *Lohengrin*. For further details on the concerts and Wagner's situation at this time, see Newman, *Life* 3, Chapter 1.

8. *Wagner an Mathilde Wesendonk*, pp. 212–13. Translation by Ellis, pp. 209–10, modified by the Editor.

9. Newman, *Life* 3, p. 7.

With his usual contempt for the critics, Wagner sent out no tickets for the Press. The journalists were there in full force, however, and their comments were almost wholly unfavourable: Wagner had for him virtually only his friend Gasperini and a writer personally unknown to him at that time—Emile Perrin, of the *Revue Européenne*, who had been Director of the Opéra-Comique, and was later to become the Director of the Grand Opéra. Azevedo complained that he had heard only two good phrases the whole evening, "and two good phrases in three hours is rather little." Another critic plaintively wondered why Wagner, instead of losing himself in abstruse harmonies and modulations, did not elect to "write music like other people": were he to do that, he would "take a high place in art." "If this is true music", cried another, "I prefer the false." "Fifty years of this music", wailed the critic of the *Ménestrel*, "and music is dead; for melody will have been slain, and melody is the soul of music." Others opined that there was the making of quite a good composer in this Richard Wagner if only he would not "reject the past absolutely" and work on a "system".

Probably the most objective review Wagner received for these concerts, but also the one that most upset him, was by Hector Berlioz, to whom Wagner had presented one of the first copies of the newly published full score of *Tristan* on January 21. Berlioz did not acknowledge receipt of the score until three weeks later, and he waited until after the third of Wagner's concerts to print his review. The *Tristan* Prelude was the last piece he discussed:[10]

> I have not yet spoken about the instrumental introduction to Wagner's latest opera, *Tristan and Isolde*. It is odd that the composer performed it at the same concert as the introduction to *Lohengrin*, considering that in both he has followed the same plan. Here again, we have a slow movement—begun *pianissimo*, increasing gradually to *fortissimo*, and returning to the dynamic level of its starting point—without any theme other than a sort of chromatic sigh, but full of dissonant chords, the cruelty of which is still further increased by long-held appoggiaturas replacing real notes of the harmony.
>
> I have read the score of this strange piece again and again. I have listened to it with the most profound attention and with an earnest wish to discover what it means. But I am forced to admit that I still do not have the least idea of what the composer wanted to do.

Insofar as Berlioz was seriously trying to be objective, his *review*—as distinct from his polemic about the "music of the future" which comprises

10. The review appeared in the *Journal des Débats* for February 9, 1860, and was reprinted in Berlioz's *A travers chants* of 1862. A recent critical edition of the latter publication was made by Léon Guichard (Paris, 1971), pp. 321–33.

more or less the second half of his article—contains a highly revealing statement of an intelligent musician's reaction to the *Tristan* Prelude when it was absolutely new. Except for this Prelude, the program consisted entirely of excerpts from Wagner's early operas—*The Flying Dutchman, Tannhäuser,* and *Lohengrin,* with nothing whatever from the intervening period. Wagner may have felt that he succeeded in making the piece intelligible to most of the audience, but he obviously did not succeed with Berlioz. What upset Wagner, however, was not so much Berlioz's review, which concludes with the above paragraph, but his well-known diatribe against "music of the future," which Wagner could not help but interpret as a deliberate and willful misunderstanding of his artistic ideas. In another passage from that same letter to Mathilde Wesendonk of March 3, Wagner confided his private view of the matter:[11]

> Berlioz has fallen victim to envy; my efforts to remain friends with him have been without success because of my music's brilliant reception, which is intolerable to him. In fact, he finds himself seriously crossed by my appearance in Paris on the eve of a performance of his *Trojans*; moreover, his unlucky star has given him a wicked wife, who lets herself be bribed to influence her very weak and ailing husband. His behavior to me has constantly wavered between friendly inclination and recoil from an object of envy. He published his review, which you may well have read, very late, yet in such a way that he was not obliged to record his impression of a repeated hearing of my music. I had to consider it desirable to reply to his ambiguous, even malicious reference to the question of the "music of the future." You will find this reply in the *Journal des Débats* for February 22.

That reply is the *Open Letter to Hector Berlioz,*[12] and Berlioz's diatribe was also a significant part of the background which led to Wagner's essay of the following summer, published in France as an *Open Letter to a French Friend* (Frédéric Villot, the curator of the Louvre) and soon afterward in Germany as *"Zukunftsmusik."*[13] In this essay, Wagner attempted to dissociate himself from that label once and for all. The

11. *Wagner an Mathilde Wesendonk,* p. 211. Translation by Ellis, pp. 207–8, modified by the Editor.

12. A German translation appeared soon afterward in the *Neue Zeitschrift für Musik* 52/9 and 10 (March 2 and 9, 1860), reprinted in Vol. 7 of Wagner's *Gesammelte Schriften und Dichtungen,* and in English translation in William Ashton Ellis, *Richard Wagner's Prose Works,* Vol. 3 (London, 1894, reprinted New York, 1966).

13. Reprinted in *Gesammelte Schriften,* Vol. 7. The best English translation is in Edward L. Burlingame, *Art, Life and Theories of Richard Wagner,* 2nd ed. (New York, 1909), pp. 132–89.

details of this controversy lie outside the scope of the present volume, but Ernest Newman effectively summarizes Berlioz's role:[14]

> * * * If Berlioz had had the smallest understanding of Wagner's aesthetic he must have known that his own version of it was the crudest parody: if he had no direct knowledge of that aesthetic he had no business to represent it as he merely imagined it to be, and, for his own ill-natured journalistic purposes, would fain have it be.

In any case, an open-minded member of the audience at the final concert, a certain Paul Challemel-Lacour, struck to the heart of the matter in a letter to a friend on February 10:[15]

> Yesterday we went to Wagner's last concert. The hall was practically full, but there were evidently many free tickets. It seems to me beyond doubt that there is something in him—power, an absolute horror of the conventional, possibly genius. This will perhaps be disputed, for there is no limit to the venality, the ignorance, the spirit of routine, in a word the infamy of our journalism—the *Débats* excepted. I saw Berlioz: he seemed to me to be applauding heartily. As for a success in the theatre, that is another matter. The Parisian public is neither musical nor religious nor artistic: it merely wants to be amused. Wagner has not descended, and for his own sake I hope he never will descend, low enough to become a purveyor to our pleasures. Another trouble is that Wagner has a system: this would be no more than an inconvenience for his talent if he merely demonstrated it in his works, but he has made himself the theoretician of it. Now nothing frightens a timid public, the slave of success and tradition, so much as the idea that someone is trying to impose a system on it. It will be in vain that Wagner has written beautiful, superb music, such as the overture to *Tristan and Isolde*: the imbeciles, that is to say the public, will always be afraid that they are going to listen to a pleading instead of to hear an opera.

The press notwithstanding, Wagner regarded his concerts as in every sense an *artistic* success, but they were certainly not a financial success. The deficit was sufficiently great, in fact, that Wagner was persuaded to give another set of three concerts in Brussels in hopes of making up for what he had lost in Paris. He gave two of the projected three concerts there on March 24 and 28, by which time it was clear that the Paris problems were being duplicated, and Wagner returned to Paris on the 29th.

Marie Kalergis eventually gave Wagner a gift of 10,000 francs to

14. Newman, *Life* 3, p. 19.
15. Translation by Newman, ibid., pp. 16–17.

offset the debts of the Paris concerts, and in early May a reading of the second act of *Tristan* was given in her honor at the house of Pauline Viardot-Garcia, who sang the female parts, while Wagner himself sang the others. Karl Klindworth, who had come over from London for the occasion at Wagner's expense, accompanied at the piano. The only guests present seem to have been Mlle Kalergis herself and Berlioz, evidently invited by Viardot-Garcia. This is all that ever came of Wagner's hopes for a production of the opera in Paris.

The most practical outcome of Wagner's Paris concerts was precisely what Berlioz had probably feared all along. As a result of Princess Metternich's intervention with the emperor, Wagner received a commission from the Opéra, something that Berlioz himself never achieved. *Tristan* was now shelved in favor of *Tannhäuser*. Meanwhile, however, Wagner had learned a crucial lesson from his Paris concerts: it had been a mistake to plunge the audience into something as new as the *Tristan* Prelude in a concert that otherwise contained only excerpts from the early operas. He would write two new scenes for *Tannhäuser*, and they would at least set his newly found compositional idiom in the context of something more familiar. And in the future, his concerts would concentrate on excerpts from his as yet unperformed operas—*Das Rheingold, Die Walküre,* and the first act of *Siegfried,* as well as *Tristan*—in order thereby to bring his audience up to date.

Wagner's Return to Germany

The imperial commission for *Tannhäuser* had the beneficial side effect of persuading the King of Saxony and his advisers to grant Wagner a partial amnesty in July 1860, whereby Wagner was allowed to return to any of the German states except Saxony itself.[1] In May 1861, just a few weeks after the third and last scandalous performance of *Tannhäuser,* Wagner went to Vienna where he attended a two-hour morning

1. The full pardon, which finally allowed Wagner to reenter Saxony, did not come through until the end of March 1862.

rehearsal for *Lohengrin* on the 11th and the first performance he ever heard of the opera on the 15th. In addition, the Vienna Opera gave a performance of *The Flying Dutchman* in his honor on the 18th. The two operas were extraordinarily successful, and on both occasions, Wagner received an overwhelmingly favorable reception from the company as well as the audience. Wagner also discovered here a group of singers that seemed appropriate and qualified for *Tristan*, and he eagerly entered into the discussions initiated by the management about a possible production of the new opera later in the year.

On his way back to Vienna in August, Wagner—primarily in order not to offend Liszt—stopped off at Weimar to attend the second *Tonkünstler-Versammlung*, held there from the 4th through the 8th. Nothing by Wagner was performed during this Congress, but the assembled musicians welcomed their colleague back to Germany after his long absence, thus making him in a sense the hero of the occasion.[2] The most significant achievement of the Congress was to establish a new formal organization with the official name of *Allgemeiner deutscher Musikverein*.

Wagner returned to Vienna in order to begin rehearsals for the projected *Tristan* production, but it soon became apparent to him that the production was not going to materialize. As Newman summarized the situation:[3]

> * * * The Press was already making it clear that it had no particular affection for either Wagner or his *Tristan*; and the Opera management, while cordiality itself with Wagner to his face, was already regretting its promises to him and only looking round for a valid pretext for not carrying them out. He was soon to realize that the far-famed Viennese charm was not much more than skin-deep. It had never occurred to the Opera people that Wagner would take quite literally their request to him to be back in Vienna by the 14th August, in order to start rehearsals for a production alleged to be contemplated in early October!

At a performance of *The Flying Dutchman* attended by the Prince and Princess Metternich, the princess presented Wagner with a silver laurel

2. Wagner's account of these events appears at the beginning of Part 4 of his autobiography, *My Life* (London, 1911), pp. 787–89. The suppressed passages from this section will be found in Ernest Newman, *Fact and Fiction about Wagner* (London, 1931), p. 199.

Another eyewitness account, not available in translation, occurs in W. Weissheimer, *Erlebnisse mit Richard Wagner, Franz Liszt und vielen anderen Zeitgenossen nebst deren Briefen* (Stuttgart, 1898), pp. 68–78.

3. Newman, *Life* 3, p. 147.

wreath as a "token of gratitude." By way of repaying her interest, Wagner requested a morning rehearsal of some passages from *Tristan* with the orchestra and some of the principal singers involved with the projected production—a rehearsal rather along the lines of the one he had attended for *Lohengrin* back in May. Luise Meyer-Dustmann was to sing the Isolde, Marie Destinn[4] the Brangäne, and Aloys Ander the Tristan. The rehearsal Wagner conducted took place on October 26, Ander in attendance "without knowing a single note of the music or attempting to sing it."[5] Princess Metternich was part of the small audience, as was also Peter Cornelius, who had coached the singers. Two days later, Cornelius sent a report about the event to Carl Tausig:[6]

> The day you wrote to me was a significant one, because at perhaps exactly the same time, the first strains of *Tristan und Isolde* were heard in the opera house. As Standhartner told me, Wagner had written a most gracious letter to the orchestra and requested this rehearsal. Beforehand we were at Fräulein Destinn's once more, and he was relatively satisfied. In addition to that, I even went through the proposed passages with Frau Dustmann on two evenings. — In that rehearsal, the orchestra achieved something unheard of. The Introduction, the first scene of Act II, the A-flat major passage in the duet, Brangäne's song, and the conclusion of the opera (Isolde) were played. Everything twice, and it all went just as it would in a final dress rehearsal. Unfortunately, Esser had to play the music for the stage-horns on the piano. — Those were two lovely hours. How beautiful it all is! I am now convinced that the opera will have the most decisive success right at its first performance. * * *

Heinrich Esser, slated to conduct the performances, retained a different impression. In a letter of the very day after the rehearsal, he told Franz Schott:[7] "Everything is brilliantly devised and composed and scored with great imagination. A pleasing invention in the musical sense is not

4. She later married a composer, Thomas Loewe, and after his death, she became a vocal coach in Prague as Marie Loewe-Destinn (see Glasenapp, *Leben* 3, p. 344, n. 2). Among her most distinguished pupils was a certain Emmy Kittl, who out of gratitude to her teacher changed her name to Emmy Destinn when she made her debut at Dresden in 1897. See Michael Scott, *The Record of Singing* [Vol. 1]: *To 1914* (London, 1977), pp. 186–89.

5. *My Life*, p. 804.

6. Carl Maria Cornelius, ed., *Peter Cornelius: Literarische Werke*, Vol. 1: *Ausgewählte Briefe* (Leipzig, 1904), p. 616.

7. Quoted in Wilhelm Altmann, ed., *Richard Wagners Briefwechsel mit B. Schott's Söhne* (Mainz, 1911), p. 22, n. 3. Esser (1818–72) had succeeded Otto Nicolai (1810–49) as conductor of the Vienna Opera and held the post until 1869.

to be found in *Tristan*, however. It is music which is actually injurious to the health of nervous people."

A certain Dr. Gustav Schönaich, who was part of the audience, later told Glasenapp[8] that Wagner had caused considerable amusement in the orchestra when he called for the beginning of Isolde's monologue by saying, "Now then, gentlemen, the final cabaletta!"

It had now been two and a quarter years since Wagner finished *Tristan*, and as prospects for the Vienna production began to seem more and more remote, his situation—particularly his financial situation—was becoming progressively more desperate. He had already sold the completed portions of the *Ring* to Otto Wesendonk and got what money he could from Schott for the publication of their piano-vocal scores. Even though Wagner had determined in Paris to do no further creative work until he had performed his recent operas (the ones since *Lohengrin*), yet another opera now seemed the only viable solution to his quandry, and he broached the new project to Schott in his letter of October 30.[9] A month later, he returned to Paris, where he finished the poem for *Die Meistersinger* toward the end of January 1862. On February 1, Wagner moved out of Paris altogether. By the 8th, he had settled in Biebrich, where, with hopes for a *Tristan* production mostly frustrated, he proposed to write the music for his new opera. Wagner's strained relations with his wife caused delay, and he does not seem to have settled down to serious composition until near the end of March. By mid-July, he had worked his way to the point where Pogner is about to introduce Walther to the masters, when a dog bit his right thumb, making it impossible for him to write for two whole months. It was about this time that Wagner sold the *Wesendonk-Lieder* to Schott for 1,000 francs.

8. Glasenapp, *Leben* 3, pp. 344–45.
9. *Briefwechsel mit Schott*, pp. 23–24.

Coupling the Prelude and
the Transfiguration

An important figure in Wagner's activities during this period was Wendelin Weissheimer, an aspiring composer and conductor who had first introduced himself to Wagner by calling on him in Zurich in mid-July 1858, about a month before Wagner had left the *Asyl* for Venice. Wagner next encountered Weissheimer in Weimar in August 1861, where both men had attended the second *Tonkünstler-Versammlung*. Weissheimer was also present at a reading of *Tristan* that took place in Biebrich in July 1862, with the Bülows, the Schnorrs,[1] August Röckel and his daughter, and Luise Meyer-Dustmann from Vienna. Finally, Weissheimer attended a performance of *Lohengrin* in Frankfurt on September 12, the first complete *Lohengrin* Wagner himself conducted.

The next day, before Wagner returned to Biebrich, he and Weissheimer discussed a concert Weissheimer proposed to give in Leipzig. It was to include some of his own compositions, and Karl Riedel, the choral conductor, Wagner and Bülow, possibly even the Schnorrs were to participate.[2] Wagner's contribution was to be his new *Meistersinger* Prelude. By early October, Wagner had definitely decided to return to Vienna and present some concerts of his own, and in his letter to Weissheimer of October 5,[3] he elicited aid in lining up copyists and supervising their work for the selections chosen for these concerts. He continued as follows:

> Now as far as *our* concert in Leipzig is concerned, I've been feeling a bit scrupulous about whether it would be worth the trouble for me to perform only this one piece, the *Meistersinger* Prelude—given the expectations of the public which, it is to be hoped, will turn out in great numbers. It seems to me that I should do something else besides. If you and others are of the same view, then I suggest the following:
> "Fragment from *Tristan and Isolde*:
> a) Prelude.

1. Ludwig Schnorr von Carolsfeld (1836–65) and his wife Malvina (1832–1904) eventually sang the title roles in the *Tristan* premiere.
2. See Weissheimer, p. 162 *ff.*
3. Ibid., pp. 176–78.

      b) Final section of the opera (without the vocal part)."

This would work in such a way that after the Prelude—just as it stands in the full score of the opera, with the half-cadence on G in the double basses—*Mild und leise* (full score page 425, 2nd system) would follow without interruption. In this way, the whole thing would consist of two nice, mutually complementary companion-pieces. The conclusion in particular was extremely effective in the rehearsal I conducted in Vienna.

    I'd entitle the whole thing

      a) *"Liebestod."* Prelude.

      b) "Transfiguration." Conclusion of the opera.

Weissheimer was delighted with the prospect of Wagner performing another piece besides the *Meistersinger* Prelude, and he consulted with both Brendel and Riedel about it. The latter were both of the opinion that since the *Tristan* Prelude had already been heard in Leipzig in the first *Tonkünstler-Versammlung*, it would probably be better to do something else [since it was a flop?], and they suggested the *Tannhäuser* Overture, always a surefire success. Weissheimer passed along their suggestion, to which Wagner wholeheartedly acquiesced, claiming that his only concern was "to make a big splash in order to earn some money."[4] The concert took place on November 1, but Wagner performed his two overtures to a nearly empty house—so much for the public which they had hoped would turn out in great numbers! Weissheimer had to rely on his well-to-do father to help him meet the deficit, and Wagner once again came away with nothing.

    Nor, of course, did anything come for the time being of Wagner's idea to couple together the *Tristan* Prelude with the final section of the opera. Meanwhile, what had happened some time before to the *Tristan* Prelude was happening now to the *Meistersinger* Prelude: it had been performed, and would go on being performed for some time to come, as a separate piece before Wagner had even finished the opera. However, there are some critical differences between the two situations. With the *Meistersinger* Prelude, Wagner conducted the first performances himself with his own ending, and—far more important—he felt confident that it would not confound audiences because of what he had earlier described to Schott[5] as the opera's "thoroughly light and popular style."

    From Leipzig, Wagner continued on to Vienna to superintend the preparations for his concerts there. At one point, even Johannes Brahms was persuaded, presumably by Tausig or Cornelius, to lend a hand

---

4. Ibid., p. 178.
5. *Briefwechsel mit Schott*, p. 23.

copying parts,[6] but he and Wagner apparently did not meet until February 1864. The concerts took place on December 26, 1862, and on January 1 and 11 in the New Year. In order not to repeat the mistake of his Paris and Brussels programs, Wagner performed only excerpts from the finished portions of the *Ring* and even the still unfinished first act of *Die Meistersinger*, though in the third concert, he substituted *A Faust Overture* and the *Tannhäuser* Overture for two *Rheingold* selections. He withheld the *Tristan* Prelude entirely "so as not to conflict with the performance of the whole work at the Opera, which was still being advertised."[7]

The first of these concerts initiated a full year in which Wagner did almost nothing except give concerts—some twenty-one in all—in St. Petersburg and Moscow, Prague and Budapest, as well as Vienna and certain other German cities. During this period, Wagner's reputation as the first of the great modern conductors really began. His next concert took place in Prague on February 8, and Wagner reinstated the *Tristan* Prelude, probably in order to play his own ending in the city which had heard Bülow's less than satisfactory ending nearly four years before. This time, Franz Gerstenkorn's report to the *Neue Zeitschrift*[8] recalled Bülow's performance, but he did not mention the difference in endings, if he was even aware of it. Just before going off to Russia later that month, Wagner gave up his quarters in Biebrich, and after his return he temporarily settled in Vienna.

It was in the second of his Russian concerts, held in St. Petersburg on March 10, 1863,[9] that Wagner finally carried out the idea he had proposed to Weissheimer and conducted the first performance of the *Tristan* Prelude with the Transfiguration. He also included the pair of excerpts when he returned to Prague for two further concerts on

6. See *My Life*, p. 847. Wagner claims that Brahms worked on a section of *Die Meistersinger*, but a curious Wagner autograph from Brahms's collection—now in the Gesellschaft der Musikfreunde in Vienna—may indicate otherwise, or it may indicate that Brahms worked on something else besides. This autograph bears the inscription, *Rheingold: No. 2*—i.e., the second selection from *Das Rheingold* used in the concerts ["*Einzug der Götter*"]. Wagner wrote out just the first few measures of the brass parts from Scene 4, beginning from Wotan's lines "[Mit] bösem Zoll / zahlt' ich den Bau!" and thus indicated for the copyist the transpositions he wanted in the parts.

7. Ibid., p. 847. Translation modified by the Editor.

8. *Neue Zeitschrift für Musik* 58/9 (February 27, 1863): 74.

9. February 26 in the Russian calendar. The Editor is grateful to John Deathridge for information about the date and program of this concert.

November 5 and 8.[10]

The last concert of this lengthy series took place back in Vienna in the Redouten-Saal on December 27, 1863, as a joint venture with the pianist Carl Tausig. Wagner now included the pair of *Tristan* excerpts, since the ill-fated production of the opera had been finally canceled the previous spring. He had originally intended to include the two forging songs from the first act of *Siegfried*, but owing to the indisposition of the tenor, he substituted the *Freischütz* Overture,[11] which excited greater interest than anything else on the program. F. P. Laurencin's report for the *Neue Zeitschrift*[12] devoted an extensive paragraph to Wagner's performance of the Weber piece and a mere two sentences of "short but pithy characterization" to the *Tristan* excerpts. He called them "truly unique things" and claimed that they were "among those very few creations that bear comparison only with the greatest ever offered to us from the entire range of artistic epochs."

Eduard Hanslick was of a different opinion.[13] He described the *Tristan* excerpts as

> discomforting music, if music at all. In the Prelude, a whining motive of five notes is pursued in "endless"[14] development, which is to say repeated— sometimes higher, sometimes lower, now by this instrument, now by that one—without any contrasting section or point of repose whatever. This chromatic wailing, with its incessant diminished-seventh chords and the overstrained sensual appetite of its orchestration, was intensely irritating to the nerves. If one had the capacity to abstract from this impression and to verify calmly, one would find the piece simply boring. The same thing applies to the noisier but musically just as impoverished final section ("Transfiguration"). We found in it the accurate translation into music of the poetic bombast which Wagner puts into the mouths of the two lovers and which reaches its culmination in the following concluding words:

> > "Liebe, heiligstes Beben,
> > Wonne-hehrstes Weben

---

10. *Neue Zeitschrift für Musik* 59/22 (November 27, 1863): 189. Gerstenkorn says very little about the pieces themselves, but he does at least list them and makes it clear that Wagner performed the Prelude and Transfiguration in both concerts.

11. See Glasenapp, *Leben* 3, pp. 444–45.

12. *Neue Zeitschrift für Musik* 60/5 (January 29, 1864): 42.

13. From Eduard Hanslick, *Aus dem Concert-Saal: Kritiken und Schilderungen aus 20 Jahren des Wiener Musiklebens, 1848–1868,* 2nd ed. (Vienna, 1897), pp. 327–29.

14. Hanslick sets off the word *unendlich* in quotation marks as a reference to *unendliche Melodie* (endless melody), a phrase which Wagner had introduced in his essay *"Zukunfts-musik."*

Nie-Wieder-Erwachens wahnlos
Hold bewusster Wunsch"!¹⁵

This is the very article in which Hanslick initiated his unfortunate attempt (echoed by many later writers) to set up Wagner and Brahms as artistic antipodes and, by extension, contemporaneous "rivals." Still clinging to his mistaken notions about "Music of the Future" in spite of Wagner's essay on the subject, which he had evidently read but not understood, Hanslick concluded the article with the following paragraph:

> After the Wagner pieces, we derived double pleasure from a new composition by Brahms, which was performed on the same day at the Hellmesberger Quartet's *soirée*. This is a Sextet in B♭ major, Op. 18, for two violins, two violas, and two cellos. We count this composition not only among Brahms's best, but altogether among the most beautiful productions of recent chamber music. The first movement in particular is of the most spontaneous freshness of invention, from beginning to end melodious, transparent, masterly in form and execution. The entire Sextet is simply and charmingly controlled in that clear, moderate, self-contented atmosphere which resounds so ingratiatingly from Brahms's D major Serenade. In their amiable beauty, such compositions are really the best critique and reply for the mighty feats of the Music of the Future. Brahms is an utter musician through and through, whereas what Plutarch reports about Damon, the music teacher of Pericles, could be said of Wagner or Liszt: "He was a sophist of the first order and seems to have hidden himself behind the name of music."

By early 1864, Wagner's fortunes had reached their absolute lowest ebb, so that in late March, he had no choice but to leave Vienna and

15. The exclamation mark at the end is Hanslick's own. It is not clear what he means by "concluding words" [*Schlussworte*]. In any case, these lines are not from the Transfiguration, but from Act II, Scene 2, just before Brangäne's first interruption. Hanslick mistakenly substitutes *Beben* for *Leben* in the first line, and he has taken the entire group of lines from the separate imprint of the poem, unaware that in the opera, Wagner reverses the order of the first two. That Hanslick did not consult the score before reviewing these excerpts is understandable: Bülow's piano-vocal arrangement had only been in print a little over three years.

If Wagner ever troubled to read Hanslick's article, which is unlikely, the conclusion of this passage can only have confirmed his own misgivings about a separate publication of the *Tristan* poem, as expressed in his letter to Mathilde Wesendonk of April 15, 1859: "It occurred to me [while reading Goethe's *Tasso*] that it was ill-advised for me to publish [the poem of] *Tristan* after all. The difference, in both design and realization, between a poem specifically calculated for music and a purely verbal poetic drama must be so fundamental that when the former is viewed with the same eye as the latter, its essential meaning must remain almost totally incomprehensible—precisely until it *has* been completed by music." [*Wagner an Mathilde Wesendonk*, p. 125.]

go into hiding. The extraordinary story of his sudden and utterly unexpected rescue by the newly ascended King of Bavaria, Ludwig II, reads like one of the most fantastic fairy tales of the nineteenth century. Even so, further problems lay ahead for Wagner—and they surfaced much sooner than anyone could possibly have anticipated—but for the time being and with a great sense of relief, he was content to settle down in Munich to complete his artistic projects and to produce his operas. On December 4, he conducted the first Munich performance of *The Flying Dutchman*, and a week later he conducted a concert in the theater, which included the *Tristan* excerpts, definite plans having already been officially formulated for a production of that opera the following spring. For this concert, Wagner used the Program Notes reproduced below on pp. 47–48, as he had probably also done in both Prague and Vienna. Additional performances of these particular excerpts occurred in two "private" concerts for the king in the *Residenz-Theater* on February 1 and July 12, 1865. Meanwhile, after a great many problems and delays, Hans von Bülow had finally conducted the premiere of *Tristan* in the *Nationaltheater* on June 10.

Coda: The Title "Liebestod"

The premiere of *Tristan* forms the real conclusion to our history of the concert excerpts Wagner extracted from the opera and performed before the opera's premiere, but the title *"Liebestod"* merits special consideration. The word (also occasionally found in the form *Liebes-Tod*) actually appears in the text of the opera toward the end of the love scene in Act II, and we have seen that when Wagner appropriated it as the title for an instrumental excerpt, he consistently and exclusively used it for the Prelude to Act I. *Liebestod* thus defines a musical representation of a "state-of-mind" or psychological reference point, which exists *before* the action of the opera we witness. In the course of the opera itself, there are several musical recalls of that particular state. Thus, in Wagner's view the opera does not culminate in *Liebestod*, but rather presents *Liebestod* by purely musical means before the curtain opens on the first act.

Nowadays, however, and in fact during most of this century, *Liebestod* has unfortunately become the title for Isolde's concluding monologue, which, as we have also seen, Wagner consistently called Transfiguration. The person responsible for this misleading change seems to have been none other than Franz Liszt, who in 1867 made a piano transcription of Isolde's monologue (with his own "concert beginning"—see below, p. 152) and called it *Isolden's Liebes-Tod.*[1] While Liszt's transcription has not been much in evidence in recent years, the change in title it effected shows how extremely influential arrangements of this sort actually were throughout the nineteenth and early twentieth centuries. That transcription, incidentally, may also be responsible for another equally drastic change in the world's view of this piece. Liszt's arrangement of the climax (mm. 1681–84) spans more than six octaves of the keyboard, requires a system of three staves for its realization, and bears the dynamic indication *fff*—

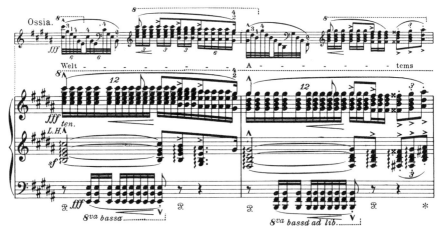

all of which effectively captures the spirit and character of most modern performances of the original version of this passage. As Richard Strauss was the first to point out[2] and one of very few to observe in actual

---

1. So it stands in Liszt's autograph, now in the Goethe- und Schiller-Archiv in Weimar. The Editor is grateful to Rena Mueller for this information.

2. In his "Nicht veröffentlichtes Vorwort zu *Intermezzo*" of 1924, in Willi Schuh, ed., *Richard Strauss: Betrachtungen und Erinnerungen*, 2nd ed. (Zurich, 1957), p. 138.

performance, Wagner's own dynamic indication in all instruments (the single harp alone excepted) is simply *forte*.

As late as 1903, Breitkopf & Härtel issued a set of parts for the Transfiguration with vocal part and still used the "correct" title (*Isolde's Verklärung*).[3] The one really odd feature of this publication is its "concert beginning"—not Liszt's—which in the piano-vocal score, included with the parts, runs as follows:

The last two of these seven introductory measures are, of course, the very two which precede the Transfiguration in the opera. The first five measures also appear in the opera, but as the conclusion of Act III, Scene 2. The version shown above corresponds exactly to Hans von Bülow's piano-vocal score of the passage from Act III, Scene 2, except for the bass-line ascent to d♭ on the last sixteenth note of m. 5. This separate piano-vocal score existed with this "concert beginning" for some time before the firm issued the orchestral parts. When they decided to do so, they obviously did not realize that these measures exist in Wagner's opera, for they got someone to score them up from the piano version. Bülow's left-hand figure in the second half of m. 2, for example, became a counterpoint for the English horn, which Wagner did not employ at all in these measures!

3. Under Plate No. Orch[ester] B[ibliothek] 1387. A copy of this set of parts, including the piano-vocal score, is in the Music Library of the University of California at Berkeley.

WAGNER'S
PROGRAM NOTES

Prelude

[with the Concert Ending]†

An old, old tale, inexhaustible in its variations, and ever sung anew in all the languages of medieval Europe, tells us of Tristan and Isolde. For his king the trusty vassal had wooed a maid he dared not tell himself he loved, Isolde; as his master's bride she followed him, because, powerless, she had no choice but to follow the suitor. The Goddess of Love, jealous of her downtrodden rights, avenged herself: the love potion destined by the bride's careful mother for the partners in this merely political marriage, in accordance with the customs of the age, the Goddess foists on the youthful pair through a blunder diversely accounted for; fired by its draught, their love leaps suddenly to vivid flame, and they have to acknowledge that they belong only to each other. Henceforth no end to the yearning, longing, rapture, and misery of love: world, power, fame, honor, chivalry, loyalty, and friendship, scattered like an insubstantial dream; one thing alone left living: longing, longing unquenchable, desire forever renewing itself, craving and languishing; one sole redemption: death, surcease of being, the sleep that knows no waking!

Here in music's own most unrestricted element, the musician who chose this theme for the introduction to his drama of love could have but one care: how to impose restraint on himself, since exhaustion of the subject is impossible. So just once, in one long-articulated impulse, he let that insatiable longing swell up from the timidest avowal of the most delicate attraction, through anxious sighs, hopes and fears, laments and wishes, raptures and torments, to the mightiest onset and to the most powerful effort to find the breach that will reveal to the infinitely craving heart the path into the sea of love's endless rapture. In vain!

† From *Richard Wagner's Prose Works*, trans. by William Ashton Ellis, Vol. 8, (London, 1899), pp. 386–7. Translation modified by the Editor.

Its power spent, the heart sinks back to languish in longing, in longing without attainment, since each attainment brings in its wake only renewed desire, until in final exhaustion the breaking glance catches a glimmer of the attainment of highest rapture: it is the rapture of dying, of ceasing to be, of the final redemption into that wondrous realm from which we stray the furthest when we strive to enter it by force. Shall we call it Death? Or is it the miraculous world of Night, from which, as the story tells, an ivy and a vine sprang of old in inseparable embrace over the grave of Tristan and Isolde?

Prelude and Transfiguration†

Prelude (Liebestod)

As suitor, Tristan transports Isolde to his king and uncle. The two are in love. From the timidest lament in inappeasable longing, the tenderest shudder, to the most terrible outpouring of an avowal of hopeless love, the sentiment traverses all phases of the vain struggle against inner ardor, until this, sinking back powerless upon itself, seems to be extinguished in death.

Final Section (Transfiguration)

Yet what Fate divided in life now springs into transfigured life in death: the gates of union are thrown open. Over Tristan's body the dying Isolde receives the blessed fulfilment of ardent longing, eternal union in measureless space, without barriers, without fetters, inseparable!

† From *The Wagner Operas* by Ernest Newman (New York, 1949), p. 205. Newman's translation modified and completed by the Editor.

THE SCORES OF
THE PRELUDE AND
TRANSFIGURATION

INSTRUMENTATION

3 Flutes (*Fl.*)
III doubles on Piccolo (*Picc.*)
2 Oboes (*Ob., Hb.*)
1 English Horn (*E.H.*) in F
2 Clarinets (*Clar., Kl.*) in A
1 Bass Clarinet (*B. Clar.*) in A
3 Bassoons (*Bsn., Fg.*)

4 Horns (*Hr.*) in F, E
(The notes marked + are to be played as stopped tones.)
3 Trumpets (*Tr.*) in F, E
3 Trombones (*Trb., Pos.*)
1 Tuba

1 Harp

Timpani (*Timp., Pk.*) [Wagner suggests 3 kettledrums rather than the usual 2, to facilitate changes in tuning.]

[16] Violin I (*Vl., V.*)
[16] Violin II (*Vl., V.*)
[12] Viola (*Va., Br.*)
[12] Cello (*Vc.*)
[8] Double Bass (*D.B., Kb.*)

N.B.: In the remainder of the opera, the clarinets and bass clarinet alternate transposition in A with transposition in B♭. Aside from stage instruments, Wagner otherwise follows the instrumentation listed above consistently, except for the addition of triangle and cymbals during the last 60 measures of Act I.

Wagner did not specify the precise number of strings in the published score. The figures given here correspond to those used for the Paris performances of the Prelude, as reported in his letter to Mathilde Wesendonk (see above, p. 28). From that point on, Wagner always considered these figures ideal, and he did specify them in the four *Ring* scores published later.

PRELUDE

Langsam und schmachtend.

feeling — slowly emotively (handwritten annotation)

greater liveliness

allmählich im Zeitmaß etwas zurückhaltend

The two different endings proceed from this point. The ending in the opera follows immediately, on p. 68; the concert ending begins on p. 70.

THE CONCLUSION IN THE OPERA

Transfiguration begins p. 76.

THE CONCERT ENDING

Immer zurückhaltend.

Immer zurückhaltend.

TRANSFIGURATION

1650

rau - schen, soll ich at - - men, soll ich lau - - schen? Soll ich

1690

Transfiguration:
Text and Translation

Isolde, die nichts um sie her vernommen, heftet das Auge mit wachsender Begeisterung auf Tristans Leiche.

Unaware of anything around her, Isolde fixes her eye with increasing rapture on Tristan's body.

Mild und leise
wie er lächelt,
wie das Auge
hold er öffnet:
seht ihr's, Freunde,
säh't ihr's nicht?
Immer lichter
wie er leuchtet,
stern-umstrahlet
hoch sich hebt?
Seht ihr's nicht?
Wie das Herz
ihm mutig schwillt,
voll und hehr
im Busen ihm quillt?
Wie den Lippen,
wonnig mild,
süsser Atem
sanft entweht: —
Freunde! Seht!
Fühlt und seht ihr's nicht?
Höre ich nur diese Weise,
die so wundervoll und leise,
Wonne klagend,
Alles sagend,
mild versöhnend
aus ihm tönend,
in mich dringet,
auf sich schwinget,

Mildly, gently,
see him smiling,
see his eyes
softly open:
Friends, behold him!
see you not?
Ever brighter
brightly shining,
borne in starlight
high above?
See you not?
How his heart
so proudly swells,
full and bold
it throbs in his breast?
Gentle breathing
stirs his lips;
ah, how calmly
soft his breath: —
See him, friends!
Feel and see you not?
Can it be that I alone
hear this wondrous, glorious tune,
softly stealing,
all revealing,
mildly glowing,
from him flowing,
through me pouring,
rising, soaring,

hold erhallend
um mich klinget?
Heller schallend,
mich umwallend,
sind es Wellen
sanfter Lüfte?
Sind es Wolken
wonniger Düfte?
Wie sie schwellen,
mich umrauschen,
soll ich atmen,
soll ich lauschen?
Soll ich schlürfen,
untertauchen,
süss in Düften
mich verhauchen?
In dem wogenden Schwall
in dem tönenden Schall
in des Welt-Atems
wehendem All—
ertrinken—
versinken—
unbewusst—
höchste Lust!

boldly singing,
round me ringing?
Brighter growing,
o'er me flowing,
are they waves
of tender radiance?
Are they clouds
of wonderful fragrance?
They are rising
high around me;
shall I breathe them,
shall I hear them?
Shall I taste them,
dive beneath them?
drown in tide
of melting sweetness?
In the rapturous swell,
in the turbulent spell,
in the welcoming wave,
holding all—
I'm sinking—
I'm drowning—
unaware—
highest love!

Isolde sinkt, wie verklärt, in Brangänes
Armen sanft auf Tristans Leiche. Grosse
Rührung und Entrücktheit unter den
Umstehenden.

As if transfigured, Isolde gently sinks in
Brangäne's arms onto Tristan's body.
Great compassion and emotion among the
bystanders.

(Der Vorhang fällt während der letzten
Fermate.)

(The curtain falls during the final fer-
mata.)

English translation for singing by
Andrew Porter
© 1981 Andrew Porter

Textual Note

This edition reprints the following scores:

Prelude with Concert Ending: Miniature score: "Partitur-Bibliothek Nr. 2375" (Leipzig: Breitkopf & Härtel, 1904, Plate 25,000).

Transfiguration: The score contained in *Fünf Vorspiele (Ouvertüren) und Isoldens Liebestod* (Leipzig: C. F. Peters, n.d., Plate 9847).

I have revised and corrected these scores to agree with Wagner's autographs as noted below. The operatic conclusion for the Prelude has been redrawn in order to avoid duplication and to minimize page turns.

PRELUDE AND TRANSFIGURATION

The definitive source for these two excerpts is Wagner's autograph full score of the opera, now in the Nationalarchiv der Richard-Wagner-Stiftung in Bayreuth. In 1923, it was published in a handsome facsimile edition of 530 copies by the Drei Masken Verlag of Munich. As indicated in my essay on Wagner's sketches and drafts (see p. 113), this manuscript actually consists of a fair copy of an earlier pencil full score for the Prelude, plus a first-draft full score for the remainder of the opera. In spite of Wagner's haste in writing much of it, the document poses no problems with regard to his intentions, since wherever errors did creep in, he corrected them carefully and clearly.

There have been countless separate issues of the Prelude and Transfiguration, but I have chosen to ignore them entirely and to list here only the few variants between Wagner's autograph and the three best printed scores of the opera. The most important of these, of course, is the first one, issued by Breitkopf & Härtel, for which Wagner's autograph actually served as the engraver's model (*Stichvorlage*), and for which Wagner himself and Hans von Bülow painstakingly corrected the proofs. The same plates, with the number changed to "R.W.v.," served also for the firm's later issue of the score in 1917, as Volume 5 of a projected complete edition of Wagner's works (reprinted 1971). For this publication, Michael Balling edited the music, Wolfgang Golther the verbal text.

Since it is so convenient and readily available, I have also taken into account the study score with Felix Mottl's performance suggestions, published shortly after Mottl's death in 1911 by C. F. Peters in Leipzig and variously reprinted by the firm itself and by both Broude Brothers and Dover Publications in New York. The only shortcoming of this score is its retention of the tenor clef for the vocal parts in that range.

Like these three scores of the opera, the present edition preserves Wagner's own disposition of the instrumental parts within a system. Wagner placed the horns with the woodwinds, rather than in between the woodwind and brass complements, and then in turn arranged horns-plus-woodwinds by register rather than by family group.

PRELUDE

44   Vla.: In the printed scores, the C♯ in the 2nd half of the measure lacks its tie to the C♯ in the next.

57   Horns in E: The Mottl score mistakenly gives F as the last eighth note.

94   Upper Horn in F and upper Horn in E: The printed scores give > instead of ———————

100   D.B.: The printed scores give f instead of sf.

TRANSFIGURATION

1668   Harp: The printed scores lack indications for arpeggiation of the chords in the treble staff.

Final measures   The stage direction, "Marke segnet die Leichen" (Marke blesses the corpses), is present in both manuscripts of the poem and also in the first imprint of the poem (early 1859), from which it was taken over into the various editions of Wagner's *Gesammelte Schriften*. But Wagner changed his mind on this point, as on many others in the text, during composition of the music, and he omitted the direction in his autograph full score. It was "restored" in the Mottl score and (by Golther) in the 1917 Breitkopf score, evidently on the assumption that Wagner did not always take the trouble to write out all his stage directions in his mature full scores. Nothing could be further from the truth. The same logic would require restoration of the direction, near the end of the third act of *Parsifal*, for the deceased Titurel to sit up in his coffin—a direction which appears in the original 1877 imprint of the poem, but which Wagner later eliminated during composition.

THE CONCERT ENDING
FOR THE PRELUDE

Once again, the present edition conforms to Wagner's autograph full score, in this case exceptionally neat and fastidious in every respect. The three-page manuscript passed into the hands of Carl Tausig, who in turn gave it to Johannes Brahms, probably sometime in 1864.[1] Along with

---

1. See Karl Geiringer, "Wagner and Brahms, With Unpublished Letters," in *The Musical Quarterly* 22 (1936): 180.

much of the rest of Brahms's estate, it is now part of the collection of the Gesellschaft der Musikfreunde in Vienna.

Unlike the autograph full score of the opera, this manuscript appears not to have been used as the engraver's model for Breitkopf's publication. In his letter of December 25, 1859 to the firm, Wagner said he would send along a *copy* from which the three additional plates could be engraved,[2] although he did not actually send anything until two months later.[3] The separate publication of the Prelude with its concert ending appeared in early May 1860,[4] but the three new plates are much less accurate than those for the printed score of the opera. Wagner probably never saw proofs for them at all, and assuming he corrected the copy he supplied, the firm was careless in making the necessary corrections. Nonetheless, this publication remained the only available full score of the concert ending until Breitkopf & Härtel's early twentieth-century edition in miniature-score format (with most of the same errors), which is reprinted in this volume. The following list details the variants between Wagner's autograph and the two printed scores.

93a	V. II: The G♯ lacks its tie to the G♯ in the following measure.
94a	V. I: B in the lower part incorrectly printed as a half note.
	Va.: Dynamic indication missing.
	Ob.: In the printed scores, the second dynamic indication (*più* ***p***) is squeezed in too early in the measure.
97a–98a	Bsn: These parts are quite thoroughly garbled. In Bsn. I, the rests in the latter part of m. 97a are omitted, and upward stems are incorrectly added to the notes in m. 98a. For Bsn. II, a ♮ is unaccountably added before the A in the first edition.
99a	V. II: Dynamic indication at the end of the measure missing.
	Va.: Dynamic indication is *più* ***p*** (rather than *dim.*) here and therefore omitted in the following measure.
101a	Clar. I: C rather than A for the penultimate thirty-second note.
102a	Clar. I: Tie for the two Cs lacking.
	D.B.: Downward stem incorrectly added to the D, indicating performance by the lower half of the divided section.
114a	Ob.: Ties for the two F♯s lacking in the first edition.
114a–116a	Trb. I & II: Printed scores give 
116a–118a	Ob.: Dynamic indications omitted for both parts. In addition, for Ob. I, the printed scores incorrectly reposition Wagner's tie as a slur between m. 116a and 117a, and omit the tie altogether between m. 117a and 118a.

2. Wilhelm Altmann, ed. *Richard Wagners Briefwechsel mit Breitkopf & Härtel* (Leipzig, 1911), pp. 182–83.

3. Ibid., p. 192.

4. Ibid., p. 198.

WAGNER'S
PRELIMINARY DRAFT

These transcriptions reproduce Wagner's corrections and revisions and, insofar as possible, duplicate his own methods of notating them. Toward the end of the Prelude where he entered a second version on top of the first, I have separated the two and placed them side by side for the sake of clarity. In any case, initial versions plus any changes are labelled with successive letters.

Measure numbers, where given, correspond to those of the Score.

Prelude

Adagio (langsam und schmachtend)

Transfiguration

weht Freunde, seht fühlt u. seht ihr's nicht

hö - re ich nur die - se Wei - se die so wun - der -

voll u. lei - se Won - ne kla - gend al - les sa - gend

mild ver - söhnend aus ihm tö - nend in mich dringet

auf   sich   schwinget   hold   er - hallend   um   mich   klingt

hel - ler   schal - lend   mich um - wal - lend   sind   es   Wel - len

sanf - ter   Lüf - te?   Sind   es   Wol - ken   won - ni - ger   Düf - te?

Wie sie schwel - len   mich um - rau - schen   soll   ich   ath - men,

An Analytical Study of the Sketches and Drafts

Wagner's method of composing the music for *Tristan* included three separate successive stages:

1. A hasty *Preliminary Draft* in pencil on small individual oblong sheets;
2. A much more carefully written and fully elaborated *Developed Draft* in ink on full-sized upright pages grouped in gatherings;
3. A final definitive *Full Score.*[1]

These three documents embodied compositional tasks sufficiently distinct and so well defined in Wagner's mind that he could shift from one to another at will, or concentrate for an extended period of time on any one of them.

In his Preliminary Draft, his primary tasks were setting his text to music and working out the essence of the purely instrumental passages. Wagner's approach to text setting involved the conception of a vocal part in conjunction with a structural bass line, and he therefore used at least two and sometimes three staves—one always reserved for the vocal part, the remainder for the bass line plus any preliminary notations of additional orchestral elaboration. Similarly, he always used at least two staves for the instrumental passages—one for the uppermost melodic line and another for the bass line—and he sometimes expanded to three staves if necessary. In passages with chorus or with two characters singing simultaneously, Wagner usually wrote out only the uppermost vocal part.

Wagner based this complete draft to some extent on earlier musical sketches, which varied considerably from one another in length and degree of elaboration, and he naturally made additional sketches as his work progressed. The few surviving examples of sketches for *Tristan* are found in the little pocket diaries he carried about with him, in the

---

1. A summary of the dates on which Wagner began and finished each act in the two complete drafts and Full Score appears on pp. 8–9. Wagner actually made a first draft of the Full Score in pencil and then a fair copy in ink—*but only for the Prelude*. He gave up the idea, presumably because of the pressure he felt to send off the score to the publisher. The rest of the Full Score is thus actually a first draft in ink. All these documents are now in the Nationalarchiv der Richard-Wagner-Stiftung, Bayreuth.

two manuscripts of the poem (Wagner's own, plus the copy made by Mathilde Wesendonk that he used to make the Preliminary Draft), but above all on occasional individual worksheets.[2] In any case, Wagner's tasks when making his Preliminary Draft are best summarized as primarily "invention"—particularly as regards the specific details of text setting—and also as "elaboration" (usually in the sense of mere extension), insofar as he based the musical fabric of this draft on earlier sketches. The degree to which Wagner elaborated the accompaniment at this stage varies considerably from one passage to another.

Wagner used this Preliminary Draft as the basis for the next stage in his procedure—a Developed Draft, in which he worked out the remaining details of the choral sections and the second vocal part for duet sections. His primary task here, however, was "elaboration" of the contrapuntal variety, for he now built up the full texture of the accompaniment from the two structural voices and whatever else the earlier draft contained. Thus, in addition to a separate staff for the vocal part, he now required at least two, and sometimes even three or more, staves for a uniformly complete presentation of the entire orchestral texture, which he worked out to the point of including the specific details of registral disposition and frequently even the instrumental doublings. The creative gap between these two complete drafts is often considerable, particularly for those passages where Wagner discarded his initial version, and in such situations, he undoubtedly resorted to intermediate sketches, of which only very few survive.

Wagner's goal in his Developed Draft was to write out the music so completely and definitively that once he had finished the document (or any passage within it), he could consider the act of original composition over and done with. From this point on, he made very few compositional changes, and in all cases he wrote them into his Developed Draft, usually in pencil to distinguish them readily from what was already there in ink. Thus, when he later used this draft as the basis for his final Full Score, he was able for the most part to ignore purely

2. The Editor has followed the line of least resistance and differentiated the two diaries connected with *Tristan* by their bindings: black-and-gold leather in one case, brown leather in the other. These diaries, both manuscripts of the poem, and all save one of the known work-sheets are now in the Nationalarchiv der Richard-Wagner-Stiftung, Bayreuth. The remaining worksheet is now in the Manuscript Division of the New York Public Library. The generosity and kindness of the late Winifred Wagner made it possible for the Editor to study Wagner's manuscripts, and his transcriptions appear in this volume with her gracious permission.

compositional questions and to concentrate on the special problems of orchestration.

On the other hand, Wagner frequently made compositional changes or reworked entire passages within the Preliminary Draft itself, and also between the completed Preliminary Draft and the Developed Draft. The Preliminary Draft, together with the surviving early and intermediate sketches, constitutes the only practical basis for studying some of the problems Wagner confronted while composing the music for *Tristan*. If we propose to do more than merely describe those problems— whether they be the tonal, harmonic, and motivic problems in the Prelude, or the problems of text setting and formal design in the Transfiguration—we must have some perspective from which to evaluate them. We can develop that perspective only through an analytical understanding of the work itself. Studying the sketches and drafts thus serves to direct our attention to particular points that merit analytical attention in the final version of the opera, and the understanding we gain through analysis in turn helps us to interpret Wagner's solutions to his compositional problems.

Meanwhile, owing to the unique historical position of *Tristan*—a single piece that marks a major turning point in the history of music— its Prelude has often served as a focus for discussions of later nineteenth-century tonal practice and harmonic vocabulary. In order to illuminate the new elements that surface in the musical language of *Tristan*, a brief review of some of the basic nineteenth-century modifications and extensions of harmony and tonality will be necessary, even though this may be surveying an already familiar terrain. Older principles remained with the system, of course, but the accretion of new ones inevitably wrought some variation in them. New ideas often resulted from the attribution of large-scale structural significance to relationships which were already implicit within the system and had served as mere foreground decoration. Much of our musical vocabulary has developed from analysis of tonal music before *Tristan*, and when we apply it to later compositions, we must be aware of the critical distinction between a term's *descriptive* meaning and its *functional* implications. For example, the word "dominant" on one level merely *describes* the fifth scale degree and, by extension, the triad or tonality based on that scale degree. In music which turns on a central axis of tonic and dominant, the *functional* implications of the word *dominant* become far-reaching indeed. Many terms are extremely problematic in the context of later tonal music precisely because of those *functional* implications, though we have no choice but to continue using most of them for basic description.

An immediately apparent principle of later nineteenth-century German tonal construction is modal mixture, the use of both the major and minor inflections of a given key. Schoenberg recognized the "transition from twelve major and twelve minor keys to twelve chromatic keys" and claimed that "this transition is fully accomplished in the music of Wagner, the harmonic significance of which has not yet by any means been theoretically formulated."[3] The terms *major* and *minor* remain useful, of course, but only for the purpose of identifying the qualities of particular triads. When we want to identify the tonality of large sections, or that of whole pieces or movements, it is best simply to refer to the key by itself and to avoid specifying mode, precisely because the "chromatic" or mixed major-minor mode is so often utilized.[4] By extension, the sense that a passage from a piece, or an entire movement, is in the major mode or in the minor mode is usually no more than an illusion, created by restricting the particular inflection of the *tonic triad* during the passage or movement in question to its major or minor form. Otherwise, the major and minor modes have by this point become equivalent and interchangeable, so that either one can substitute for the other. Where both forms appear in alternation, local voice leading, in terms of the specific voice or voices carrying the third of any triad, is the mechanism which controls the triad's actual mode.

It seems strange nowadays that the tonality of the *Tristan* Prelude can ever have been seriously disputed. When Hans von Bülow constructed his own ending for the excerpt, he clearly never considered any alternative to A, and his letter about it to Wagner shows that he was also aware that the Prelude "seems to shift between major and minor."[5] Wagner's concert ending concludes in A, with the major form of the tonic triad. In 1924, Lorenz declared that the Prelude was unequivocally in A minor,[6] and he summarily dismissed Guido Adler's earlier and much more suggestive idea that the introduction had not a single tonic, but that instead it fluctuated between A minor and C major/

3. Arnold Schoenberg, *Theory of Harmony*, trans. Roy E. Carter (Berkeley, 1978), p. 389.

4. Many early twentieth-century theorists—Hugo Riemann, Alfred Lorenz, and even Ernst Kurth, for example—continue to insist upon the independence of major and minor keys, and that insistence occasionally lands them in considerable difficulty.

5. The complete passage from Bülow's letter appears above, p. 14.

6. See below, p. 214, n. 21.

minor.[7] Curiously, neither Lorenz nor Adler took A *major* into account, even though the first root-position A triads are all major ones (mm. 22, 24, and 44), and even though Wagner changed the signature to A major at m. 43.

Alongside the older diatonic principle of voice leading arises the new principle of semitone voice leading, which may very well be the logical outgrowth of the single semitone difference between the major and minor forms of a triad. Except at moments of harmonic stability, which always—but not exclusively—occur at points of structural artic-ulation, *linear* considerations (with either diatonic or semitone voice leading, or both in alternation) more and more take precedence over *harmonic* ones. This principle of semitone voice leading—if a given voice moves or "resolves" at all, it moves by semitone—underlies the new possibilities for resolution of the V[7] sonority, all of which assume equivalent significance in this period:

Example 1

The first of these progressions is the most familiar and characteristic cadential progression in tonal music. Semitone voice leading governs all the others. 1b is of particular interest because with semitone voice leading, either the major or minor form of the triad can appear. Enharmonic respellings of the V[7] sonority in progressions like 1b and 1c permitted its description as an augmented-6th chord (or German 6th), a functional differentiation that maintained the much greater importance of dominant function in resolution 1a. In music before *Tristan*, these progressions usually had only "decorative" significance at best—mere foreground progressions with no larger harmonic or tonal significance. Later on, however, music often turns on these equally valid "meanings" or resolutions for the one sonority. This change reflects the typical historical process of evolution in musical language: a phenome-non originates as a merely decorative addition to the prevailing idiom and is gradually elevated to the level of structural import. As a harmonic entity with a linear source, the V[7] sonority itself is a striking case in point. It seems to have begun life with the addition of a merely decorative

7. Guido Adler, *Richard Wagner: Vorlesungen gehalten an der Universität zu Wien* (Mun-ich, 1904), p. 274; 2nd ed. (Munich, 1923), p. 282.

passing tone to a triad in the sixteenth century. With the rise of the tonal system during the seventeenth, however, it attained significance as a harmonic dissonance which, together with its resolution, reflected the larger tonal polarity of dominant and tonic.

As simple chordal juxtapositions, these semitone paradigms can work as progressions in either direction, and the 7th does not necessarily need to be present in the initial sonority. Progression 1b, for example, can also take the form shown in 2a, which concludes with the minor triad:

Example 2

2b is the equivalent form which concludes with a *major* triad, and 2c shows a possible harmonic representation of the same thing. In progression 2b, the moving voice actually proceeds by whole tone rather than by semitone and can thus be regarded as the "diatonic" equivalent of 2a.

The two triads in progression 2a differ from each other by only a semitone, the same difference that exists between the major and minor forms of a single triad. Just as the major and minor forms of any triad can substitute for each other, so also can either of the two triads in 2a substitute for each other in local situations, even including internal cadences like that of m. 17 of the *Tristan* Prelude, where an F-major triad substitutes for the A-minor one. The immediate local progression thus moves *upward* by semitone, E⁷–F, analogous (in the opposite direction) to progression 1c. The name *deceptive cadence* for such a progression emanates from a time when it was merely decorative. Progressions of this type are central hallmarks of the new system and work in an absolutely consistent and logical way with semitone voice leading, and it is therefore misleading to continue using the term *deceptive cadence* with its implicit suggestion of temporary departure from "normal" harmonic progression.

This brings us to the question of cadences in general. The V–I progression in Example 1a remained a viable cadential progression throughout the nineteenth century, particularly for internal cadences involving secondary keys. Meanwhile, however, another cadential pattern became increasingly prominent—that of *minor* IV–*major* I as shown in Example 3a. Like progressions 2a and 2b, 3a juxtaposes two triads of opposite mode and at the same time preserves semitone voice leading.

Example 3

3b illustrates the possibility of using both modes of the subdominant triad, while 3c shows a characteristic melodic feature—the ascent of the uppermost voice to the 3rd of the tonic triad—in combination with progression 3a. 3d presents another common variation, which begins with the tonic triad itself, adds the 7th, which converts the tonic locally to V^7 of IV, changes the mode of IV (in accordance with 3b), and finally resolves back to I. The typical plagal progression in 3e—*major* IV–major I—is the "diatonic" variant of 3a, since one voice moves by whole tone rather than by semitone. Finally, the V–I cadential progression in 3e simply reverses the order of 3a, still reflecting the principle of semitone voice leading, since the cadential tonic is in the minor mode.

3a and 3e taken together, and also 3d, demonstrate a principle of reciprocal function characteristic of the musical idiom of the later nineteenth century. In much the same way that the progressions in Examples 1 and 2 can move in either direction, so any two elements brought into harmonic or tonal juxtaposition have not one but rather two possible relationships. If we take the simple case of C and G, for example, G can function (and usually does function) in relation to C as its dominant, but on the other hand, it is also possible for C to function as G's subdominant:

C G
I← V

or IV→I

Earlier music tended to subordinate the subdominant, particularly on the large scale, to the crucial dominant–tonic projection. In later nineteenth-century music, however, if either one of the two possible relationships between C and G appears at all, the other interpretation of the relationship between them will eventually be exploited as well, at a different point in the piece, perhaps, or even on another level of the structure. Accordingly, progression 3d is often played out on a large scale without the defining tonic pedal point, particularly in codas, and by the end of the century, it is almost a cliché of the style. The final measures of many eighteenth-century pieces use progression 3d on a much smaller scale, retaining that defining pedal point, and this is another excellent example of how an element already implicit within the system is modified and expanded in the later period.

The elevation of additional resolutions of the V^7 sonority to structural equivalence with the V^7–I resolution is a major factor in eroding the strength of the dominant *function*. At the same time, the dominant has come to be so closely associated with the tonic itself—often to the point of being a mere linear extension of I, or even a substitute for it—that its value for providing effective tonal *contrast* is seriously undermined. The older structural polarity of tonic and dominant thus gradually gave way to a new system with polarities based on the interval of a 3rd. For any given tonic, there are four possible thirds—the minor and major 3rds above, and the minor and major 3rds below. Extension beyond these particular 3rds in either direction can be accomplished in two different ways. The first possibility is to progress on to V (in the upward direction) or to IV (in the lower direction):

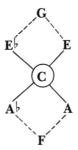

In this case, the tonality based on V frequently *functions* not as the dominant but rather as the III of III. Similarly, the tonality based on IV often *functions* not as the subdominant but rather as the VI of VI.

The alternative is to work along an axis of 3rds of the same quality (major or minor), perhaps even to the point of making a complete circle of major or minor 3rds:

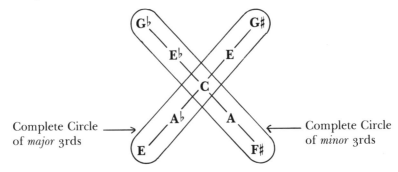

The tonic notes of the circle of minor 3rds form a diminished-7th chord, while those of the circle of major 3rds form an augmented triad. These two sonorities are still further examples of how decorative phenomena from the earlier system later achieved some semblance of structural significance.

Wagner did not invent the features we have reviewed, nor is *Tristan* the first work in which they appear. From this perspective, Wagner's historical position is that of synthesizer rather than inventor, and his essential contribution consists in the application of these principles on a larger scale than had been previously attempted. *Tristan* is his first work to present these new relationships systematically. The role of Liszt's influence on Wagner's "harmonic" thinking during the 1850s undoubtedly had the practical effect of increasing his awareness of the possibilities inherent in the principle of semitone voice leading.[8] Certainly that principle seems to dominate the first 17 measures of the *Tristan* Prelude, where the only other interval Wagner uses is the 3rd (and its complementary 6th). In addition, however, *Tristan* takes a major step beyond what we have examined so far, and we can now turn to its innovations.

Analyses of the Prelude customarily accept it as a separate self-contained work, even though Wagner gave it the special label *Einleitung* in his full score—the only opera in which he used this designation for the orchestral preface to a first act.[9] Presumably he wanted us to regard it not as an overture to the whole opera, nor as a "ritornello" for the music of its opening scene, but rather as a "slow introduction" to the large symphonic design that follows. Some background about the tonal structure which that Prelude prepares is therefore in order.

The new feature in *Tristan* with the most far-reaching consequences for large-scale organization is the pairing together of two tonalities a minor 3rd apart in such a way as to form a "double-tonic complex." The pairing of A and C for the whole of Act I may well have grown out of the traditional close relationship between A minor and C major, but the double-tonic idea goes well beyond merely beginning in a minor key and concluding in its relative major, as in Chopin's Scherzo in B-flat minor, Op. 31, and his F-minor Fantaisie, Op. 49. In some ways,

8. See above, pp. 21–22.

9. Wagner had used the term just once before—for the orchestral introduction to the third act of *Lohengrin*—and he used it only once again—for the opening of Act II of *Tristan* itself.

the new concept plays upon that very closeness, but we are now dealing with the "chromatic" mode of A and the "chromatic" mode of C. The two elements are linked together in such a way that either triad can serve as the local representative of the tonic complex. Within that complex itself, however, one of the two elements is at any moment in the primary position while the other remains subordinate to it. The Prelude establishes the close duality between A and C, and this complex serves as the controlling tonic for the entire first act, which both begins (in the Prelude) and ends with the A/C complex. While A is the primary member within the complex through most of the Prelude, Wagner prepares the eventual shift of emphasis to C in the final section of the Prelude itself, which in turn prepares C as the central tonic (paired with E♭) for the opening dialogue between Isolde and Brangäne. C attains the primary position within the tonic complex in the concluding sections of the act, and at the end Wagner deliberately sets Tristan's final speech apart from its context so that it forms a cadence in A, and then juxtaposes that cadence in A directly against the final orchestral cadence in C.

The harmonic embodiment of this double-tonic complex is a chord like 2c, but transposed up a minor 3rd so that it combines the notes of the A minor and C major triads (see Example 7 below). Wagner reserves this sonority until shortly before the end of the act, where he lets it appear for the first time at the conclusion of the short love duet that follows the drinking of the potion. The function of this major triad with added 6th should not be confused with the function of the added-6th chord in twentieth-century popular music, which acts simply as a decorated triad (a triad with an extra nontriadic note). The actual notes of the two chords are the same, but this double-triadic sonority functions here as the harmonic representative of the double-tonic complex at work throughout the structure.

Once the major triad with added 6th attains an important position in tonal vocabulary, the principle of modal mixture suggests a corresponding form in the minor mode:

Example 4

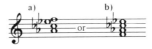

This is the so-called *Tristan* chord, and 4b is the spacing used as the basis for its familiar description as a half-diminished 7th chord. A more appropriate description is "minor triad with added 6th," because it maintains the analogy with the *major* triad with added 6th, because the word *triad* is actually part of the description, and finally because it relates most easily to the actual sound of the chord. This description also seems justified by the ways Wagner treats the chord in its original form and by the ways he alters it. We can describe the *Tristan* chords in the first two phrases of the Prelude, then, as an A♭ (G♯)-minor triad with added 6th and a B-minor triad with added 6th. At the beginning of the love duet near the end of Act I when these phrases return, Wagner expands them into symmetrical units of seven measures each and actually replaces the earlier *Tristan* chords with the straightforward A♭ and B triads, changing their mode to major:

Example 5

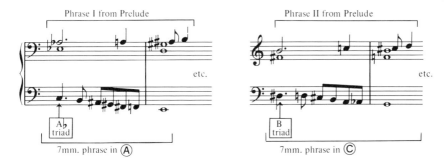

At the beginning of Act III, Wagner presents the spacing of 4a, intensified by the violins' open G string for the added 6th:

Example 6

However he spaces the *Tristan* chord, Wagner consistently treats it as a local dissonance, which usually resolves with semitone voice leading. The chord is to some extent referential, and therefore it serves to focus at least one level of large-scale dissonance, which we might regard as "resolving" to the *major* triad with added 6th as a local consonance in the cadence to the love duet—with the same symmetrical spacing as that of the first two *Tristan* chords from the Prelude:

Example 7

Most commentators regard the *Tristan* chord in the first phrase of the Prelude as a somehow significant phenomenon—worthy, at any rate, of its long-familiar label—but then proceed to regard its G♯ as resolving to A. They thereby interpret A as the actual chord note and reduce the *Tristan* chord to a mere passing foreground event. Wagner, on the other hand, seems to have taken considerable pains to make the listener perceive G♯ as the chord note, if only by holding it a full five times longer that the A which follows it, and by treating that A as a passing tone on the way to B. From this point of view, then, the fundamental progression is that of 8a rather than 8b:

Example 8

We could also argue that an inherent beauty of music is that it can in fact do two things at the same time, and this may well be so in the present instance. Thus, we have a striking example of two different but equally appropriate interpretations: 8b deals with the situation as a purely local event, while 8a takes into account the chord's large-scale structural implications. We shall see that the very move from G♯ to A, responsible for the two different interpretations, constitutes an essential motivic idea underlying this piece. As an aside, we might note that progression 8a is consistent with the principle of semitone voice leading, since the two voices that move by minor 3rd engage in simple voice exchange of the two common tones.

Another innovation in the musical language of *Tristan* is the treatment of the V^7 chord as a temporary local consonance, as shown in either progression of Example 8.[10] Elaborate periphrasis on the nature of consonance and dissonance lies outside the scope of this study, and we shall content ourselves with the practical but admittedly circular definition of dissonance as something that requires resolution, and consonance as anything that can be used to resolve a dissonance. There are of course varying degrees of consonance in earlier music, where only the triad provides resolution, though the root-position triad is a stronger consonance than either of its inversions, and ultimately only the *tonic* root-position triad is strong enough to provide the final cadence for a composition. As far as *final* cadences are concerned, the latter principle prevails through the later nineteenth century as well, but there are now two new sonorities that can function in certain local situations with varying degrees of secondary consonance: 1) the major triad with added 6th, which as we have seen actually appears in an internal cadence; and 2) the V^7 chord. With these two examples at hand, we may well believe that the later nineteenth century ought to be looked upon as a period which expanded the concept of *consonance*, rather than as a period which expanded the treatment of dissonance.

Still another innovation in *Tristan* is what we might call the *indirect* method of exposition, wherein certain fundamental tonal and motivic elements first appear by implication rather than by explicit statement. If we return once more to the set of harmonic paradigms in Example 1, we note that the V^7 sonority acts as a dissonance in each one. The operative principle there was that the V^7 sonority, when treated as a dissonance, is just as apt to resolve with semitone voice leading as it is to resolve to a triad whose root is a perfect 5th below that of the original V^7. On the other hand, when the V^7 sonority functions as a local consonance, it does so by way of *implying* (but not actually stating) resolution 1a. The dominant is in fact so intimately bound up with its tonic that it can suggest or present it by implication and thereby substitute for it.

The concluding V^7 sonorities in the first two phrases of the Prelude thus imply the triads (and, by extension, the tonalities) of A and C,

10. Kurth approaches this idea with a somewhat different perspective. See below, p. 190.

which act as the double-tonic complex governing the structure of the whole of Act I. The double-tonic complex of this act, in other words, is presented at the outset, but *indirectly*—by implication, rather than by direct successive (or simultaneous) statement of the two triads. The third phrase continues to the V^7 of E, thus completing an outline, *by implication*, of triads based on the three notes (A–C–E) of the primary member of the tonic complex, the A-minor triad.[11]

When Bülow exclaimed to Draeseke that the *Tristan* Prelude had "not a single pure triad,"[12] he was clearly exaggerating, but insofar as he was referring to *tonic* triads, he had a real point, since the density of tonic triads is far lower in the *Tristan* Prelude than in most earlier compositions. Schoenberg expressed the point more precisely when he noted that "A minor, although it is to be inferred from every passage, is scarcely ever sounded in the whole piece. It is always expressed in circuitous ways; it is constantly avoided by means of deceptive cadences."[13]

The indirect method of exposition also applies to at least one of the most significant motivic underpinnings of the opera—the semitone between A♭(G♯) and A♮. The first three notes in the cellos (A–F–E) constitute another main motive of Act I (Motive *x*), but the initial presentation with its leap of a *minor* 6th is not the primary form. The initial A♮–F–E never returns at its original pitch level again throughout the remainder of Act I, but recurs instead in the form A♭–F–E.[14] Thus, the Prelude begins with a chromatically altered form of this motive, and the primary form with its leap of a *major* 6th first appears in Phrase II (See Example 9 on facing page). The motivic "tension" between A♭(G♯) and A♮ is thus implicit in the very opening note, though we naturally do not perceive it as such until later on, when the A♭ in this motivic context has been established. At the climax of the Prelude (mm. 80–83), the cellos (doubled here by horns) recall this motive, not once but three times in succession, with A♭ rather than A♮. Isolde

11. This point is also discussed by Edward T. Cone in his article "Sound and Syntax: An Introduction to Schoenberg's Harmony," in *Perspectives of New Music* 13/1 (Fall–Winter 1974): 23–24.

12. The complete passage from Bülow's letter appears above, p. 13.

13. Schoenberg, *Theory of Harmony*, p. 384. In this passage, Schoenberg blurs the critical distinction between the key and its tonic triad. What he evidently means is that the *key* of A minor is to be inferred from every passage even though its *tonic triad* is scarcely ever sounded, and that while the *key* is expressed in circuitous ways, the *tonic triad* is constantly avoided.

14. In fact, the only time the A♮–F–E form ever appears in the opera is near the end of Act II, at the conclusion of King Marke's monologue.

Example 9

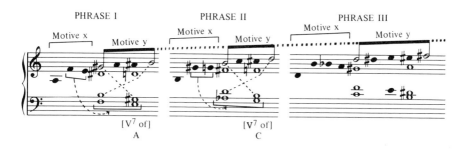

THE OPENING UNIT

actually sings the motive, also with A♭, just before she drinks the Potion
("Ich trink' sie dir"). One rationale for this semitone alteration of Motive
x on its first appearance is that it melodically outlines progression 2a
and thus prepares the cadence of the opening unit in m. 17, where the
F-major triad substitutes for an A triad.

Wagner scored Motive *x* for cellos, whereas he could perfectly well
have given it to the first violins. This unusual scoring draws attention

to the register of the motive and assists in playing out the tension between G♯ and A♮, which occurs when the initial cello A is transferred up to the oboe's initial G♯ at the beginning of Motive *y*. In the new register, this G♯ in turn moves to A. In Phrase II, the primary form of Motive *x* uses B as its first note, which shifts up a full octave to B in the answering clarinet (Motive *y*), so that in spite of the clarinet's immediate move from B to C, the semitone tension between B and C is not so strong as that between G♯ and A. As for Phrase I, there is some evidence that Wagner may have intensified this tension between the A of Motive *x* and the G♯ of Motive *y* by using the cellos' open A string.[15]

In addition, the cellos' descending semitone, F–E, in Motive *x* returns an octave lower as the bass line for Motive *y*. In strict parallel with this, Phrase II duplicates the G♯–G♮ semitone in Motive *x* an octave lower as the bass line for Motive *y*.

The cellos initiate Phrase II with the *major* 6th, B–G♯, and this interval complements the minor 3rd (G♯–B) chromatically linearized by the oboe in Phrase I, Motive *y*. At the same time, these two notes are part of the V^7 of A with which Phrase I concluded—an important device for maintaining continuity in this opening unit. Except for the difference between the major and minor 6ths of Motive *x*, then, the Prelude begins with two symmetrical phrases, and the first implies A while the second implies C. The double-tonic complex is thus presented *by implication* in two symmetrical phrases.

Phrase III also begins with a major 6th, in parallel with Phrase II, but otherwise the exact symmetry of Phrases I and II now breaks down. Motive *x* and Motive *y* each have an extra note, the *Tristan* chord appears in a new spacing, and the bass line for Motive *y* does not duplicate any portion of Motive *x*. With the addition of these extra notes, Wagner has also upset the rhythmic parallel he established between Phrases I and II. Motive *x* does not even begin in the same part of the measure, and the sophisticated treatment of rhythm evident here successfully obscures

---

15. The witness is Emmanuel Chabrier, who, at a performance of the opera in Munich, is said to have "burst into sobs of despair before even the first note of the Prelude. To his friends who enquired whether he was ill he could only reply, 'Oh that open A on the cello! Fifteen years I've been waiting to hear it!' " (Quoted in Edward Lockspeiser, *Debussy: His Life and Mind*, Vol. 1 [London, 1962], p. 95, n. 1.) We can but hope that poor Chabrier was not disappointed.

The Editor is grateful to Jenny Kallick for the suggestion that once cellos typically had a metal A string (the others being gut), playing the first note of the Prelude on the open string would have been quite logical.

any sense of regular recurrent metrical pattern. This treatment of rhythm became more and more pervasive in Wagner's later style, and this very short example seems to represent its actual beginning, for there is nothing quite comparable in the second act of *Siegfried* or earlier.

If we examine Phrase III more closely, we see that the extra note in Motive *x* creates a retrograde duplication of the melodic notes from Phrase I/Motive *y*:

Example 10

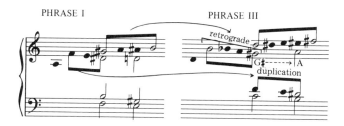

After Motive *x* arrives at G♯ and becomes the alto voice of Motive *y*, it does not descend a semitone in parallel with Phrases I and II, but instead *ascends* to A and is thus consistent with the G♯–A motivic idea. In addition, the tenor voice of Motive *y* duplicates the three descending notes, F–E–D♯, from Phrase I, Motive *x*.

The extra note in the melodic line of Motive *y* brings Phrase III to a termination on F♯ rather than F♮ (E♯). So far, then, the melodic line of Motive *y* has ascended chromatically from G♯ to B in Phrase I, from B to D in Phrase II, and now from D to F♯ in Phrase III. This melodic ascent constitutes nothing other than a chromatic linearization of the *Tristan* chord from Phrase II,[16] where it resolved to (the V⁷ of) C.

Phrase I's transfer of the A in Motive *x* to the G♯–A of Motive *y* prepares the comparable but *linear* octave transfer that takes place over the course of the first 16 measures. An interruption of this process occurs in mm. 12–15, which nonetheless serve to intensify the approaching change of register in other ways. First, Wagner repeats Motive *y* from Phrase III an octave higher, then returns to the original register and stresses the extra note in Motive *y* by stating just the last two notes

16. Milton Babbitt also noticed this point. See below, p. 290.

of that motive (E♯–F♯) in the violins, doubled at the lower octave. He then shifts back to the winds, which repeat those same two notes an octave higher, also with octave doubling.

The cadence of the opening unit begins with the same E♯–F♯ back in the original register in the violins, now harmonized within the V^7 of A. The violins complete the process of chromatic ascent up to G♯, an octave above the G♯ with which the oboe began in Phrase I. The process of octave transfer is now complete, and after the arrival at G♯, the line leaps a minor 3rd up to B, repeating once more that very interval chromatically linearized in Phrase I, Motive *y* and again in retrograde in Phrase III, Motive *x*. From this B, the line resolves down to A. Thus, the initial G♯ is transferred up an octave, where it finally resolves to A, after linearizing the *Tristan* chord from Phrase II along the way. We have noted that the harmonic presentation of this particular *Tristan* chord in Phrase II resolved to (the V^7 of) C, whereas the linear presentation of the same chord resolves to A. This distinction between linear and harmonic presentations is frequently at work in later nineteenth-century music, but the process is rarely arbitrary: the difference here reflects the two members of the double-tonic complex, A and C.

Meanwhile, the bass line of the cadence (E–F) reverses the semitone progression of the bass line from Phrase I, Motive *y* (F–E), which in turn was prepared an octave higher in Motive *x*. Thus, the sense of upward octave transfer is duplicated in the opposite direction in the bass line.

Example 11

Two horns, the first doubled by oboes, are added to the scoring for the cadence, and these two new parts together create a V–I cadence in A. The first horn line prefigures the melodic termination of the cadence by leaping from G♯ to B just before the violins complete their chromatic octave ascent. This voice arrives at A (in the same register as the A from which the chromatic ascent began) simultaneously with the leap to B in the violins. The lower horn part moves directly from E to A, even though the actual harmonic progression involved is E⁷–F, the F-major triad "substituting," (as we have noted) for an A triad (see Example 2a). At the moment when the violins fall back to A, the A in the lower horn part is taken over by the cellos—the same A with which they initiated this opening unit.

   Wagner's first complete sketch for the opening seventeen-measure unit survives on a worksheet now in the New York Public Library:

Example 12

Perhaps the most extraordinary feature of this sketch is its very first note—not A, nor even $A^\flat$ ($G\sharp$), but rather B. In fact, Motive *x* in each of the first two phrases begins with a tritone rather than a 6th. In addition, the first measure of the cadence (m. 16 in the score) occupies two measures in this sketch rather than just one, and it also has a sixteenth-note pick-up which Wagner later eliminated, perhaps in order to strengthen the dissonant effect of the E$\sharp$ against the E⁷ harmony. When Wagner made this sketch, he was actually expanding an earlier sketch in his Black-and-Gold Diary:

Example 13

PHRASE II
Final version

The second measure of this fragment corresponds in essential outline to Phrase II, Motive *y*, while the first measure begins with the tonic C itself. Leaving aside that initial C, the melodic idea in the first measure contains the essence of Motive *x* as developed at the beginning of the New York sketch: the diminished 4th of the earlier sketch became a diminished 5th in the later one, while a descending semitone follows in both versions.

Wagner thus began with Phrase II, the phrase in C, and extrapolated from it a parallel phrase in A for the beginning of the New York sketch. When he in turn elaborated that sketch into a complete version of the Prelude in his Preliminary Draft, he incorporated there the changes he had decided upon, and the opening seventeen-measure unit assumed its final form *in abstracto*.

Wagner obviously did not begin work on the Prelude with the final form of Motive *x* already defined, and in the New York sketch, the interval of a 6th first appears in Phrase III. The motive evolved gradually, and Wagner eventually transferred it back to the first two phrases. When he expanded the diary sketch, he clearly had two ends in view: 1) two phrases exactly parallel—one in A, the other in C; and 2) in each phrase, a transfer of the first two notes of Motive *x* to the two lower voices of the ensuing *Tristan* chord. The latter point would seem to negate Mitchell's assertion that in Phrase I "the diminished 5th outlines an obvious supertonic chord,"[17] first of all because no referential tonic has yet been established or even suggested as the basis for such an interpretation, and secondly because the two notes of that interval in fact become the lower two notes of the *Tristan* chord that follows. The tritone beginning for Phrase II (D–A♭), on the other hand, serves

17. William J. Mitchell, "The Tristan Prelude: Techniques and Structure," in *The Music Forum* 1 (1967): 178.

two of the same purposes as the eventual major 6th (B–G♯): either interval picks up two notes from the V⁷ chord of the preceding phrase, and either interval duplicates two notes in the *Tristan* chord that follows. The tritone beginning for Phrase II does not complement the chromatically linearized minor 3rd from Phrase I, Motive *y*, however, and this feature emerges in the New York sketch only in Phrase III, where the major 6th (D–B) finally appears.

Wagner did not alter the initial B in Phrase I to A♭ (G♯), which would have presented the primary form of Motive *x* at the very outset and would also have retained the absolute parallel of the first two phrases. Instead, he decided on A♮, which evidently has something to do with the cadence of the unit (m. 17), where an F major triad substitutes for the A minor one. All essential details of this cadence are present in the New York sketch, except for the condensation of its first two measures into one. The upper horn counterpoint appears, but its resolution to A is delayed and occurs simultaneously with the analogous melodic resolution to A in the violins.

The final version of the opening is thus dependent not simply upon the minor 6th (A–F), but on the whole of Motive *x* (A–F–E), which, as we have seen, outlines progression 2a. Wagner's changes came about not only as an attempt to derive a central motive, but also, in the case of Phrase I, as an attempt to reinforce the implication of A as tonic and to prepare the opening unit's cadence. At the same time, he established another large-scale means of maintaining the tension between the A♮ of the very beginning and the A♭ (G♯) of the same motive on its reappearance at the climax of the Prelude (mm. 80–82). Mitchell observed the "vital motion of a in the final version, as it moves to its successor, g♯¹, in [the *Tristan* chord],"[18] and Wagner did not exploit a parallel tension in either Phrase II or Phrase III, though he might easily have done so, and this seems convincing evidence that he did indeed wish to place special emphasis on the specific pitches A and G♯.

If we saw the New York sketch in isolation, we might wonder why Wagner broke off the way he did, with just the first three notes of the melody for the next unit. As we might suspect, he had already jotted down that melody in its complete form in his Brown Diary (see Example 14 on p. 134). The New York sketch shows, however, that Wagner has already decided to reverse the strong and weak accents by beginning this melody in the middle of the measure.

18. Ibid.

Example 14

Whereas the first unit's uppermost line presented a *chromatic* linearization of a *minor* triad with added 6th, the second unit now presents a *diatonic* linearization of a *major* triad with added 6th, A–C–E–G, precisely the chord which represents the double-tonic complex. The ascent from A to C is clear enough, though the C on the downbeat of m. 18 is dissonant with the harmony. The ensuing D, which provides the local resolution for C, is dropped down to the D below so that it is not an integral part of the ascending line. The same thing happens at the beginning of m. 19 where the E is harmonically dissonant, and the resolving D is once again descended to, so that it also stands outside the upward movement of the line. Meanwhile, the C in the middle of m. 18 is harmonized with a C-major triad in second inversion, and the arrival at G in m. 20 coincides with a second C-major triad, this time in *first* inversion. The first two triads from the double-tonic complex in the Prelude are thus C-major triads, but neither one is in root position. The diatonic scalar ascent by 3rds is broken once G is reached, though in the purely intervallic sense the ascent continues one step further to B♭. From B♭, the line descends and arrives at the first *root-position* triad from the tonic complex on the downbeat of m. 22—an *A-major* triad, however, not a C triad. Once Wagner presents tonic triads, he clarifies their relative position—A as primary, C as secondary—within the complex by presenting the C triads first, but not in root position, and then proceeding to a *root-position* A triad. The remainder of this second unit of the Prelude continues on to still another root-position A-major triad in the second half of m. 24.

Wagner's Preliminary Draft for this second unit shows some odd variants from the final version. The sketch from the Brown Diary (Example 14) has G in the bass at the beginning of the second measure, and the C-major triad is clearly implied. In the Preliminary Draft, however, the bass in the middle of m. 18 has a G♯ instead of the G♮, so that the harmony is an augmented triad rather than the C-major triad. In the second half of m. 24, Wagner seems first to have preferred the A-major triad in second inversion and evidently wondered about whether to present the root in the bass at all. Finally, his instrumental abbreviations in the Preliminary Draft in mm. 17–18 show that he intended to begin the second unit with the cellos, just as he had done in the first unit, but the violas (*Br*) were to continue the new melody halfway through m. 18, and against their melody he supplied the beginning of a counterpoint with which the cellos were to continue. This phrase assumed its final form in the Developed Draft, where Wagner rewrote the lower parts in accordance with the familiar version and gave the entire main melody to the cellos.

Another problematic passage in the Preliminary Draft begins at m. 70, a passage not yet worked out in its final form. Mm. 70–73 of the Prelude actually extend to six measures in the Draft, since Wagner attempted to weave in the entire material of Phrases II and III from the beginning. He had begun with Motive *y* from Phrase I in mm. 68–69, since the harmony of the end of mm. 67–68 would not permit the use of Motive *x*. When he later revised the ensuing passage, he cut Motive *x* out of Phrases II and III as well, and this enabled him to eliminate a full measure in each case.

Wagner had already decided not to include the interruption (mm. 12–15) in this recall, but instead to elide from m. 11 into the second half of m. 16. This compression of material as a climax approaches is characteristic of Wagner. He realized in this instance that a recall of both Phrases II and III, even in combination with the new motive of this passage, would be psychologically static, an effect inherent in the very nature of a complete literal recall. He thus withheld complete recapitulation of the opening unit until the final section, where it could effectively support the process of transition to a lower level of musical intensity. Since Wagner wrote out the Prelude from beginning to end in the Preliminary Draft, he may not have foreseen, when he reached this passage (mm. 70–73), precisely how he would accomplish that later transition. Once he had worked out the conclusion, however, he could look back and see that a complete recall of the first three phrases in mm. 68–73 not only undermined the effect of the climax, but also that the final pages of the Prelude devoted altogether too much space to literal repetitions.

For the passage beginning at m. 74, the Preliminary Draft contains the same three basic elements as the final version: the cello melody in the middle of the texture with a new continuation, plus chromatically descending and ascending counterpoints above and below. Wagner's original idea was to begin the cello melody in the middle of the measure, as in m. 17, and he wrote it out in that position. But the contrapuntal combination did not work out, and his solution to the problem lay in shifting the entire melody back half a measure and making a few adjustments in the counterpoints to accommodate the shift. Wagner indicated to himself what he had to do by drawing new barlines for the cello melody. This additional act of compression served to intensify the approach to the climax even further, since the entrance to the cello melody now anticipates the melodic resolution of the preceding phrase (B–A). The cello melody itself continues differently after reaching B♭, and Wagner later condensed this new continuation by eliminating the two half-measures bracketed in the transcription. In both versions, the melody's original conclusion with A-major triads does not appear. Wagner begins the process of harmonic transition to C in this passage, first by reinforcing the texture of mm. 74–76 with a timpani roll on C, and then by phasing out that portion of the cello melody most unequivocally associated with A.

This new continuation culminates in an expanded return of the opening unit in mm. 82–94. In the Preliminary Draft, Wagner planned to begin this return with Phrase I, Motive *y* and to omit the first appearance of Motive *x*, just as he had done in the comparable recall he originally drafted for the passage just before m. 74. When he revised this later recall in his Developed Draft, he first expanded it by anticipating Phrase I, Motive *y* with two rhythmically and melodically altered statements of it in the trumpet (mm. 81–82). Later on, Wagner realized the full implication of what he had done there and added to the Developed Draft in pencil an additional counterpoint for the cellos (now doubled by horns) in the form of three statements of Motive *x* from Phrase I (A♭ replacing A♮).

In this recall, Wagner extended both Phrase I and Phrase II with a literal retrograde of its own Motive *x*. The retrograde version had already become an important motive in its own right in the bass beginning at m 28, but it now assumes the rhythm as well as the melodic contour of the first segment of the cello melody (see Example 15).

The cello melody itself returns once more in mm. 94–100, but Wagner now reharmonizes it and varies it with still another continuation which initiates the final phase of the transition to C. In mm. 101–6, Phrase I and Phrase II make their last appearance before the curtain opens, and a timpani roll on G is added to Motive *x* in both phrases. In addition, the bass line of Phrase I, Motive *y* does not move to E, so that the concluding harmony of Phrase I, accompanied by G in the timpani,

Example 15

Extension of Phrase I
(mm. 84-85)

Extension of Phrase II
(mm. 87-88)

is now altered to the V^9 of C. In his Preliminary Draft, Wagner has two versions of the phrase in mm. 100–3, the second written on top of the first. The transition to C had been accomplished by this point, and his first thought was simply to present two statements of Phrase II, one in the original register and then another an octave lower. Wagner realized only later on that he could rework the final chord of Phrase I in such a way as to present the V of C, rather than the V of A.

Wagner conceived the concluding melody for cellos and basses in notes of equal value, except for the prolonged final A♭ and G. This melody features an arpeggiation of the notes from the *Tristan* chord in Phrase I, and in his Developed Draft, Wagner grafted onto this arpeggiation the rhythm of Motive *x*:

Example 16

Tristan chord from Phrase I
(mm. 107-09)

Rhythm of Motive *x*

The arpeggiated version resolves to G (= V of C), whereas the chordal version at the beginning of the Prelude had resolved to the V^7 of A. It may in fact have been the resolution of this arpeggiation which suggested Wagner's reinstitution of Phrase I in mm. 100–3, with its new termination on the V^9 of C rather than the original V^7 of A. This manipulation of Phrase I to suggest C rather than A is an idea Wagner carried a step further at the end of Act I, as the curtain falls, where the whole of Motive *y* is subsumed within the V^7 of C:

Example 17

We have noted that two essential elements underpinning the Prelude are the double-tonic complex of A and C, and the motivic tension between $A^\flat$ (G#) and A♮. These two elements are eventually made explicit in Scene 2, shortly after the second appearance of the Sailor's Song. To a foreshortened recall of the opening of the Prelude up through Phrase III, Motive *x*, Wagner appends a phrase with two discrete segments:

Example 18

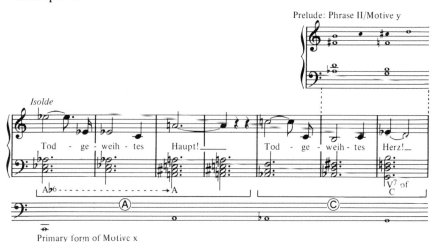

The bass line for this phrase corresponds exactly to the bass line of Wagner's initial sketch (see Example 13). It is also the primary form of Motive *x*; the two segments explicitly contrast A and C, but while a complete root-position triad amplifies A, C is still only implied by its V^7. This V^7 chord is approached directly from the same *Tristan* chord that had preceded it in Phrase II of the Prelude. By this means, Wagner supports the primary position of A within the tonic complex.

Lorenz regarded this phrase as the "resolution" of the *conclusion* of the Prelude[19] and consequently used it to mark the end of the first "period" (structural unit) in Act I, ignoring altogether the complete cadence in C some 50 measures further along. When Wagner actually begins to tip the tonic balance in favor of C later on in Act I, he does use this phrase as a cadence just before the transition to Scene 5. Now, however, he actually spells out C rather than merely implying it:

Example 19

Meanwhile, the A triad in the first segment is approached from another complete triad on A♭. Wagner thus makes explicit the motivic significance of A♭–A♮ and defines the local importance of A♮ by presenting that triad in root position, while the A♭ triad is in first inversion. With this first segment, then, the A♭–A♮ motive is elevated to the level of *harmonic* amplification, and at the midpoint of Act II, Wagner carries the process a step further. Here, it operates on the level of large-scale *tonal* contrast, for Wagner juxtaposes a large section in A♮ with another in A♭. Once A♭ is established and Tristan begins to sing, his vocal line picks up with another arpeggiation of the *Tristan*

---

19. Alfred Lorenz, *Das Geheimnis der Form bei Richard Wagner*, Vol. 2: *Der musikalische Aufbau von Richard Wagners "Tristan und Isolde,"* 2nd unaltered ed. (Tutzing, 1966), pp. 29–30.

chord from Phrase I of the Prelude, which Kurth was evidently the first to point out.[20] In addition, however, the arpeggiated *minor* triad with added 6th is supported in one measure by a harmonic presentation of the corresponding *major* triad with added 6th:

Example 20

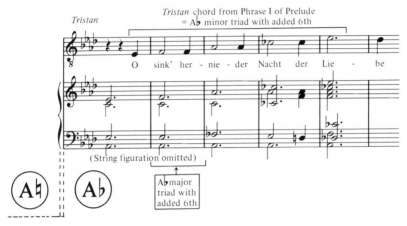

The Transfiguration is primarily a recapitulation of two passages from the concluding portion of the love scene in Act II. Wagner begins by recalling the first of two parallel strophes which precede Brangäne's second interruption. The later recapitulation of just *one* of two or more parallel strophes is a noteworthy technique, since it also became a common procedure with later nineteenth-century symphonic composers. The strophe from Act II begins with a characteristic four-note motive harmonized with an $A\flat\,^6_4$ triad and arrives at a $B\,^6_4$ triad in its penultimate measure. The second passage Wagner recalls—the last 100 measures of Act II, Scene 2—*begins* with a $B\,^6_4$ triad (and the same four-note motive), and Wagner was thus able to unite the two passages by eliding the two $B\,^6_4$ triads. After this second recall, Wagner continues with new material in the form of an extended cadence culminating in one final appearance of Motive *y* from Phrase I of the Prelude, whose new extension concludes the opera with what Richard Strauss called "the most beautifully scored

20. Ernst Kurth, *Romantische Harmonik und ihre Krise in Wagners "Tristan,"* 2nd ed. (Berlin, 1923), pp. 86–87.

final chord in the history of music."[21]

Wagner made several revisions in his original text[22] for the Transfiguration, and except for a single couplet, the text assumed its final form in his setting in the Preliminary Draft. The structure of this revised text, plus the tonal references Wagner wrote as reminders in Mathilde Wesendonk's manuscript copy of the poem,[23] appear in outline in the left-hand column of the chart on page 142. As far as the musical setting is concerned, Wagner treated it as if constructed in four parts. He organized Parts I and II on the principal of a recurrent couplet functioning as a verbal refrain and expanded its third appearance at the end of Part II. On the other hand, Parts III and IV (12 lines, plus 22 reduced from the original 24) are continuous and more rhapsodic in character.

When Wagner set this text in his Preliminary Draft, he altered his compositional procedure with regard to the foundational role he customarily assigned to the vocal part (in conjunction with bass line). Because this section involves a substantial musical recall, Wagner's task here was to adapt a new text to music already composed. For most of Parts I through III, he simply adapted the new words to the already existing vocal line or chief instrumental melody—hence his statement after the change to the B-major signature, "Here even children can make themselves an accompaniment!!" In Part IV, on the other hand, he constructed a new vocal part as an additional counterpoint to the earlier orchestral texture and also to his new continuation.

In the Preliminary Draft, Wagner gave the three refrains different vocal settings, and for the first and third, he also composed an entirely new accompaniment which duplicates nothing whatever from Act II. Wagner thus decided to let the first and third refrains remain outside the scheme of recapitulations he had devised for the bulk of the monologue. For the second refrain, however, he transferred the original Act II vocal line to the orchestral texture he was recalling and gave Isolde a new vocal line instead—the one instance in Parts I through III

21. In his essay of 1933, "Zeitgemässe Glossen für Erziehung zur Musik," in Willi Schuh, ed., *Richard Strauss: Betrachtungen und Erinnerungen*, 2nd ed. (Zurich, 1957), p. 124.

22. The original version of Wagner's text for this passage appears in his *Gesammelte Schriften und Dichtungen*, Vol. 7, 4th ed. (Leipzig, 1907), pp. 79–81.

23. These "tonal indications" were merely Wagner's reminders of the passages he would recall from Act II and do not reflect an attempt to lay out an abstract tonal design in advance. Similarly, verbal indications of keys in the Preliminary Draft either substitute for an actual signature or serve as reminders of where to reposition a new signature in the Developed Draft.

FORMAL PLAN OF THE TEXT

ORIGINAL SETTING   FINAL VERSION
(with Wagner's tonal references
from the manuscript of the poem
he used for the Preliminary Draft)

PART I   PART I

> 4 lines

"seht ihr, Freunde,   "seht ihr, Freunde,
säh't ihr's nicht?"   säh't ihr's nicht?"

> 4 lines

"seht ihr, Freunde,
säh't ihr's nicht?"   "seht ihr's nicht?"

PART II   PART II

H-dur
> 8 lines

"Freunde, seht!   "Freunde, seht!
fühlt und seht ihr's nicht?"   fühlt und seht ihr's nicht?"

PART III   PART III

E
> "Höre ich nur,"
>   *etc.*
>
> 12 lines

PART IV   PART IV

> "Heller schallend,"
>   *etc.*
>
> 22 lines

where he composed the vocal line as a new counterpoint to the music drawn from Act II.

The chart on page 144 presents an outline of the two passages recalled from Act II and compares Wagner's basic formal design for the earlier setting with that for the final version (which emerged in his Developed Draft). He adapted Part I—two groups of 4 lines, each followed by the refrain—to Tristan's strophe preceding Brangäne's second interruption, and he retained its 6/8 metrical arrangement. After adapting the first 4 lines to Tristan's vocal part, Wagner inserted two new measures (bracketed in the transcription) for the first refrain, then picked up where he had left off with the Act II strophe and continued adapting his new text to the earlier vocal part until he reached the refrain once again. This is the point where Wagner shifted the earlier vocal part to the accompaniment and wrote an entirely new vocal line as counterpoint to the thus modified texture. The two appearances of the refrain divide the original strophe into two separate sections, and except for the two newly composed measures for the first refrain, the musical fabric of Part I is exactly the same in the Preliminary Draft as in the final version.

Part II, in both versions, begins at the change to a B-major signature, and Wagner's first setting becomes much more problematic. In Act II, the final B-major portion of the duet contains two passages that begin with the main motive harmonized with B_4^6. In the final version, Part II begins with the *first* of these two passages and continues straight through to the end of the scene, but the Preliminary Draft picks up from the *second*. Wagner proceeded with the same method he had followed in Part I and adapted the 8 lines of Part II to one or the other of the original Act II vocal parts or primary instrumental melody. He also eliminated some of the internal repetitions conditioned in Act II by the presence of both Tristan and Isolde. He then composed five entirely new measures (bracketed in the transcription) for the third (expanded) refrain.

For Part III, Wagner returned to the music from Act II and back-tracked to the spot he had indicated in Mathilde's manuscript of the poem, which begins with the same 4-note motive on E_4^6. Once again, he set the first 10 lines to whichever of the Act II vocal parts best suited the new words. For the last 2 lines, he composed three new measures (bracketed in the transcription) and elided the last word of Part III (*klingt*) onto the beginning of the music for Part IV, thereby obscuring the formal division between Parts III and IV.

(References for the music from Act II are to the study score published by Broude Brothers and Dover. 387/1 = measure 1 on p. 387. For the final version of the Transfiguration, measure numbers correspond to those in the Score in this volume.)

Act II	387/1–388/5	410/2–411/8	411/9–415/5	415/6–421/2	421/3–427/5
	$\frac{6}{8}$ (A♭$^6_4$)	$\frac{2}{2}$ (B$^6_4$)	(E$^6_4$)	(B$^6_4$)	
First Setting (Preliminary Draft)	PART I $\frac{6}{8}$		PART III $\frac{2}{2}$	PART II	PART IV (same setting as final version)
Transfiguration					
Final Version	PART I $\frac{4}{4}$	PART II $\frac{4}{4}$		PART III	PART IV
Transfiguration	mm. 1621–1631	mm. 1632–1648		mm. 1649–1663	mm. 1664–1680

After the first few measures of Part IV, Wagner changed the method he had been following so far and for the most part ignored the Act II vocal parts altogether. Instead of simply adapting the new text to an earlier vocal line or instrumental counterpoint, he copied out the melody and bass line of the orchestral texture from the final portion of Act II, Scene 2 and added the new continuation along those same lines. In turn, he constructed an essentially new vocal part as a counterpoint to what he had written out. The Preliminary Draft for Part IV corresponds exactly to the final version up to Isolde's last note, except that Wagner duplicated the 2/2 meter from Act II. Ultimately he changed the whole monologue to 4/4 meter—scarcely surprising in the case of the 6/8 strophe for Part I, since the Preliminary Draft shows one passage where he seems to have slipped unawares into duple meter *in the vocal part* for four measures.

When Wagner revised Parts I through III, he also removed the new music he had composed for the first and third refrains. He retained the *text* of the first refrain intact, however, and his readaptation of it to music from the original strophe shifted the remainder of the text for Part I ahead by two lines. Thus, the Act II strophe now concludes with the second group of 4 lines, and Wagner repositioned the second refrain at the beginning of the music for Part II. In assigning this new structural position to the second refrain, he eliminated its exact parallel with the first refrain by shortening it to one line—the only change he made in the version his text had assumed in the Preliminary Draft. He also adapted the third refrain to music from Act II, but he retained its position at the conclusion of Part II, which thus both begins and ends with modified refrains, now so different from each other. In the final version, then, Wagner abandoned the original symmetrical refrain structure he had built into the text for Parts I and II in favor of the purely musical principle of recapitulation. We have noted that when Wagner began the new setting of Part II with the *first* B-major passage from Act II, he continued from that point straight through to the end of the scene, but he retained the excisions of internal repetitions he had made in the earlier setting of Part II. The music Wagner had used in the Preliminary Draft for the 8 lines of Part II now appears as the setting for the first 7 lines of Part III.

Wagner's new continuation following the end of the second recall begins at m. 1681 and provides a final resolution of the major triad with added 6th in the harmonic context of a cadential IV–I progression:

Example 21

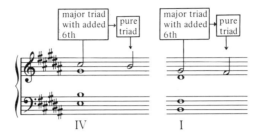

The added 6th is now treated as a long-sustained appoggiatura to the 5th of the triad. He then reinforces the cadential character of the passage by converting IV to the minor mode in mm. 1688–89. Isolde's last note remained D♯ even in the Developed Draft, and as a much later afterthought, Wagner took a pencil and entered the change to the high F♯, so that the conclusion of the vocal line foreshadows the terminal high F♯ for the violins. The Preliminary Draft already includes the violin ascent to the high F♯, but Wagner approached it chromatically from the E♯ below. His change to a diatonic ascent through the first five notes of the B-major scale was conditioned in part by his eventual decision to add one last recall of Motive *y* from the opening phrase of the Prelude. In revising this progression for its new context, Wagner added a B pedal point to the whole motive and replaced the E[7] of the earlier progression with an E-*minor* triad, which now initiates a characteristic minor IV–major I cadence in B. In this extension, the melodic line continues its ascending pattern, but now diatonically from B to D♯. Wagner decided to include this recall of Motive *y* before he reached this passage in his Developed Draft. His sketch for the new version, in its final form, stands alone on the otherwise blank *verso* of the last sheet from his Preliminary Draft for the opera:

Example 22

VIEWS AND COMMENTS

Unless specified otherwise, all numbered footnotes in the following essays are those of the authors.

DONALD FRANCIS TOVEY

~~~~~~~

Wagner in the Concert-Room†

Composer, pianist, lecturer, and one of the most articulate writers on music in the English language, Tovey is best known nowadays for his *Essays in Musical Analysis*, which cover a wide range of subjects from many different critical and analytical perspectives. In the following extract, he makes an eloquent plea for performing the *Tristan* Prelude with Wagner's concert ending, evidently unaware—as many still are—that coupling the Prelude (with its operatic conclusion) to the Transfiguration was Wagner's own idea. Tovey's observations about the vocal part in the Transfiguration continue to hold wide currency in many quarters, but they probably bear reexamination in the light of Wagner's Preliminary Draft (reproduced above) and of Leonard Meyer's analytical points (see pp. 297–302).

In the middle of the nineteenth century there was one main reason why the teaching of musical composition fell into bad ways. This was the delusion that musical art-forms exist in a generalized state and can be grasped as in a bird's-eye view. In the later nineteenth century another delusion arose, and both are now prevalent. This other delusion arose from the persecution and the triumph of Wagner. Both the persecutors and the Wagnerians argued without knowledge of any genuine principles of musical composition, and both sides were in unconsious agreement that, whether Wagner could or could not compose, he did not, as a matter of fact, do so. It is as absurd and as essentially underbred to complain of the "vogue" of Wagner as to complain of the "vogue" of Beethoven. But extracts of Beethoven as accompaniments to cowpuncher films are not more artistic than Wagner concerts of selections which, like Mr. Punch's early classification of

† From *Essays in Musical Analysis*, Vol. 6 (London, 1939), pp. 102–4. Reprinted by permission of Oxford University Press.

149

trains, consist of (*a*) those which start but do not arrive; (*b*) those which arrive but do not start; and (*c*) those which neither start nor arrive. With the vogue of such concerts and the approval of them by critics, the last vestiges of popular and academic instinct for composition disappeared. It has now been decided to ordain that Wagner shall be out of fashion. To this I move an amendment. Let it be decided that Wagner is a composer; and that until the arbiters of musical fashion have shown themselves capable of recognizing the difference between a composition and a scrap-book the public that goes to hear Wagner's music-dramas shall be allowed to enjoy its normal and healthy activity of understanding Wagner's music through his drama without fear or favour of fashion. How grave the destruction of all critical and academic standards of composition has become through the acceptance of inartistic Wagner excerpts may be seen from a recent example when a highly educated writer on music contributed to a musical journal some interesting and important remarks upon the prelude to *Tristan*, in which he assumed that in the concert-room it was inseparable from the *Liebestod*, and accordingly had no complete key-system. No doubt to the general public key-systems are academic technicalities which concern only teachers of harmony. Similarly, to repeat one of my favourite illustrations, the distinction between the nominative and accusative is an affair for grammarians. But the general public will miss something of material interest to it if the translators and producers of a tragedy in a foreign language do not know who killed whom; and a piece without a key-system or with an incoherent key-system does not give the naïve listener the same coherent impression, or even the same tuneful impression, as he will get, without any knowledge of theory, from a piece that has a key in which it begins and ends. Now the excellent critic who wrote so well about the prelude-and-liebestod monstrosity betrayed that he did not know that Wagner wrote a page, one of the most beautiful in all his works, that finishes the prelude in its proper key and makes it as coherent and as exact in its proportions as any movement by Bach. The critic was thus quite unaware that the modulations which lead to the rise of the curtain upon the first act are a powerful and subtle dramatic catastrophe in their proper place.

This orthodox view of Wagner's later style is no better than a conviction that Wagner's mind was a mush. Here we see a reverential Wagnerian actually unaware that Wagner did his best, and an absolutely perfect best, to make the *Tristan* Vorspiel a coherent piece of music in

A minor ending in A major, with a sense of tonality strengthened, instead of being weakened, by what has been happily called his "chromatic iridescence" at its highest power. Most unfortunately, it happens that the catastrophic darkening to C minor upon which the curtain rises at the beginning of the play makes a grammatically correct join with the dark chords from which Isolde's dying utterances emerge into a key not only different from, but totally destructive of the harmonic basis of the prelude. What do we gain by joining these two pieces in the concert-room? For those who know the whole music-drama we gain the opportunity of listening to a quotation from the end of the opera after we have heard the uncompleted prelude. We can, if we like, imagine that the rest of the three acts are past. But we do not gain the living or dying presence of Isolde herself, because the problem of how to represent the voice-part in a purely instrumental performance is solved by the sublimely simple process of leaving it out. Liszt, in his wonderful transcription of the *Liebestod* for pianoforte, did not go quite so far, inasmuch as he contrived to represent no less than seven independent vocal notes and a grace-note near the beginning: *seht ihr's Freunde? Seht ihr's nicht?* For the rest, it is a remarkable symptom of an abnormality in Wagner's art that, though the voice inevitably dominates the attention whenever it is heard among instruments, and though the vocal writing of Isolde's *Liebestod* is perfect both in declamation and singability, it is so little essential to Wagner's invention that Isolde's *Liebestod* is a complete piece of music without Isolde at all. She is singing for sixty-eight bars, and in twenty-five of these she is able to deliver the main theme, constantly broken, sometimes quite awkwardly, by pauses and other necessities of declamation. For the other forty-three bars she is descanting in counterpoints, of which, as I have already remarked, Liszt has been able to preserve seven notes and a grace-note. How much of these counterpoints does any one, except the singer, remember? Surely her last notes should be memorable? They are the right notes in the right declamation; they easily penetrate the orchestra, and they will do justice to the most golden of voices. How many music-lovers can quote them? They have never been heard in the concert-room, except when a singer was engaged; but I should not be surprised if many of the music-lovers who go to every stage performance of *Tristan* found themselves unable to quote them.

If we wish to use Isolde's *Liebestod* in the concert-room as a quotation, just as we might enjoy an eminent actor reciting a soliloquy from

Shakespeare, we cannot object to doing the *Liebestod* without Isolde. It is no case of Hamlet without the Prince of Denmark. The only possible objection to playing the *Liebestod* as an instrumental piece is that it begins nowhere. Liszt's pianoforte transcription remedies this by four magnificently powerful and subtle introductory bars[1] which ought obviously to be used in the orchestral version. For the rest, not only is the *Liebestod* a mere quotation in the concert-room, but it owes most of its power in the opera itself to the fact that it is there a quotation from the love-duet in the second act. There is one reason why Isolde's vocal part in it is so fragmentary. In the original duet both she and Tristan are much more centred upon the real themes of the music.

*   *   *

1. Liszt's "four magnificently powerful and subtle introductory bars" run as follows:

[*Editor*]

ERNEST NEWMAN

~~~~~

[*The Prelude*]†

In contrast to Tovey, Newman regarded the Prelude and Transfiguration as making "an admirably rounded whole, musically and psychologically." Author of the standard English biography of Wagner—for its time the greatest biography in any language—Newman spent much of his time as a music journalist. The following selection is from *The Wagner Operas*, as fine an introductory "textbook" as any ever written about a major composer's major masterpieces. Newman approaches Wagner's music as a metaphor for the drama by noting the occurrences of *Leitmotive*—the means by which, in one form or another, most opera lovers have come to know Wagner's works for the last hundred years or more. The most enlightened spokesman for this familiar approach, Newman cautions in his Overture to the book that "it is a cardinal error to suppose either that the musical tissue of a Wagner opera is made up simply of a pinning together of motives, or that, in most cases, any one label can be found that will cover all the uses and meanings of any one motive."

* * *

There is here no attempt, as in the Prelude to the *Mastersingers*, to epitomise the stage action and the characters of the opera. Wagner concentrates on the inmost essentials; the Prelude is the slow musical elaboration of a single bitter-sweet mood. For convenience' sake we have to attach labels to the "motives" upon which it is constructed, but the reader must be warned against interpreting these too literally. As a rule the commentators have decided upon a label from a hint given by the words or the situation with which a motive is associated on its first appearance in the opera. But we shall go hopelessly wrong if we allow

†From *The Wagner Operas* (New York, 1949), pp. 207–15. Reprinted by permission of Alfred A. Knopf, Inc. and the Estate of Ernest Newman.

that particular association to occupy our minds each time we hear the motive; it may undergo all kinds of metamorphoses and take on all shades of meaning as the drama goes on.

It is easy for the casual listener to get a false notion of the opening bars of the Prelude:

No. 1

The melodic line seems to be a continuous one, running from the opening A in the lower clef to the final B in the higher. But in reality there are two motives here: the first (No. 1A), extending from the opening note to the D sharp of the second full bar, is given out by the 'cellos in the upper register of the instrument, where the tone has a peculiar poignancy; the other (No. 1B) comes out in the penetrating timbre of the oboes, over a woodwind harmony of bassoons, cor anglais, and (in the second bar) clarinets. We shall call No. 1A the Grief or Sorrow motive, though it must be understood at the outset that its expression in the course of the opera is too multiple and too complex for it to be always tied down to the connotation of a single word: it has in it at various times something of longing, of pain, of hopelessness, of resignation, and many things more. No. 1B is called by some analysts the motive of Desire, by others the motive of Magic, for no better reason than the fact that when it is first heard in the opera Isolde is speaking of her mother's craft in the brewing of magic potions. Our own rough-and-ready label for it will be Desire, with which the magic art of Isolde's mother necessarily has a certain external connection. But it must always be borne in mind that, as has been pointed out in the foregoing pages, Wagner never intends to imply that the love of Tristan and Isolde is the *physical consequence* of the philtre, but only that the pair, having drunk what they imagine to be the draught of Death and believing that they have looked upon earth and sea and sky for the last time, feel themselves free to confess, when the potion begins its work within them, the love they have so long felt but have concealed from each other and almost from themselves. Nor will the reader need to be reminded that this motive No. 1B was committed to paper in December 1856, before a word of the scenario of the opera had been written. Consequently there is no warrant whatever for identifying it literally, as we were taught to do at one time, with the "magic" of Isolde and her mother: for Wagner it stood primarily for the predestined yearning of the lovers towards each other.

He himself, in a letter of March 1860 to Frau Wesendonk, has given us a clue to the complex of emotions the motive symbolised for him. He is in Paris, unhappy and sick to the depths of him with a sense of loneliness and alienation from his environment, and looking forward wistfully "towards the land of Nirvana". But Nirvana, it appears, becomes identical in his mind with Tristan, and Tristan and himself with the Buddhist theory of the origin of the world—the troubling of the primal cloudless heavens by a breath that swells and swells and finally condenses into our visible world in all its "inscrutable and impenetrable variety"; and he gives us the key to his meaning by quoting the music of our No. 1B, in a way that shows that he identified it just then with the "breath" out of which the cosmos has condensed. In a word, it is Desire, for ever expanding and retracting, for ever seeking to realise itself and for ever being frustrated.

Repetitions of No. 1 at various pitches and in various colours lead to a sforzando which introduces two new motives:

No. 2

The first of these (A) relates particularly to the Anguish of Tristan; the second (B) is generally described as the Look (or Glance) motive, from the fact that it first appears in the opera at the point in the first act where Isolde tells Brangaene how her resolve to avenge herself on the slayer of Morold melted away under the glance that the sick Tristan had turned on her. No. 2 emerges insensibly into a third motive of a similar cast, which the commentators associate with the love philtre:

No. 3

A half-passionate, half-mournful development of this is broken at one point by the reiteration of figures of this type:

No. 4

which answer each other in different registers and colours. In his letter of December 1859 concerning the concert close to the Prelude, Wagner tells Frau Wesendonk that she will "recognise ivy and vine in the music, especially when you hear it in the orchestra, where strings and wind alternate with each other". He was referring to the antiphonal figures shown in No. 4. But it would be the height of folly on our part to take all this too literally. The ivy-and-vine legend plays no part whatever in Wagner's drama. It may have pleased him and Frau Wesendonk to associate privately No. 4 (and themselves) with ivy and vine, but nowhere in the opera has the motive any such connotation; and here in the Prelude it depicts simply one more phase of the yearning of the lovers.

A point that should not be overlooked is the bass line (B, C, D sharp) in the fourth and fifth bars of No. 3. It wells up and subsides ominously in the double basses, bassoons and bass clarinet, and symbolises Death (or Fate). It is curious that Bülow, who made the first piano arrangement of the score, should have failed to see that these three notes constitute a definite motive; otherwise he would not have altered Wagner's slurring of them in the arbitrary way he does here and elsewhere.

Wagner now works up to his climax by way of a new motive:

No. 5

which incorporates in itself more and more insistent reminiscences of No. 1B. The culmination is heralded by a fortissimo enunciation of No. 2B in increasingly complex harmonic forms, and with a terrific fortissimo in the full orchestra the climax is reached and passed. The fortissimo quickly subsides to a piano; the orchestra dwells sadly upon echoes of No. 1, No. 2B and No. 4, and the music gradually ebbs away into a heaving figure in the 'cellos and basses * * * that prepares us for the sea setting in which the opera will open.[1]

The Prelude is a perfect specimen of musical form at its most consummate, not a schematic mould imposed upon the "thematic material" from the outside but a form that has come into being simply as the outcome of the ideas. Once more, as in the Prelude to *Lohengrin*, Wagner unconsciously obeys that natural law of structure that brings in the climax at a point about two-thirds of the time-distance between the beginning and the end. This is not only good art but ordinary experience; while it takes a long time to scale a mountain, the descent may be accomplished in half or a third of the time. Some conductors ruin Wagner's perfect design by pumping an accelerando into the music during the long crescendo that leads up to the climax. Wagner, who, though some conductors will receive the news with incredulity, knew infinitely better what his music was about than they will ever do, has not specified a single change of tempo during the prolonged ascent to the peak-point. He prescribes a slight holding-back after the peak has been reached, which is entirely in keeping with the general law of descent after a toilsome climb. The Prelude—and the same is even more true of the Liebestod—is far more tremendous in its tension when the

1. Example 6 has been omitted. [*Editor*]

ascent is not hurried in order to get a conductor's effect of "increasing passion", a cheap showman's trick upon which Wagner used always to pour out his scorn. The last thing he wanted was that his music should reach the hearer not as he had conceived it but as it appears after it has passed through the distorting and sometimes vulgarising medium of a conductor's mind. As early as 1852 he had written to a friend, "I don't care in the least whether my works are given or not: all I am concerned with is that they shall be performed as I conceived them. Whoever can't and won't do that may leave them alone." Upon tempo he always laid the utmost emphasis: it was his constant complaint during his last years that he did not know a single conductor who could be trusted to find unaided the correct tempi for any of his works.

Let us now glance for a moment at the ending he himself devised for use when the Prelude is to be played in the concert room without the Liebestod. His instinct for form told him that in the first place the terrific climax would have to be dispensed with, since the goal was now different and the descent from the peak-point was going to be accomplished in a new way. With the closing scene of the opera in his mind the ebb of the psychological tide of the Prelude would necessarily have to be brought about in terms of that "Verklärung". So Wagner cuts out the original climax, which had come in the Prelude in bars 83 and 84.[2] In bar 82 the trumpet and trombones had given out No. 1B. He begins his new close at this point: he swiftly dissolves the fortissimo into a diminuendo, cuts out bars 83 and 84, and continues quietly, as in the original, with bars 85 to the first half of 94. Here begins the short "Verklärung". A change in the latter part of bar 94 serves to introduce a motive of ecstasy that had appeared in the opera for the first time in the opening scene of the second act:

2. Newman has quite thoroughly garbled the situation here. At the beginning of Wagner's piano arrangement of the concert ending, made for Mathilde Wesendonk and sent to her with his letter of December 19, 1859, appears the inscription "82 measures"— indicating, as Newman correctly inferred, that Mathilde should play the Prelude intact up through m. 82 and then continue with what Wagner had written out for her. Newman was evidently familiar with the concert ending only from the facsimile of this document included in the volume of Wagner's letters to Mathilde. And because he followed Lorenz's bizarre numbering of the measures, which assigns the number 1 to the initial eighth-note pick-up, Newman is one measure off in his analysis of this passage. The printed scores, which he obviously had not seen, show quite clearly that there is no change whatever in the Prelude until the second half of m. 93.

Incidentally, a comparison of Wagner's piano arrangement with the printed score shows immediately that Wagner himself did *not* count the Prelude's initial upbeat as m. 1! [*Editor*]

No. 6

* * * The remainder of the new matter consists almost entirely of wistful broodings upon this theme, until at last it assumes the form in which it plays a dominant part in the closing stages of the Liebestod, with the poignant No. 1B piercing through the texture at the finish, as it does at the end of the opera. * * * Wagner ends his arrangement, however, not in B major, as in the final bars of the opera, but in A major, thus rounding off the A minor in which the Prelude had begun.

A final word on the Prelude may not be out of place: it may help to clarify for the reader the whole problem of Wagner's use of "motives". We are compelled to attach labels to these, for otherwise we could not refer to them in our discussion of a work; but some of these labels have done considerable harm by bringing up in the listener's mind the same too literal connotation each time the motive appears. There are Wagnerian motives, of course, the meaning of which is virtually unchanging; they are definitely associated with a particular character (such as the Beckmesser or the Gutrune motive), or with an object that is at once physical and symbolic, and therefore static (such as the Spear motive in the *Ring*). But Wagner's conception and employment of motives varied with the nature of the work he had in hand; and when, as in *Tristan*, stage action and external reality count for very little and psychological states for virtually everything, the import of a motive can rarely be pinned down throughout to any particular person, object or episode. The motives are sensitive, plastic musical materials, on a par with those of the symphonist, with which the composer weaves a fabric of thought and emotion of a kind that can exist only in music.

Now the Prelude to *Tristan* was not written, as most introductions to operas are, after the completion of the work, when the composer has the whole of his thematic material before him and can select from it just what seems to him best suited to epitomise the contents of the whole work. The *Tristan* Prelude contains no motive specifically correlated with the second and third acts, for the simple reason, among others, that Wagner had not even begun formal work upon these when the Prelude was written.[3] He commenced the music of the first act on the 1st October 1857; and apparently he began with the Prelude. As his own programme note shows, it is in no way dramatic or pictorial: it expresses the incessant projection and recoil upon itself of a single emotion—that of longing without satisfaction and without end. Even if the opera had never been written the Prelude would still be a perfectly organised piece of mood-music that requires no "explanation" outside itself, a symphonic epitome, as it might be, of an unwritten drama. When Wagner was composing it the separate themes of it had probably no such precise meanings for him as the labels we attach to them are apt to suggest. When the time came for him to embody them in the opera, each of them would necessarily be associated on its first appearance with this, that or the other psychological point of the moment. But it is an error to assume, as the commentators have been inclined to do, that because at this point or that a motive is first heard in connection with certain words or a certain situation it relates specifically to that sentiment or that situation whenever it occurs later in the opera, or, before that, in the Prelude.

Our Nos. 2B, 1B and 4 are cases in point. Because No. 2B first appears in the opera when Isolde tells Brangaene how the sick man looked up at her from his couch and the sword fell from her hand, the analysts have agreed to call it the Look motive, with the result that people innocently read that too definite meaning into it each time it occurs in the Prelude and in the opera. The truth is that it is a musical theme of generalised import, the expression of the love that Tristan and Isolde were fated from their birth to feel for each other; it is only the dramatic exigencies of the text that lead to its first putting in an appearance when Isolde recalls the outer circumstances of their realisation of this fatality. So with No. 1B: there is no necessity, and indeed it is misleading, to tie the meaning of this down to the "Magic" of Isolde's mother merely because it is first given out by the orchestra when Isolde says bitterly, "O futile art of the sorceress, that only balsams can brew!", and is heard again later when Brangaene says to Isolde,

3. Wagner also composed the Preludes to *Die Meistersinger* and *Parsifal* before he began "formal work" on the music of those operas. [*Editor*]

"Hast thou thy mother's arts forgot? Think'st thou that she who knows all secrets would have sent me with thee into a strange land without counsel?"—by which she means the philtre that is to ensure Isolde the love of King Marke. The true psychological significance of the potion has already been dwelt upon in the foregoing pages: it is not the prime cause of passion but the symbol of it. To think of the philtre in its material sense on each of the many occasions when the motive recurs later in the opera—for instance, in the prelude to the second act, or in the subtle transformation it undergoes in the introduction to the third act * * * —is to fall into the rankest absurdity.

Again, although Wagner, in his letter to Frau Wesendonk, lets his fancy play upon the ivy and the vine in connection with our No. 4, we must not suppose for a moment that he originally shaped the theme with the intention of setting up any such permanent connection in the listener's mind. For him it was simply another aspect of the predestined passion of the pair. He uses it, for example, when, after drinking the philtre, they fall at last into each other's arms:

No. 7

Here any association of it with ivy and vine would manifestly be out of place.

* * *

ROGER SESSIONS

~~~~~~~~~~~~

[The Opening Bars of the Prelude]†

Unlike most of the other distinguished American composers of his generation, Sessions studied in Germany between the wars, rather than in Paris. In the following extract, he begins with a presentation of the analytical view of the Prelude's opening measures widely accepted as standard, at least in America. A crucial feature of this analysis is its view of G♯ as an appoggiatura to A, which is thus regarded as the actual chord tone of the first harmony—an interpretation not effectively challenged until Mitchell's analysis (see pp. 242–67). Sessions's analysis serves as a basis for an intriguing discussion of musical aesthetics, with specific commentary on the nature of musical expressivity and its "emotional" impact on the listener.

* * *

In analyzing these measures we must not forget that we are dealing with living materials, and that such analysis has therefore to do only with the effect which the music produces, not necessarily with the conscious intentions of the composer. The music is a *gesture*, the result of at least as many complex forces, impulses, and experiences, both individual and general, as every other gesture. Like every other gesture it is essentially indivisible, and while we can, obviously, note certain of its elements, we must nevertheless remain constantly aware of the fact that we are not thereby revealing its whole or even its essential meaning. Analysis, whether technical, historical, or—according to the latest fashions—psycho-sociological, may reveal some of the effects which art produces and some of the means through which these effects are produced. Beyond this it remains mere speculation, certainly without artistic and possibly without scientific validity. For art consists neither of devices, supposed "influences," or mere reflections of the artist's inner life.

With due consciousness of such limitations, then, let us examine

† From "The Composer and His Message," in Augusto Centeno, ed., *The Intent of the Artist* (Princeton, 1941), pp. 113–25. Reprinted by permission of Princeton University Press.

the passage in question.

Its four well defined sections are indicated in the present text by brackets. If the third bracketed section seems disproportionately long, it is nevertheless obvious that the repetition of the same notes in measures 11, 13, 14, and 15 illustrate clearly to the eye what is still clearer to the ear—the fact that these measures serve to prolong and intensify this musical moment, without introducing any essential changes. Measures 12 and 13, to be specific, repeat at a higher octave the two preceding measures, while measures 14 and 15, in the same two octaves, recall the concluding beat of the phrase and thus prolong still further both its harmony and its expressive effect. I shall refer presently to this prolongation and to its expressive significance.

Each of the four bracketed parts is based on the same musical phrase. This does not mean that the phrase is literally repeated or that, even in the second phrase, it is literally transposed. It means however that the general outlines, the accent, the inflection, are in each case so similar as to leave no doubt in the hearer's mind that each successive phrase is a repetition, with equal or greater intensity, of the same musical gesture.

Let us look, then, at the phrase itself in its original form. Note the long F of the 'cello at the beginning of the first measure, and the long G♯ of the oboe at the beginning of the second. Each of these notes is extraneous to the harmony, and each creates a feeling of suspense which is not resolved till the very end of the measure. The expression of the F is enhanced by the long crescendo which is so familiar to all who have heard this music; the G♯ by an accent and by the dissonant chord which accompanies it. In the third measure the dissonant A♯, again, slightly delays the note, B, which belongs to the harmony.

The effect may be grasped more vividly by looking at the underlying harmonies themselves:

The three notes in question—F, G♯, and A♯—not only give the melodic line flexibility and a certain degree of freedom; they also, by delaying in each case the entrance of the expected harmonic note, draw special attention to that note, and thus intensify both the note itself and the harmony which supports it. Above all, they help in these instances by their very length to create and sustain a feeling of suspense, which is the essence of the expression to which I referred above.

Let us look further, however, at the harmonies themselves. They form what musicians know as an "uncompleted cadence" in the key of A minor. This means that to the normal musical ear they produce the effect of a question which is left temporarily, at least, unanswered. We expect, after the last of the chords quoted in the preceding example, the chord of A, and in its minor form. * * * Why this is so I shall not attempt to explain here. The answer leads into the most fundamental problems of music, esthetics, and even acoustics. Let me draw attention, instead, to the paramount importance of the final harmony in each phrase. Its position as the conclusion of the phrase makes of it inevitably, by the fundamental laws of rhythm, the goal of the harmonic impulse and thus the point at which the harmonic expression of the phrase is, so to speak, accumulated.

In the present case it may be observed that this final chord—E, G♯, D, B—leaves the hearer temporarily at least in a state of suspense, and that this is further enhanced by the long pause which follows. The E on which the chord is based is known to musicians as the "dominant" of A; among the tonal relationships which the composer, through the technical means at his disposal has set up, the E, at the interval of a fifth above A, is second in importance to the A itself; and through these relationships, the listener has been given the almost instinctive desire, or at least the expectation, that the A will follow in the bass, along with the upper notes which complete its chord.

What does follow, I shall not describe in complete detail. The same processes within this phrase are repeated in their essentials in the two following phrases. The 'cello in each case takes its note from the final harmony of the preceding phrase, and each statement in its turn intensifies, through sheer repetition in the first case, through slight variation in the second, the expression of the initial gesture. But what is more important is the binding principle which, far more than the so-called "thematic development" of the phrase itself, welds the whole passage into a single gesture of much larger proportions.

In other words, the expressive meaning of these seventeen measures is embodied in a design which makes of them a single unit. It is fairly easy, for example, to follow the upper voice from each phrase to the following one, which begins with the same note on which its predecessor left off; the ear follows without difficulty the connection between the B in measure 3 and that in measure 6, between D in measure 7 and that in measure 10. It recognizes, in the first two notes (E♯–F♯) of measure 16, the notes of the preceding measures, to which I have already drawn attention. A closer examination of the passage as a whole would reveal other connections of the same type, attributable not so much to the "technical" prowess of the composer as to the absolutely unhampered and consistent intensity of his musical thought.

These, however, are only details in their relation to a large harmonic design, itself a prolongation of the "dominant seventh" harmony of A minor, to which reference was made above. I have already referred to the fact that the harmonic sense of a phrase reaches its point of greatest concentration in the final harmony of the phrase; and no clearer illustration of this fact could be given, than the passage included in the third bracket, where the final harmony is prolonged by repetition, first together with the measure which resolves into it (12–13), and then, by a double repetition of the melodic pattern of this final measure itself (14–15).

The emphasis on this harmony underlines the fact that we have here reached, so to speak, the harmonic climax of the whole passage—the moment of greatest tension. What has happened? The answer to this question may be grasped in the clearest fashion by repeating in close succession the final harmonies of the three phrases, the significance of which I have already noted. It will be seen that the basic notes of these harmonies progress in two successive steps from E, which we have already defined as the "dominant" of A minor, to B, the upper fifth and quasi-dominant of E, and that if taken together they form the chord of E minor, with B as its culminating point. The B harmony therefore creates, so to speak, a new level of expressive suspense which is intensified or, in the langauge of sheer design, *underlined*, by the prolongation, described above, of the harmony in question.

mm. 3   7   11-15   16   17

The expressive process becomes quite clear in measure 16 where the entrance, *forte*, of the original E chord brings a temporary sense of resolution; a closing, so to speak, of the harmonic circuit. These sixteen measures may in fact be considered as a vast elaboratioin of this harmony, the "dominant seventh chord" (E–G♯–B–D) of A minor. This harmony, in other words, is developed in such a way that its inner structure is utilized with a maximum expressive effect, constituting not only the coordinating center, but the very expressive essence, of the passage in question.

I have dwelt at such length on the harmonic aspect of the passage simply because it is the most difficult to describe in words which convey a meaning except to the technically initiated. No less important to the whole effect is the steady upward unfolding of the chromatic scale, beginning with G♯ in measure 2, moving first from G♯ to B, B to D, D to F♯, and then through G♯ in measure 16. These sixteen measures may thus in a sense be considered, through this chromatic traversal of a complete octave, as in the upper or melodic voice, an elaboration of the G♯. This melodic effect is in actual fact, of course, inseparable from the harmonic effect already described. The G♯ is not only an ingredient of the dominant seventh E, G♯, B, and D but in a sense its most active ingredient, since it is the so-called "leading-tone" of the key—i.e., the tone directly below the key note or tonic, and one which, as musical theorists are wont to say, always tends upward to this key note—in this case of course A. In other words this G♯ in the upper voice enhances in the greatest measure the expressive effect of the "dominant seventh" harmony.

Both the chord and the G♯ find their resolution in measure 17. Here, however, one may observe another harmonic principle, which dominates the whole prelude, and which embodies still further the expressive principle of suspense. As I have pointed out, the expected resolution is, in the case of the G♯, the "tonic" A, and in the case of the "dominant seventh" chord, the tonic chord of A minor as illustrated above. By means of what is called the "deceptive cadence," however, the suspense is prolonged and heightened through the substitution of another harmony—in this case the chord of F—while the G♯ is resolved to A (preceded by B) in quite normal fashion. Examination of the whole Prelude will reveal the fact that the expected resolution never takes place, and careful analysis would show a profound connection between this fact, and the expressive impact and character of the whole.

I have brought forward this illustration in order to show certain aspects of what I have called "movement" in music, and in doing so, I have touched upon the question of musical expression. What is it, actually, that music expresses?

Let us consider for a moment the music to which I have just referred. It is associated in Wagner's drama with a definite situation, with definite characters—hence we are accustomed to say it "expresses" the tragic love of Tristan and Isolde. Is it, however, the music that tells us this? Does it tell us anything, in any definite and inevitable sense, of love and tragedy? How much of what is implied in this definition of its content is there by virtue of its association with the drama? Is this association an inevitable one, or is it in the last analysis arbitrary?

The music certainly tells us nothing specifically about Tristan and Isolde, as concrete individuals; in no sense does it identify them or enlighten us regarding the concrete situation in which they find themselves. Does it tell us, then, specifically, anything about love and tragedy which we could identify as such without the aid of the dramatic and poetic images with which Wagner so richly supplies us?

It seems to me that the answer in each case is, inevitably, a negative one. There is, in any specific sense, neither love nor tragedy in the music.

I have attempted a description of this music in terms of movement. I have tried to point out how intimately our musical impulses are connected with those primitive movements which are among the very conditions of our existence. I have tried to show, too, how vivid is our response to the primitive elements of musical movement.

Is not this the key both to the content of music and to its extraordinary power? These bars from the Prelude to Tristan do not express for us love or frustration or even longing: but they reproduce for us, both qualitatively and dynamically, certain gestures of the spirit which are to be sure less specifically definable than any of these emotions, but which energize them and make them vital to us.

So it seems to me that this is the essence of musical expression. "Emotion" is specific, individual and conscious; music goes deeper than this, to the energies which animate our psychic life, and out of these creates a pattern which has an existence, laws, and human significance of its own. It reproduces for us the most intimate essence, the tempo and the energy, of our spiritual being; our tranquility and our restlessness, our animation and our discouragement, our vitality and our weakness—all, in fact, of the fine shades of dynamic variation of our inner life. It reproduces these far more directly and more specifically than is possible through any other medium of human communication.

*   *   *

DERYCK COOKE

The Creative Imagination as Harmony†

Cooke is best known to music lovers nowadays for his performing version
of Mahler's Tenth Symphony and for *I Saw the World End*, his unfinished
and posthumously published study of Wagner's *Ring* cycle. *The Language
of Music* was based on Cooke's belief that European tonal music constituted
by tradition a language of artistic communication analogous to that of
verbal speech. In his preface, Cooke explains that the book "attempts to
isolate the various means of expression available to the composer—the
various procedures in the dimensions of pitch, time, and volume—and to
discover what emotional effects these procedures can produce; but more
specifically, it tries to pinpoint the inherent emotional characters of the
various notes of the major, minor, and chromatic scales, and of certain
basic melodic patterns which have been used persistently throughout our
musical history." Cooke assumes a characteristic expressive meaning for
certain intervals, particularly for those other than thirds, fourths, and
fifths. In the following extract, he also attempts to elucidate the feature
of *Tristan* so often paid lip service—expressive harmony.

For our example of the functioning of the creative imagination in
the harmonic field, let us take that celebrated case of harmonic innovation, the opening of the *Tristan* Prelude, since there is nothing
melodically or rhythmically individual about it at all.

Wagner's conception of *Tristan and Isolde* was, in his own words,
that of "a tale of endless yearning, longing, the bliss and wretchedness
of love; world, power, fame, honour, chivalry, loyalty, and friendship
all blown away like an insubstantial dream; one thing alone left living—
longing, longing unquenchable, a yearning, a hunger, a languishing
forever renewing itself; one sole redemption—death, surcease, a sleep
without awakening." The Prelude he conceived as "one long succession
of linked phrases" in which "that insatiable longing swells forth from

† From *The Language of Music* (Oxford, 1959), pp. 187–94. Reprinted by permission
of Oxford University Press.

the first timidest avowal to sweetest protraction. . . ."[1] It is clear that
the emotion which motivated this conception must have been a very
powerful one, and it is not surprising that it gave rise to an inspiration
of such a revolutionary nature that it bewildered and alienated many
on a first hearing:

Example 1

Here, the melodic element is not in the least individual: the opening
three notes, before anything else happens, are that well-worn basic
term, the arched minor 5–3–2–1, in D minor, disappointed of its natural
conclusion on the tonic; and the four rising chromatic notes on the
oboe, in A minor, are a common "yearning" feature of Mozart's style.
In fact, we can find them in the Andante of his String Quartet in E♭,
K. 428, in the exact form in which Wagner used them; and this quotation
will also reveal that the rhythmic element of the *Tristan* inspiration is
not new either:

Example 2

Strangely enough, by thus putting the music into the same key as the
Tristan Prelude, we can see clearly that the essential core of the latter's
harmonic element is not new either; yet it was precisely in the harmonic
field that Wagner's creative imagination exerted itself so powerfully
indeed that whenever the harmony of Ex. 1 turned up again in post-
Wagnerian music (as it often did) it immediately evoked the cry of
"Tristan!" Where, then, lies the decisive creative act? Clearly in the vital
sharp fourth (D♯), in the sounding of it in conjunction with the major

1. Wagner, programme-note for performance of the Prelude in Paris, 25 January
1860 (quoted in Ernest Newman, *Wagner Nights*, p. 219) [*Author*]; American edition: *The
Wagner Operas*, p. 206 [*Editor*].

seventh (G♯) and the minor sixth (F♮), and in placing the result in a new and revolutionary tonal context, which will become clear as we proceed. (It is not intended to suggest that Wagner consciously or unconsciously "gingered up" this passage from Mozart: such a progression was very much part of his tradition, and may have reached his unconscious from the work of composers like Spohr and Liszt.[2]

The best way of describing the functioning of this particular inspiration is as follows. Wagner's conception of the work, given above, must have stimulated certain of the most expressive tonal tensions to materialize from the D minor/A minor key-area of his unconscious: these were, naturally enough, the "tragic" minor third, the "anguished" minor sixth, the "hopeless" minor second, the "mournful" minor seventh, the "pathetically longing" fourth, and (most significantly) the "violently longing" major seventh. As we might expect, the "joyful" major third and sixth were not called upon, nor was the *tonic*—a most extraordinary omission, but only a natural outcome of the original emotion, the infinite longing that can find no satisfaction. (The dominant—context of flux—was naturally drawn on, of course.) The creative imagination integrated the above six tonal tensions into a new harmonic complex of unprecedented intensity, dovetailing into it a pair of familiar melodic progressions (one already connected with the type of harmony) and animating the whole complex by means of a familiar rhythmic impulse (also connected with the type of melodic-harmonic progression). In this instance, the "high tension" of the composer's emotion did not reside specifically in a particular state of animation nor in a particular sequence of outgoing and incoming emotion, and so its current was not converted into new patterns of rhythmic or melodic tensions; what it did reside in was the phenomenal psychic intensity of the feeling, and it was thus naturally transformed into a vital new pattern of harmonic tensions (absorbing certain well-worn melodic tensions) corresponding to that psychic intensity. (In actual fact, there *was* something unusual about the state of animation—the abnormally low level of physical vitality; and consequently there was something new about the rhythmic impulse—its extreme slowness; but this creative act in the rhythmic sphere was submerged entirely in the extraordinary harmonic innovation, and in its own special potency towards the harmonic-melodic

2. See the opening of Beethoven's *Sonata Pathétique* as the probable unconscious source: three slow, isolated phrases ending in *appoggiatura*, the last half-repeated; melody of bar 5 (cf. Prelude, bars 18–19); melody and harmony of bars 7–8 (cf. Ex. 1: almost complete identity at the *end* of the Prelude—in C minor). Cf. also Adagio, bars 5–6, with Prelude, bars 25–8.

complex). Once again, the current of the composer's emotion was transformed into a form of *musical energy*, this time consisting of interacting melodic, harmonic, and rhythmic tensions—otherwise a vital melodic-harmonic-rhythmic phrase.

The expressive power of an essentially harmonic inspiration, like that of an essentially melodic one, can be related back to the tonal tensions themselves, and to the general effects of rising and falling pitch—naturally so, since the tonal tensions move the hearer in the same way whether they are used successively or simultaneously, the only difference being that in the latter case they can enhance one another's effect by their sympathy or repulsion (hence the "psychic depth" of harmony).

How exactly does the *Tristan* progression function expressively? As we have said, the key of the first three notes is D minor, and we have an upward (outgoing, passionate) leap from the lower dominant over the tonic to the "tragic" minor third, which is emphasized by rhythmic accent (here we begin to feel the special potency of the rhythmic impulse). The minor third falls to the second, which obviously functions as a passing-note, a neutral intermediate note; though there is a sense of the "anguish" of the minor 3–2 suspension, which is to be revealed retrospectively as a minor 6–5 in A minor. At this point, the melodic line has had most of the effect of the arched minor 5–3–2–1 of "restless sorrow"[3] * * *; indeed, with a lesser romantic composer, or even with Wagner himself in his earlier days, it would probably have materialized as the complete term, in some such way as the following:

Example 3

This routine piece of romantic expression conveys well enough a sense of restless sorrow (arched minor 5–3–2–1), and of anguish (minor sixth in harmony) shot through with sad longing (2–1 and 8–7 suspen-

3. Cooke here refers the reader to a group of melodies based on the figure:

                                                                [*Editor*]

sions in minor key), but not of "endless yearning." If we flatten the E♮ at the beginning of the second bar, the feeling of hopeless anguish characteristic of the minor second enters in, but we still have no feeling of "endless yearning." No attempt had ever been made to express this peculiarly romantic emotion in music before, and so audiences were conditioned by tradition unconsciously to expect some such purely sorrowful D minor continuation as Ex. 3 (especially at the beginning of a work); and it was against the background of their expectation that the famous *Tristan* chord, introducing the unfamiliar emotion for the first time in music by "reaching out" harmonically in a way hitherto unknown, achieved its revolutionary effect. For us it has inevitably lost its freshness, but some trace of the original shock can be recaptured by playing Ex. 3 twice, followed by Ex. 1.

What happens when the *Tristan* chord enters? The E of the melody, the normal second of D minor, falls to E♭ (D♯), the "hopeless" minor second; and this note is harmonized as though it were a new *tonic minor*, by the melancholy secondary seventh chord on its supertonic (F), a chord which derives its gloom from the presence of the anguished minor sixth, C♭ (B♮). So far, so intensely sad; but the eventual resolution of the chord reveals it retrospectively as a complex of tensions *on the sharp side of the dominant key of A*: the F in the bass is the anguished minor sixth of that key; the D♯ is the "violently longing" major seventh of its dominant, E; the G♯ is the "violently longing" major seventh of A itself; and the B is the dominant of the dominant, having a stiffening, binding effect. So that the chord is compounded, as indeed it sounds to be, of anguish and violent longing in conflict, and of mystery, too, for its character is tonally ambiguous; its effect is emphasized by rhythmic accent (the rhythmic impulse's "potency" at work again).

When the chord resolves, what happens? The violently longing G♯, major seventh of A, is resolved upwards (onwards, outwards) to its tonic, which can provide no satisfaction since it is functioning merely as an unaccented passing-note; the melody moves on upwards chromatically (outwards, yearningly) on to the hopeless minor second, B♭ (A♯), which is accented by rhythmic means (the potency of the rhythmic impulse again) and harmonic means (it functions as a dissonant accented passing-note); this note resolves upwards (still outwards) on to the major second, B♮, whose natural longing is left unsatisfied, a desire open towards the future, as the upper note of a dominant seventh chord of A. Of the previous chord, the minor sixth (F) has carried out its normal, anguished resolution on to the dominant (E); the strong dominant of the dominant (B) has fallen to its major third (G♯), which is not at all joyful, since it functions also as the longing major seventh of A: and the violently longing major seventh of the dominant (D♯) has fallen semitonally (sadly) to its mournful minor seventh (D), which also functions as the pathetically longing fourth of A. So that this final chord is compounded, as it sounds to be, of pathos and longing combined.

This analysis of the expressive effect of each separate note can be confirmed by playing the progression over and over at the piano and concentrating on each note in turn. During a performance, of course, we cannot, and do not want to, listen like this with the analysing ear of the intellect: we are simply moved by the general effect (in which, however, every one of these details plays its indispensable part). This general effect is: (a) passionate leap from lower dominant up to minor third; (b) pathetic minor 3–2 suspension; (c) intensely poignant, mysterious chord, felt at first as a melancholy chord in "depressed" key of the minor second, but revealed retrospectively as chord of anguish and violent longing completely overshooting the nearest legitimate object of desire (the dominant key), and falling back wearily towards it, exhausting its tension by (d) a "resolution" on to the pathetic longing of the dominant seventh chord *in* the new dominant key, which is by implication the dominant minor (we have attained the nearest object of desire, but have found no kind of satisfaction in it); (e) there is no resolution, but instead the phrase is repeated twice, higher each time, and still without resolution on to any tonic. In each case, we are left with the major second, expressing its "longing in a context of finality"—but there is no finality. Any better way of conveying "endless yearning" and "a languishing forever renewing itself" has yet to be discovered.[4]

To complete the picture, we should note that volume, tone-colour, and texture all play their parts. The opening melodic leap begins *pianissimo* (determined by the emotion behind the conception—"the first timidest avowal") and is on the "expressive" unaccompanied cellos, which swell out on the sustained note in a rhetorical *crescendo*. The tense *Tristan* chord enters at the climax of the cello *crescendo*, and is emphasized not only by rhythmic accent and the change from melody to harmony,

---

4. As is well-known, Schopenhauer's philosophy of the Will partly conditioned the conception of *Tristan*, and the Prelude is clearly an unconscious expression of the emotional reality at the heart of Schopenhauer's central concept: the idea that life is a chain of unfulfilled desire, owing to the fact that desire, each time that it is satisfied by the attainment of what one has been longing for, moves on immediately to attach itself to a new "unattainable."

but by louder volume, the change from string to woodwind texture, and the bitter tang of the actual woodwind sonority, caused by the scoring. Finally, the sense of partial release conveyed by the "resolution" on to the final unresolved chord is enhanced by a *diminuendo.*

The process whereby the creative imagination breeds new harmonic inspirations is clear enough, if we glance at Exs. 1 and 2: it vitalizes the well-worn harmonies of tradition by changing and adding notes, and by placing chords in new contexts; by fertilizing them with rhythmic impulses possessed of a special potency towards them; and by letting them fertilize familiar melodic terms. But exactly how this is achieved is another of our ultimate mysteries—though the objection might be made that there is no mystery here at all: melodic and rhythmic inspirations may come unbidden and ready-made from the unconscious, but harmonic inspiration can be (and often is) quarried out by the composer consciously at the keyboard. Melody and rhythm are primitive, elemental, natural impulses; but harmony has been a consciously-willed, complex invention of Western European man—there is always something intellectually calculated about it.

This is an illusion caused by the fact that harmony is the youngest of the three primary means of musical expression, and still bears clear traces of the intellectual work put into its creation. Everything had to be created once, including melody and the basic terms, and rhythm and the basic rhythmic impulses; but whereas these have become unconscious habits in the long course of time, the organization of the harmonic element of a composition still demands a conscious effort from most composers. But harmony has been used entirely instinctively by the great improvisers, such as Mozart and Beethoven; and it seems that both Debussy and Delius were able to sit at a piano and pour out a creative flood of "inspired" harmony. In any case, if a composer does have to search out his harmonic material painfully at the keyboard, he is hardly indulging in an intellectual activity: he is groping. For what? Something that will prove satisfying. To what? To his particular expressive need, which is a matter of feeling, of emotion, of the unconscious. We do not know how the inspiration for the opening phrase of *Tristan* came to Wagner; but even if he stumbled on it at the piano, as has been suggested, after laborious trial and error (in much the same way as Stravinsky discovers his own highly emotive harmonies to-day), it was still left for his creative imagination to select, from the random offerings of his groping fingers, the sound that he had already vaguely imagined as being apt for the expression of the insatiable longing of romantic love. He was really doing no more than Beethoven often did when he wrestled with his melodic-rhythmic inspirations, "trying them out" in different forms as sketches on music-paper. In such cases, the flash of inspiration will function as the flash of recognition.

Whether it acts in the melodic, rhythmic, or harmonic fields, the creative imagination remains an unanalysable force, in its power to produce new shapes out of old for the embodiment of new emotions.

ANALYTICAL ESSAYS

Unless specified otherwise, all numbered footnotes in the following essays are those of the authors.

The Prelude and
the "Tristan Chord"

ARNOLD SCHOENBERG

~~~~~~~~

[*From* Theory of Harmony]†

In an essay of 1931 called *National Music*, Schoenberg stated that his
teachers had been "primarily Bach and Mozart, and secondarily Beethoven, Brahms, and Wagner." More specifically, he claimed that from
Wagner he had learned
> "1. The way it is possible to manipulate themes for expressive
>   purposes and the art of formulating them in the way that will
>   serve this end.
> 2. Relatedness of tones and chords.
> 3. The possibility of regarding themes and motives as if they were
>   complex ornaments, so that they can be used against harmonies
>   in a dissonant way."

The following extract reflects more on what Schoenberg *taught* than on
what he *learned* from Wagner. It is from his *Theory of Harmony* (1911;
revised and expanded edition, 1922), an outgrowth of the periods of his
active teaching in Berlin. His translator notes that he aimed "at a systematic
pedagogical presentation rather than a systematic theory."

In themselves these [vagrant] chords do not require * * * lengthy
discussion, for they are indeed not particularly complicated. But since
they play a great role in Wagner's harmony and since so much has been
written about them, I, too, am compelled to take a position with regard
to them. (I do not know those writings but have only heard of them.)
The chord in Example 1a, transposed a minor third higher and

† *Theory of Harmony*, trans. Roy E. Carter (Berkeley, 1978), pp. 257–59. Reprinted
with permission of The University of California Press and Faber and Faber Ltd.

enharmonically altered (1b), is known to everyone as the so-called "Tristan Chord."[1] To be sure, this chord does resolve to E, thus is analogous to Example 1a. The continuation should then be that in Example 1b, that is, should indicate e^b minor [or $d\sharp$]; but Wagner treats the E as the dominant of a minor (1c). There has been much dispute over the question to which degree that chord belongs. I hope to contribute to the disentanglement of this question, but I think I can best do so if I give no new derivation. Now, we may regard the $g\sharp$ as a suspension going up to a, in which case the chord has the form shown in Example 1d, or it would also work to call the a a passing tone going (through $a\sharp$) to b; or we may yet assume the very worst: namely, that the "Tristan Chord" is actually derived from e^b minor (1e) (if it absolutely must be derived from something) and, being a vagrant chord, is reinterpreted and taken to a minor. (The latter seems to be the most extravagant interpretation. But it is not, for a minor and e^b minor actually have in common not only this chord, but simpler ones as well. For example, the VI of e^b minor is identical with the dominant of the dominant of a minor, the secondary dominant on II; and the Neapolitan sixth in a minor is V in e^b minor; moreover, the Neapolitan sixth of e^b minor and the V of a minor are the same chord.) Which of these interpretations [of the "Tristan Chord"] we adopt seems an indifferent matter once we have seen how rich the relationships among keys become, however remote these keys, once vagrant chords create new routes and new modes of travel. Of course I do not actually wish to say that this chord has something to do with e^b minor. I wanted only to show that even this assumption is defensible and that little is actually said whenever one shows where the chord comes from. Because it can come from everywhere. What is essential for us is its function, and that is revealed when we know the possibilities the chord affords. Why single out these vagrant chords and insist that they be traced back at all cost to a key, when no one bothers to do so with the diminished seventh chord? True, I did relate the diminished seventh to the key. That relation is not supposed to restrict its circle of influence, however, but should rather show the pupil systematically its range of practical possibilities, so that he can find out through inference (*Kombination*) what his ear has recognized long ago through intuition. Later, the pupil will best take

---

1. Cf. Schoenberg's analysis of the opening of the "Prelude" to *Tristan* in *Structural Functions of Harmony*, p. 77, Example 85a. [*Translator*]

Example 1

all these vagrant chords for what they are, without tracing them back
to a key or a degree: homeless phenomena, unbelievably adaptable and
unbelievably lacking in independence; spies, who ferret out weaknesses

and use them to cause confusion; turncoats, to whom abandonment of their individuality is an end in itself; agitators in every respect, but above all: most amusing fellows.

Once we abandon the desire to explain the derivation of these chords, their effect becomes much clearer. We understand then that it is not absolutely necessary for such chords to appear just in the function their derivation calls for, since the climate of their homeland has no influence on their character. (Moreover, as will be shown later, this same characteristic can be proved true of many other chords, where one would not suspect it at first.) They flourish in every climate; and it is now understandable how another form of this chord in *Götterdäm-merung* is resolved the same way (Example 1f) and leads to *b* minor. My first derivation (1a) is then confirmed after all by another example from Wagner; for Example 1g, the schematic reduction of the quotation in 1f, is without doubt a form of the function shown in 1a, transposed a half step down. I am not saying, however, that that is the derivation; for this chord appears in the music of Wagner with a great variety of other resolutions:

Example 2

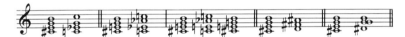

etc., and it is easy to add yet many others. But as these examples show, the chords of resolution are principally those whose tones may be reached by chromatic steps; or they are other vagrant chords, whose origin and relation do not require elaborate demonstration in the voice leading.

The following observations should guide the pupil in his own efforts to find resolutions for such vagrant chords: since here close attention to the sequence of degrees, the root progressions, often does not assure control over the quality (*Wert*) of a progression, control through the melodic lines [voice leading] could be substituted, as has indeed been frequently reiterated. Thus, in general, the best connections of simple chords with vagrants or of vagrants with one another will be those in which the second chord contains, as far as possible, only tones that appeared in the first or are recognizable as chromatic raising or lowering of tones of the first. * * *

HUGO LEICHTENTRITT

~~~~~~

Tristan und Isolde: Prelude†

Musical Form first appeared in 1911, the same year as the first edition of
Schoenberg's *Theory of Harmony*, but Leichtentritt added his analysis of
the Prelude to the book only in its second edition of 1921. Leichtentritt
is a direct product of the German *Formenlehre* tradition responsible for
most of the formal categories familiar today. This school looked upon a
musical "form" as something primarily defined by means of melodic
repetition and gave little if any consideration to its tonal construction or
principles of harmony. They paid special attention to what they regarded
as the primary building blocks for these forms: first, the *motive*; secondly,
phrases, based on or embodying a motive, of varying lengths and types
of construction; and finally, large sections built up from any number of
phrases. Leichtentritt thus stands closer to Alfred Lorenz than to any of
the other authors represented in this volume, and Lorenz's analysis
of the Prelude includes a critique of Leichtentritt's (see p. 216–17).

The prelude to Wagner's *Tristan und Isolde* presents certain difficulties
of analysis because the intentional avoidance of full cadences, which are
replaced by deceptive cadences, obscures the structure of the piece for
the listener. The result is the so-called "unending melody," which as a
stylistic element has perhaps never been employed with greater mastery
than in this piece. Compared with the forms based on division by means
of cadences, this piece is distinguished by the absence of all "transition
groups" leading over from one theme to another, as occurs in the sonata
and the rondo. The strictly thematic melos does not stop for even a
single measure; it entirely scorns introductions and transitions before
the entrance of certain melodic phrases. The ear hears an unbroken
chain of melodic phrases; it perceives only a difference in intensity, in
color, in accumulation of sound, but not a difference in melodic
character. Nevertheless, the inquisitive mind can perceive the planned
structure of the piece. Its first two measures state two closely related

† From *Musical Form* (Cambridge, Mass., 1951), pp. 355–58.

and yet essentially different motifs, exhausting the entire thematic material for the 110 measures.

Motif *a* with the leap of a sixth, followed by a chromatic descent; motif *b* chromatically ascending. Motif *b* is later heard in two variants:

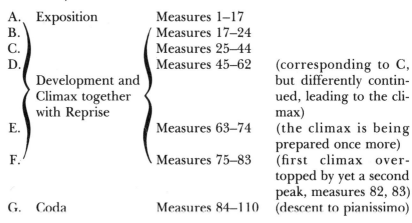

and

An analysis of the structure follows:

A. Exposition	Measures 1–17	
B.	Measures 17–24	
C.	Measures 25–44	
D.	Measures 45–62	(corresponding to C, but differently continued, leading to the climax)
Development and Climax together with Reprise		
E.	Measures 63–74	(the climax is being prepared once more)
F.	Measures 75–83	(first climax overtopped by yet a second peak, measures 82, 83)
G. Coda	Measures 84–110	(descent to pianissimo)

Notice the period-like correspondence of parts C and D to the very original use of the reprise: Measures 66–71, 75–78 correspond to measures 1–12, 17–21, but they lead up to an outburst of the highest ecstasy, whereas the earlier measures start softly, filled with longing. Also E and F have a certain correspondence to A and B. Furthermore, the coda G is an even more precise reprise of the introduction A with but slight variants. A striking feature is the phrase (measures 17–21), which returns three times in identical form in different places, but each time with greater passion and forcefulness: measures 33–36, 58–62, 74–77.

These repetitions occur at exactly equal distances: measures 17, 33, 58, 74, in symmetrical disposition, sixteen, twenty-five, and sixteen measures from each other, in addition to which there are the seventeen measures which precede the first appearance of the phrase. Almost arithmetically exact multiples of eight measures are manifest here: sixteen, sixteen, twenty-four, and sixteen measures, an architectural idea, like a conspicuous ornament which is built into a façade at regular distances. Moreover, the dynamic element in this piece is used more intentionally and more frequently than usually, not only as a coloristic effect, but also as a constructive, formal element. The surging and ebbing motion, manifest already in the elementary motifs of the first two measures, is the real dominating motif of the entire structure. Of these, the surging motion receives preferential treatment. Compared with it the ebbing away gives the impression of a short breathing pause before the still stronger onslaught to follow. The aesthetic balance is brought about in the coda: after the most powerful outbreak, a sudden collapse follows; the entire coda is dominated by diminuendo. The curve of intensity of the piece (disregarding for the sake of clarity slight deviations, passing sforzati) would look like this:

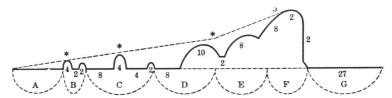

at * the episode *c* enters four times with growing intensity.

The mutual relations of the single sections may be made evident by the following:

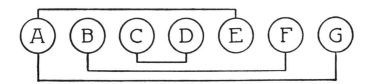

AG, AE, BF, CD belong together in one way or another. The entire piece represents a short exposition, followed by a long development section, led to the highest climax with interruptions. In this development the same melodic episode appears four times at exactly equal distances. A slightly sketched-out reprise is worked into the climax. The development in itself is also symmetrically constructed (CD). The coda corresponds to the introduction, somewhat extended, its energy spent as it comes to the close. Though the piece appears to be very novel and thoroughly original, it nevertheless makes use of many traditional and well tried means, such as two-bar phrases, frequent sequences, cautious modulation. Besides the main tonality A minor, the piece employs only the closely related keys C major, E minor, A minor, F sharp minor.

*   *   *

ERNST KURTH

[*The* Tristan *Prelude*]†

One of the most significant and influential voices in early twentieth-century music theory, Kurth was really the first analyst to attempt a systematic exposition of principles of tonal composition in its later phases, using as his starting point Wagner's *Tristan*. His treatise defies easily comprehensible English translation, since he developed a unique vocabulary which draws as much upon conceptions derived from the psychology of perception and from physics as upon familiar musical terms. An excellent introduction to some of Kurth's other analytical applications is the article by Patrick McCreless, "Ernst Kurth and the Analysis of the Chromatic Music of the Late Nineteenth Century," in *Music Theory Spectrum* 5 (1983).

*   *   *

In order to adduce the basic theoretical features of chord forms and associations in the first measures of the Prelude, it is best to consider

† From *Romantische Harmonik und ihre Krise in Wagners "Tristan,"* 2nd ed. (Berlin, 1923; reprinted Georg Olms Verlag, Hildesheim, 1968), pp. 45–53, 62–67, and 318–27. Translated by the Editor and included with permission of the publisher.

first the separate phrases by themselves, and then later their overall relationship. In this way, several theoretical principles are revealed. First of all, the root progressions of each of the chord groups are really based on very simple cadences, in which the individual chords themselves are chromatically altered. The first [appears in mm. 1–3].

The basic form of the first cadence is $B^7–E^7$, i.e., a dominant–tonic cadence whose termination is in turn the dominant chord of the Prelude's tonality, A minor. The progression of these chords is saturated with neighbor-note alterations. The melodic tension of the fifth (*f♯*), the lowest voice of the chord *b–d♯–f♯–a*, is intensified in the direction of the following *e*, so that *f♯* appears in the chord in the lowered form of *f♮*. The *g♯* of the upper motivic voice enters in the chord with the tension of a free chromatic neighbor-note alteration toward the chord tone *a*. With the resolution, another appoggiatura-like chromatic element appears in the new chord as the chromatic passing tone *a♯* before the *b*. (Here the voice leading *d♯–d*, for example, proves that chromatic voice leading generally presses forward.)

The principles of alteration apparent in the *Tristan* chord itself show that it is founded on intensification and on manifestations of inner dynamism, and only secondarily—i.e., only in its immediately perceptible expression—based on an increase and duplication of chordal impulses. Technically, it is based on freely entering chromatic neighbor notes, which take the place of pure chordal elements. These neighbor notes enter at the same time as the chord itself and do not need preparation to define them as chromatic passing tones. They are directed with their tensions exclusively toward a specific continuation.

On the other hand, it is characteristic of alteration technique that chromatic transformations of an original primary form are not arbitrary recolorings of the chordal statement, but are always linked to melodic continuation of a chromatic nature. For example, the *f* occurs in the B^7 chord only with respect to the following *e*, as an expression of the total tension building toward the resolving chord, E^7. A leading tone is created, and the intense climactic tension in the driving progress of the basic scale, pushing forward from leading tone to goal tone, is transferred to the chord tone which here strives downwards. The chromatic transformations consequently result in the saturation of chords with tensions of motion, reproducing the historical process which led to alteration all along. While the energy of these tensions is absorbed into the chord, a potential energy state suffuses the whole chord, so that as a whole, it seems to express definite strivings. Kinetic energy changes to potential energy which in turn pushes out from the chord toward resolution in motion. The fusion of tones for a total perception of the chord also absorbs their individual tensions and allows them to permeate the entire chord. As far as a single tone is concerned, its acoustic-physical vibrations as well as its energy states radiate into the whole chord to which that tone belongs, but the energy states are much more essential for music than the vibrations. Every possibility of harmonic reinterpretation for a chord rests on them, particularly the possibility that the tension state, passing from single tones into the chord as a whole, will henceforth be derived from other tones, i.e., resolved in another way corresponding to the "reinterpretation." Since only the altered tones imply a specific continuation, there are various possible resolutions for the whole chord. In instrumental music, however, a technique had already developed before Wagner, in which such altered tones were no longer tied to a resolution of tension in one and the same voice. Instead, the technique is pursued hypothetically, distributing tension tones and resolving tones among different voices and even different registers.

It is typical of this style that, in the present case, the alterations apply not only to several tones of the chord at once, but simultaneously in downward and upward directions. Consequently, in the first chord there is a tendency for tension-chord energies to press outwards, whereby a characteristic chordal impulse for expansion toward the resolving chord arises, with the effect of release and exhalation after the pressure of alteration. However, the opposite situation also occurs in which a tension sonority presses toward contraction.

A remarkable phenomenon of music underlies this. That intensive feeling of expansion does not depend on large distances between tones, or on distant positions. A simple chord could be distributed over several octaves, but the powerful and forceful feeling of expansion would not be resolved. The musical impression does not depend on tones and actual sound, but on psychic energies manifest in and permeating the actual sound. In the first chord, for instance, the feeling of expansion originates not in the absolute distance between the tones, but in the pressure indicated by the distance. The musical effect is not determined by something materially present, but at all times by the will, and that phenomenon characterizes harmony in its remotest relationships, de-termines it completely, and also manifests itself again and again in the most diverse ways in melody, the art of form, and aesthetics generally; for music is based on tensions.

A glance at the technique of Haydn and Mozart shows that even in clear, early Classical harmony based on triads and seventh chords, the initial permeation of chords with alterations applies above all in the outer voices, intensifying them as leading tones toward the subsequent chord. Since this leading-tone intensification almost always makes the two outer tones tend toward the root of the subsequent chord and thus away from each other toward the octave, augmented sixths are produced predominantly between the outer voices,[1] as for example:

Example 1

1. On this basis, the so-called augmented-6th chords and four-three chords, etc., appeared more and more frequently yet unnecessarily retained their special labels in music theory. These superficial names contributed significantly to a gradual obfuscation of the essential thing—their organic origin. How helplessly music theory confronted "alterations" almost thirty years after the genesis of Wagner's *Tristan* is shown, for example, by the first serious attempt to explain the chords of *Tristan*: Karl Mayrberger, "Die Harmonik Richard Wagners an den Leitmotiven des Vorspieles zu 'Tristan und Isolde,' " in *Bayreuther Blätter* 4 (1881): p. 169 ff. [separate reprint, 1883]. Mayrberger still retains Sechter's "hybrid chords" (*Zwitterakkorden*) and explains each altered chord as a combination of elements from two different chords. This stubbornness regarding the chordal substance itself is interesting because it characterizes a broad process of historical development in music theory. We see how this theory attempts with emotional persistance to hold together what flows apart according to its nature, and how blindly it struggles against acknowledging vitally effective processes which here represent not chordal combination but rather chordal replacement. About the first chord in the Prelude, Mayrberger says (p. 171), "The initial chord is a hybrid chord whose tone *f* derives from A minor, and whose tone *d♯* is derived from E minor," and remarks in addition, "By hybrid chord the author intends the same thing earlier [!] called an *altered chord* and not a chord from the expanded minor system. That the first designation is more correct follows from the fact that such a chord belongs exclusively to neither the one tonality nor the other, hence is actually [!] something of a hybrid."

How late general recognition of the essence of alteration procedure revolutionized theory is shown by the explanation of the initial chord in S. Jadassohn, *Melodik und Harmonik bei Richard Wagner* (Berlin, 1899), one of the few writings on Wagner's harmony to appear so far. Here, for the first chord and its resolution, a *fourfold* tonal alteration is constructed, since a chord is assumed for each melodic tone, with alterations besides. Since then, much has been written about the *Tristan* chord, but we seldom find a correct explanation of it, especially since it is often interpreted as an alteration of the II of A minor. This corresponds neither to its essence as a tension chord nor to its function in analogous harmonizations, e.g., the immediately following one. Its chief emphasis derives from its dominant character in relation to its resolving chord.

A vestige of this emphasis on the outer voices can be seen even in the most extreme alteration style.

Another technical characteristic to be considered here is the resolution of the Tristan chord's seventh, the *a* at the end of the measure. The downward effect originally implicit in the dominant seventh is completely overcome by the melodic tension of upward chromatic movement extending beyond that pressure toward downward resolution. This characterizes the forward drive of chromatic energy in the intensive alteration style, and it is also characteristic that this seventh is not placed on the accented part of the measure corresponding to the weight of chordal dissonances and appoggiatura dissonances, as it would have been in earlier harmonic styles. On the contrary, its short occurrence on the final weak part of of the measure quite characteristically represents the utter conquest of downward-directed pressure of dissonance by upward-yielding motion.[2]

As to sevenths, however, an additional technical feature is prominent in this first chord of *Tristan*—namely the peculiar phenomenon that after the preceding alteration dissonance, the second chord enters as a resolving seventh chord. Considering its effect, it is a resolution which approaches the impression of a consonant chord. In the *Tristan* style, seventh chords and even ninth chords are treated in a manner reserved for triads in the Classical harmonic style. This peculiarity is related above all to the emergence of the alteration technique in such a way that the significantly greater tensions of altered sonorities make the dissonances of seventh and ninth chords seem much more straightforward and mild, so that when they follow the former, the latter in effect resolve tension. In technique as well as in effect, seventh and ninth chords have advanced to a position previously held only by consonant triads. * * *

This characteristic is technically important in still another respect if we consider the tension chord itself, the first chord, B^7. That is to say, it emerges that its seventh, *a*, the uppermost tone, is treated as an integral and fully blending chord tone for which a chromatic neighbor-note adjustment can occur freely. The fact that the effect of tension in the *g♯* is brought against the chordal seventh, *a*, shows how this is perceived as belonging to the basic structure and original framework of a chord formation.

---

2. Kurth added this paragraph in his second edition, in response to Lorenz. See below, p. 222. [*Editor*]

We see how the roots of chords in every respect extend out beyond the triad.

The next two harmonizations of the same four-note chromatic Love motive can be explained analogously. In mm. 6 and 7, the chords likewise present a dominant cadence: D^7–G^7. In the D^7 chord, the *a* is intensified as a leading tone (*a$^\flat$*) toward the *g*, and the dominant seventh *c* is a freely entering chromatic neighbor-note adjustment (*b*). In the resolving chord, the chromatic appoggiatura *c$\sharp$* before the fifth of the chord occurs with the chord's entrance in the motivic statement. Everything else also corresponds exactly to the earlier phrase.

The third harmonization of the motive (mm. 10–11), taken by itself, is no longer based on a dominant cadence, but on a subdominant one: E^7–B^7. From the chord *e–g$\sharp$–b–d*, the *e* appears with a free appoggiatura-like chromatic neighbor-note adjustment (*f*), driving downward in linear progression. Furthermore, in place of the *b*, there is a chromatic neighbor-note adjustment *c* which moves forward to the *b* only with the resolving chord.

For all their directness, the first three chord progressions seem rather strange on first hearing and also on first technical consideration, but their roots actually form very simple cadential progressions, through which the chromatic line of the Love motive is forced. Distortion of the underlying primary chord forms originates in their permeation throughout with tensions of motion. Another general feature of the intensive language of altered harmony stands out even more clearly in passages like these opening measures where short statements sound disconnected by themselves. Two or even several consecutive chords belonging together are set off from the flow of the music like separate waves, and they present the relationship of tension chord and resolving chord in such a way that the concept of resolving chord should be considered in relative terms, for it need not present an acoustically absolute resolution such as a consonant triad. Such waves often flow turbulently and irregularly into each other. On the other hand, the purely chordal-acoustic degree of dissonance cannot be considered for a chord's function as a tension chord, precisely because the tension effect of alteration is not chordal in nature, but depends on the energy of driving motion. The function is energetic. Chordally, a strong dissonant darkening can occur at the same time but this does not need to be the case, whereas a lot of the most intensely altered chords which have the most shattering effect are identical in their outer form to relatively simple chords not strongly dissonant in themselves, and perhaps not even dissonant at all. The latter situation occurs especially often in Wagner's harmony and would be disconcerting if we were to seek the essence and effect of alteration in chordal phenomena, instead of in an energy which strives against those phenomena and leads to their inner disintegration.

From this, an essential feature of the concept of dissonance follows. In high Romanticism, dissonance not only undergoes a shift through the new-style behavior of seventh and ninth chords, but is based from the outset on the distinction between purely chordal veiling of dissonance on the one hand, and the dissonant energies originating in tensions of melodic motion on the other. The path from Classical tonality to the harmonic style of *Tristan* is based primarily on the powerful pressing forward and swelling up of the linear perception of dissonance beyond the chordal perception of dissonance. Even the elevation of seventh and ninth chords to the function of resolving chords and to triadic treatment is only an expression of it, and therefore in this development instead of talking about an *advance*, we ought rather to talk about a displacement, since the acoustical dissonance of seventh and ninth chords suffers a significant loss in intensity. Even that is only a feature of the inner transformation which everywhere in Romantic music originates below the surface of the sound in psychic creative energies.

If we propose to analyze a complicated language of altered harmony, those correlated partial exchanges of tension chords and dissonant chords should always be set apart first and reduced to their basic forms. The wider tonal relationship unifying them into larger passages stems only from these simplified basic progressions * * *.

*   *   *

It is well known that in the language of altered harmony the combination of [alteration tensions] with so-called enharmonic reinter-pretations has great significance.[3] This phenomenon is simple in tech-nique, but we can get to the bottom of it in theory only if we understand it in the context of the interweaving of energetic and chordal impulses, which releases all harmonic procedures and possibilities. For as already mentioned, the enharmonic transformation of a chord is only the expression of a transformation of the relations among its inner forces. The *Tristan* chord shows this transformation and, what is more, it shows that transformation in a most intuitive relationship with the chord's

---

3. With this, one should think not only of the equality of chords with all their tones, e.g., C♯-major and D♭-flat major triads, etc., but primarily of the reinterpretation of individual chord tones, which produces an altered significance for the whole chord.

symbolic meaning in the poem and in the musical and dramatic realization as a whole.

The first three measures of the Prelude present a complex of *Leitmotivs*, from which the solo Desire motive of the minor sixth and the ascending chromatic Love motive are directly contrasted as melodic figures, while the *Tristan* chord itself extends over the music of the work in far-reaching symbolic significance and deserves the designation *Leitmotiv* in an even more meaningful sense. The chord dissociates itself from the chromatic Love motive, whose harmonization it originally forms, and takes part in the composition as a motivic idea by itself.

This thought must lead to the elevation of the alteration-based sonority to purely chordal importance, i.e., to giving it its own existence which eliminates dependence on linear tensions and relationships and gives its chordal form independent significance. That emerges technically in the enharmonic transformability of the chord. We see this change, together with the ideological content Wagner imparts to it, most clearly when we consider the chord's characteristic development during the Prelude.

Its dominating position not only is implied by frequent occurrence, which discharges its basic permeating character over the entire symphonic music of the piece, but also it represents the decisive point in the Prelude's architectural design. This manifests a very broadly planned but continuous intensification up to a climax of the utmost symphonic power (m. 83), which quickly dies away after its long and suspenseful development and leads toward the quietly ebbing conclusion. Wagner himself commented on the ideological content of this design, and in these commentaries the last stage of intensification is particularly significant and points directly to the harmony as the real symbolic content of that climax. If we view the intensification design up to this final statement (about m. 74) as a whole, then the introduction by itself presents fragments separated by fermatas and the longer rests, and these fragments are formed from the three motives mentioned. Only from m. 16 on do continuous flow and consistent musical development occur at all. The long-extended tempo first acquires decisive animation at the beginning of the A-major section, which continues in impulsive intensification with the appearance of the motive from m. 62 and its lashing upbeats in the strings. Out of this passage there develops soon after the return to A minor the highest and last intensification up to the subsequent climax (mm. 83–84), hurricanelike in its concluding measures.

From this summit beginning in m. 84, the tension, compressed to the point of stupefying intensity, dissipates quite rapidly, and the Prelude's subsequent short termination again has the shortwinded uniform melancholy motives of the opening, which sound as disconnected here as they did there and quickly breathe their last.

While all the means of compositional technique, dynamics, and orchestration work together toward the breathless ascent, a remarkable harmonic idea appears in the last part of the intensification. The fortissimo chord in the climactic measure is reiterated at full strength in the preceding measures. The last and most turbulent waves of intensification surge in each time against that same chord as against a dam, as if to break through its structure and expand into new formations, but without being able to break out of it, until it collapses in the climactic measure. For here, only the external strength of the chord dies away toward the second half of the measure, whereas the chord itself remains self-contained. The chords of both halves of the measure are identical; they are different only in enharmonic notation. The climactic chord *f–ab–cb–eb* is note-for-note identical to the form in the second half of the measure, *f–b–d♯–g♯*, and that is the return of the introduction's first chord, so that the development comes full circle. The architectural construction of the Prelude consequently manifests the extremely peculiar phenomenon that the entire intensification, including the richest harmonic developments, drives with all its might toward that very chord at the culmination which also opened the work with an incomparable atmosphere of melancholy. The chord, tonally built up in thirds, toward which the intensification accumulates, collapses in this measure into the dismembered longing of the beginning.

Bülow's piano-vocal score * * * expresses the enharmonic reinterpretation of the chord, since he distinguishes the two halves of the measure orthographically, which not all versions do. With Wagner himself the reinterpretation of this measure is even more interestingly represented. The score does not manifest the two enharmonic chords separated into the two halves of the measure, but interspersed with each other. The orchestra produces at the same time *eb* and *d♯*, *ab* and *g♯*, *b* and *cb*, not even separated by instrumental groups, but mixed together to such an extent that, for example, the strings alone and the winds alone contain notes from both kinds of notation. Thus the enharmonically altered tones suddenly permeate the chord, which appears in the midst of a deep darkening into the tonal area of B♭ and makes the strident effects of alteration surge up from within—an effect which produces the particular additional fascination that in practical performance strings as well as winds always involuntarily play the notes written with sharps a little higher in pitch than the corresponding ones written with flats.[4] With the differentiation of the two types of notation (presumably inspired by Wagner himself, but with his approval in any case), Bülow merely expresses in his piano score the enharmonic equivalence in an obvious way.

Example 2

The entire symbolism of the chord becomes evident in the Prelude's remarkable construction. Wagner himself repeatedly formulated the poetic content of the *Tristan* Prelude with its total passionate intensification:[5] "the unfulfilled sorrowful love-longing, swelling up from the sweetest impulse to violent force, and impossible of fulfillment, sinks back again into itself in infinite longing." This should be understood as symbolic of the musical design, with its highest dynamic culmination but without a bursting of its unresolved tensions—which, strange to say, Wagner never states, and which again empties into the same melancholy dismembered chord from which it began. In his program note for a concert performance in Paris (1859), Wagner writes an explanation of the long-articulated powerful intensification: "In vain! Its power spent, the heart sinks back to languish in longing. . . ." With the phrase "in vain," the whole content of that climactic measure seems summarized, as it flows into the first chord from which the world of the Prelude and of the entire drama grows. At the same time, the motivic sense of the Tristan chord itself is stamped therein with complete clarity. The longing incapable of fulfillment and the tragedy of the whole poem are symbolized in it. Therefore, the Tristan chord is a "motive," and what is more, the first and most far-reaching *Leitmotiv* of the whole music-drama, in a certain sense more than any melodic shape. Reflections

4. Involuntary modifications in pitch made by performers also express tension—a psychic urge upward or downward—and not a refinement in hearing, as is frequently supposed. [*Author*]

Since the tonal system is based on equal-tempered tuning, and would in fact not be possible without the assumption of absolute enharmonic equivalence, it is very much open to question whether such modifications in pitch are justified at all in tonal music. [*Editor*]

5. *Gesammelte Schriften und Dichtungen*, Vol. 12, 5th ed. (Leipzig, n.d.), p. 344. [*Author*] See above, p. 48. [*Editor*]

from this chord illuminate the entire music. In fact, ideologically as well as technically and stylistically, its alteration character seems already condensed on its first appearance into an embryo which serves as a starting point and center for infinite expansion. If we consider that in Wagner's *Tristan* the chromatic Love motive distinctly defines the entire *melodic* style, then both its melodic and harmonic styles appear concisely prepared at the very beginning of the Prelude.

*   *   *

The Prelude to the first act of *Tristan*, taken as a whole, can be regarded as a tonally complete structure, even though in its last measures it turns from the main tonality of A minor to C minor. Apart from this final modulation leading into the first scene with its new key intact, tonal unity is present up to m. 94. The first fifteen measures by themselves show a special type of development and constitute one of the largest-scale ideas in all tonal music. Along with a bold and novel loosening of tonal relationships, they present an image of the power to unify independent and seemingly remote harmonic formations in a simple manner. The separate statements of the main chromatic motive are disconnected by the loosening of harmony as well as rhythm and melody and separated by *fermata*-like rests.

As far as the relation of individual resolving chords and tension chords is concerned, we have already discussed their harmonization, and the motivic units can accordingly be understood as two dominant cadences followed by a subdominant cadence. The resolving chords are consistently major triads with a minor seventh—i.e., dominant-seventh chords on the roots *e*, *g*, and *b*. The relation of these fragments to each other and their arrangement into a tonal pattern is based on this. For if we consider the roots of these resolving chords, they form by themselves the minor dominant of the tonic, A minor. In each case the termination of the main motive gradually builds up the relationship of the E-minor chord—not directly, but in such a way that each of its tones acquires the function of a root in the cadential resolving chord. The E-minor chord is not made perceptible, but it latently supports the structure of the first thirteen measures, since a resolving chord is successively constructed on each one of its notes. Meanwhile, the tonal loosening goes so far that even these tonally related roots no longer serve as the basis for triads.

Consequently, from the tonal point of view, these first two measures of the Prelude form nothing more than a broad dominant upbeat. The whole section can be summarized as a minor dominant considerably extended in proportions and thereby internally loosened. We should not overlook the way the melancholy tenderness of the minor dominant settles immediately over this whole introductory section in accordance with the poetic atmosphere. Even mm. 14 and 15 are still part of it, serving as repetitions of the last half-cadence, E⁷–B⁷, which dies away like an echo and is reduced in texture to unisons. After this large and extremely individual dominant upbeat, the Prelude from m. 16 on seems chiefly developed in simpler tonal relationships, from that moment when the main melodic line no longer sounds disconnected in individual statements of the chromatic Love motive, but is given continuous expansion.

But the loosening in the tonal amalgamation up to that point produces a series of chords also to be regarded in relation to the main tonality. The first resolving chord, following an inserted secondary dominant, is the dominant, E⁷; the second, G⁷, is VII, the dominant of the relative major (in its context V once again); the third, B⁷, is the dominant of the dominant, with reference to which it follows an inserted subdominant (IV). These are the functions of the separate chords in relation to the central tonic chord, A minor. But this would be an analytical rather than a synthetic method of interpretation, for while it is certainly an expression of the chordal relations under consideration and the proof of a central unification, it is not the description of their genetic relationship, which is what produces this succession of functions. The musical conception derives from the broad statement of a dominant upbeat which gradually gives rise to the root progression *e–g–b* with the three resolving chords. This feeling of dominant harmony determines the development, but not directly those chordal functions (dominant, dominant of the relative major, secondary dominant) which are actually produced only by that basic feeling of a minor dominant indicated in the roots of the individual resolving chords. Externally, as regards the chordal images actually under consideration, both methods of interpretation are in fact identical, yet they conceal a different and even contrary background. They result, of course, not only from this difference between the analytical and synthetic points of view, but from opposite perspectives which * * * come into conflict with each other for all tonal processes of disintegration. Consideration of the chordal functions by themselves determines the coherence of the three resolving chords and reinforces the loosened harmonic development in terms of its tonal foundation, whereas the decentralizing processes lead to complications revealed by explanation of the dominant development contained in the roots of the resolving chords. In the process of tonal loosening evident here, whole chords themselves no longer represent directly the minor-dominant character of the introductory measures. Instead, that character merely lies dormant in the roots of the resolving chords, the second and third of which are formations built on the tones *g* and *b*, paralleling the first motivic termination on the dominant-seventh chord, E^7. Since from here on the main motive is continually transposed and these pitches stand together in a fixed arrangement, the newly emerging process of resolution approaches the principle of the *sequence*, which is not specifically tonal.

We encounter the analogous idea of an extension of tonal relationships again if we look ahead to a passage from the end of the Prelude—the statements of the chromatic Love motive directly following the climax at m. 83, before the Prelude's modulation to C minor. Dominant-seventh formations are consistently used: in m. 84, the resolving chord is E^7, then in m. 87, G^7, following an altered secondary dominant, D^7. The next two resolving chords both follow altered secondary dominants: A^7 in m. 90 and C^7 in m. 91. The principle of tonal coherence is this: first the roots of the resolving chords are *e* and *g*, hence dominant once more; then the root progression *a* and *c* appears and is thus related to the tonic as separate statements of triadic notes, but now only the first two.

The beginning and the end of the Prelude accordingly have a technical as well as an artistic principle in common. The resolution of the continuously flowing main melody into separate sighing statements of the chromatic Love motive is expressed in the harmonization which contrasts an expanding resolution in regard to tonal coherence with the closed tonal developments of the intervening passage, mm. 16–84. If we proceed from the principle of tonality itself, then the measures already discussed from the beginning and end of the Prelude prove to be a strong loosening, a weakening of the stability of tonal unity. On the other hand, if we examine the Prelude as a work of art and a construction unto itself, then the lines of development at the beginning seem much more a consolidation of separate tendencies into tonality, and at the end a return to the loosening away from tonality.

The peculiar technical principle underlying this is a tangible destruction of tonal centralization, and this destruction is not accomplished randomly, but as the extension of tonal relationships. Notes related to a central tonic are not only widely separated and interrupted by intermediary developments, but are the more subliminally perceptible since they occur as support for chords no longer even consonant. One step further, and tonal relationships would dissolve into a free play of chords and separate independent formations. This kind of development consequently depends on the isolation of individual notes which bear a clear relation to the tonic when unified—here, for example, notes which belong to the dominant chord—so that they can become in the most diverse way bases of a hazy tonal development. In them the last vestiges of tonality disappear, while in the path of expansion mentioned by previous writers, whole chords still maintain their simple cadential structure spanning large intermediary developments.

It is clear that even this basic idea has countless possible variants, and that furthermore, this idea, with its strongly undermining character, which obscures unified relationships, represents a specifically Romantic direction of development associated only with later epochs. Not until after Wagner is it given free reign.

The Prelude shows a highly important type of development in the passages intermediary to the main development, which begins after the introductory measures and leads to the climactic measure and its continuation already identified. The picture seems simpler here, and it is a characteristic example of how tonal development stretches into extensions and variation sections. With this we can soon recognize the definite regularity with which simple dominant and subdominant digressions alternate with each other. The whole unusual tonal conception, however, is already apparent after the first third of the prelude.

The measures after the introduction begin tonally. This continuous development begins in m. 16, and from there on the chords of the main tonality are very easy to understand and not difficult to follow in the score: V^9–VI—IV^7–III–IV^7–(V)–III. ((V) refers to the second half of m. 19, where *g–b–d* should be understood not as VII of *a* but as the secondary dominant of the subsequent relative major, III.) After this chord, there is a turn to the subdominant, D minor, easily brought about since III of A = VII of D. This turn to D minor lasts two measures and proceeds through the chords D minor: VII–IV–VII^7–I–II^7–V. (The second half of m. 21 should be understood as II, where the chord, ostensibly E♭ major, is *e–g–b♭–d*. The *e♭* in the upper voice is a chromatic passing tone to *d*; in the inner voice *e♭*, actually *d♯*, is a leading tone appoggiatura to *e*. The apparent E♭-major chord operates dissonantly as a tension harmony with only the form *e–g–b♭–d* as a resolution. Therefore it should not be understood here as a Neapolitan-sixth chord of D minor.)

Without touching on the tonic, this whole turn to the subdominant leads directly to a longer dominant passage. It is reached with the first chord of m. 22, again in a quite simple way, with the principle of common scale degrees: V of D = IV of E. With regard to the large-scale tonality of A minor, the whole succeeding dominant section is now counterbalanced against the whole preceding subdominant one.

The formations of this E-major section are not very easy to distinguish. The chord in the second half of m. 22 is *a♯–c♯–e–g*, with the tone *d♯* a leading-tone adjustment toward *e*. The chord enters as an inserted diminished-seventh chord before the succeeding B-major chord of m. 23, whose second half is then *d♯–f♯–a–c♯*. Consequently the chord progression from m. 22 to m. 24 reads E: IV–(VII⁷)–V–VII–VI–(V⁷)–IV. It should be noted that the A-major chord of m. 24 appears within a dominant section and thus does not have significance as a tonic changed to the major mode. In the following passage, the harmony of the whole of m. 25 is again *d♯–f♯–a–c♯*, that of the whole of m. 27 *f♯–a♯–c♯–e*. The third, *a♯*, appears in the melodic voice covered by the appoggiatura *b*, which resolves only in the next measure, but in the form *a*, while the end of m. 27 produces the *a♯* still in an inner voice. The second half of m. 28 is the diminished chord on degree VII, *d♯–f♯–a–c*. Accordingly the chord progression of m. 25 to m. 30 is E: VII⁷–I–VI⁷–(V⁷)–V–VII°–V–IV. Saturation of the passage with chromatic passing tones, appoggiatura adjustments, etc., is unusually strong throughout.

In m. 30, a longer subdominant passage is again directly contrasted with the section in the dominant, also without reference to the main tonality. This oscillation from the dominant region to the subdominant is also linked to the chord IV of E, which equals V of D minor.

The D-minor passage up through m. 36 is particularly easy to understand once we have exposed the chordal framework under the many chromatic distortions. In m. 32 the chord is *d–f–a*, even in the second half of the measure, and *f♯* and *d♯* should be understood here only as passing tones. In the whole of m. 33 the harmony is c–e–g, while the $g\sharp$ in the second half is a passing tone. The first chord of m. 34 should be regarded as a secondary dominant to the subsequent seventh chord on G. Hence the chord progression of mm. 30–36 is D minor: V–V^7–I–VII–(V^7)–IV^7–VII^7–iV–VII–I.

The following measures of the Prelude (36–41) break through the tonality in a sequence which * * * leads (41–44) to the transition to the A-major section. * * *

If we survey the basic principle by itself, without getting lost in details, the tonal development proves to be expanded here, in that larger proportions and entire structural units have reference to the overall tonality, just as individual chords do in smaller relationships. The dominant and subdominant chords can still be recognized as the nucleus of these deviations, however. The loosening of tonal coherence is less extensive here than in the remarkable technical conception of the first fifteen measures and is of quite a different sort. The diametrical opposition of passages seems intensified here by the fact that throughout, the clarifying turn to the dominant effects the brighter major code (E major), while the turn to the subdominant on the other hand effects the minor mode (D minor).

The simple principle evident here of an oscillation of entire long passages between dominant and subdominant regions is capable of enormous expansion, of course, since it can undergo enlargement both with regard to the prolongation of these excursions and with reference to the tonal distance traversed. The Romantic development, as opposed to the Classical, singles out the second means of expansion above all— an unfolding of tonality which spreads out in undulations of increasing distance on both sides of the line of the main tonality. Moreover, the Romantic movement intensifies the restlessness of harmonic language, since these digressions alternate much more quickly than in the more regular, balanced Classical style. At the beginning of the Prelude, as already discussed, the restriction to the two dominant keys follows the large-scale design which Wagner, with his great skill at intensification, sets in motion, first through tranquil revolutions before proceeding to violently agitated developments. It is clear that this entire harmonic principle represents an enlargement of the cadence, while whole structural units rather than simple tonal chords revolve around the tonic. It is just as clear that in this way an intensification of tonal separation in terms of distance corresponds in general to the intensified chromatic

chordal oscillations, even in the framework of short chord progressions—
something that also characterizes Romantic development. Since the
trends toward enlargement and growth incorporate all the principles
latent in the simplest cadence as developmental impulses for harmonic
motion, we can apprehend this technique as a generally applicable
principle, albeit based on the infinitely variable model of the cadence.
At the same time, we should consider further how in the last measure
before the turn to the section in the major, an intensification and definite
restlessness of development begin with the entrance of sequences in
place of tonal linkings, and moreover, these sequences drive the harmonic motion forward in shorter units. From this first third, however,
we get a glimpse of the large-scale tonal conception of the Prelude.

Now while this whole design of dominant and subdominant modulatory sections in the first part of the Prelude is, by itself, nothing
novel that transcends Classicism, something aside from what is immediately apparent must be considered technically as well as stylistically
important. The circling back and forth between dominant and subdominant regions occurs each time without a return to the main tonality in
between. The general trend of Romanticism toward loosening and
luxurious expansion of tonal spheres in the larger forms inclines toward
letting deviations in tonality overrun the tonic. Here in the Prelude this
tendency seems intensified to an extreme and becomes all the more
noticeable when the deviations themselves do not lead far away at all.
With each of the chains discussed, the tonic is simply traversed without
being dwelt upon, and it is remarkable how in this process the A-major
chord always seems just an intervening chord (IV of E = V of D), as if
a chord representing the greatest possible negation of the tonic, A
minor, should be chosen for the unification of opposing regions.

Chordal harshness, as well as external distortion of tonal unity,
increases, but the feeling of the central tonic does not disappear. In
this respect, however, the beginning as well as the whole of the *Tristan*
Prelude displays one of the greatest peculiarities in all music. Even
though the tonality is clearly A minor, its tonic chord does not occur
even once, not even in a distorted alteration form. In this total avoidance
of the tonic chord lies that restlessness that symbolizes great longing.
An enormous tension is built upon the chord; if it were to appear, it
would necessarily have the effect of an explosion. Wagner avoids it and
presents a tonic chord only in the section in the major. That A-major
chord enters in m. 44, shortly after the beginning of the section in the
major, as an extremely powerful eruption, intensified, moreover, by its

highly chromatic manner of presentation * * *. The A-major form of the triad is briefly touched upon twice more in the course of the Prelude (m. 50 and m. 65), but there it is alluded to as the related scale degree in a modulatory section, as was the case in m. 24. Thus, in spite of the external identity of sound, no feeling of the tonic is produced. Even in the later section of the Prelude (m. 71 *ff.*), in the minor once more, the tonic chord does not appear even once. Similarly, the conclusion turning toward C minor (from m. 95) does not produce the C-minor chord even once. Thus the A-minor chord does not appear in the entire Prelude, and space is given to a tonic effect only once, and that is in the excursion to the major. Even if one disregards the individual chord forms variously distorted by auxiliary tones and alteration, the tonality at first sight seems replaced by a construct of chaotic chord progressions. No wonder that at the appearance of *Tristan* musicians pulled out their hair! Despite this, there is no confusion here, but absolutely logical unity and clear tonal structure. Even the impression of the tonality, A minor, with its absolute individual coloring is characteristically invoked. A minor is already sounded in the introductory measures (1–15) through a disguised and greatly relaxed dominant upbeat, then maintained as the mediator between oscillations in dominant and subdominant tonal feeling, extending into the later sections which intensify in further easily recognizable modulations. The chordal root is rigorously concealed in the Prelude.

The Romantic principle seems driven to an extreme. The significance of the chord is quite supplanted by the significance of *tension*. The chord is no longer required when only the willful striving directed toward it is present. This suffices for the perception of tonality and the tonic—not only suffices, but is its representative to a much higher and more intense degree.

For the third time in the history of western music, we can almost speak of a new concept of tonality. The first concept was linear, based on the scalar prototypes of the church modes. With the development of polyphony, it dissolved, after a centuries-long battle between church modes and the natural mode of perception (individually reflected in almost all works of art), into the harmonic concept of tonality, which found its fullest ripening in Classical tonality. It was based on the two opposite basic chords, major and minor. Then perception of tonality, like the musical sensibility in general, forced itself beyond the chord again. Line—chord—tension—these are the three basic impulses in the changing perception of tonality.

The concept of tonality in the *Tristan* Prelude should be designated as characteristically Romantic—not as if there were many pieces on which it is stamped in such an extreme fashion, nor as if it had somehow been consciously elevated to a new principle. But it manifests the basic feeling and the psychological foundations of Romanticism carried to their last logical consequence. In the development of tonality, the transition from the perception of chordal background to the perception of tension initiated both in the individual tone, as well as in the further unfolding of all harmonic characteristics, appears here with the greatest brilliance.

* * *

ALFRED LORENZ

The Prelude†

Lorenz is known primarily for his analyses of Wagner's later operas in terms of conventional formal categories. Although he recognized tonality as an important determinant of musical structure, he often subordinated it to the principle of melodic repetition. His conceptions of harmony and tonality are rooted in the theories of Hugo Riemann, who oriented all harmonic phenomena to tonic (T), dominant (D), and subdominant (S) functions. Whenever a distinction is necessary, Riemann qualified his three basic chord symbols (T, D, and S) with ° before the letter to indicate the minor mode, or with $^+$ after the letter to indicate the major mode. A lower-case p is added after the basic symbol to indicate the "parallel" major or minor mode, which for Riemann actually meant what we nowadays in English call the *relative* major or minor (Tp, Dp, and Sp).

Another group of closely related triads are the *Leittonwechselklänge* ("leading-tone change chords"), triads of opposite mode generated from the original ones by changing only one of the notes a semitone. The sign $\succ$ is superimposed upon the symbol when the original triad is in the

† From *Das Geheimnis der Form bei Richard Wagner*, Vol. 2: *Der musikalische Aufbau von Richard Wagners "Tristan und Isolde"* (Berlin, 1926; 2nd unaltered ed., Tutzing, 1966), pp. 12–28 and 194–96. Lorenz's chapter on the Prelude appeared earlier in the *Zeitschrift für Musikwissenschaft* 5/9–10 (June–July 1923): 546 *ff.*, under the title, "Die formale Gestaltung des Vorspiels zu Tristan und Isolde." Appendix III from the book deals with the "*Tristan* chord". Both selections included with permission and translated by the Editor.

minor mode, so that with an A-minor triad as starting point, $\digamma$ designates an F-major triad. When the original chord is in the major mode, the sign $<$ is added to the symbol, so that if the starting point is C major, $\digamma$ designates an E-minor triad. Finally, $\mathcal{D}$ is Riemann's symbol for the dominant of the dominant (or secondary dominant), while $\mathcal{S}$ indicates the subdominant of the subdominant. The best introduction to Riemann's theories is William C. Mickelsen's *Hugo Riemann's Theory of Harmony: A Study* (Lincoln, 1977).

Lorenz curiously calls the initial eighth-note pickup measure 1, and his measure numbers are thus one off throughout the Prelude. I have changed Lorenz's measure numbers to agree with those in the Score.

Prelude? Wagner labeled it "Introduction" (*Einleitung*) in the score and with good reason, as we shall see in the course of our investigation! The practice of talking about the "*Tristan* Prelude" has become so common, however, that in the circles most familiar with Wagner, people— including even Richard Wagner himself—have not been able to shake off this habit.

This composition has already brought forth many studies—numerous essays in particular to decipher the famous first chord. But not one of the authors has attempted to discover the actual formal structure of this fascinating blossom from an inexhaustibly rich imagination. Writers have mentioned articulations only incidentally and have in general been content to discover a vast dynamic intensification which collapses at the climax. In this way they have characterized only a rather general poetic impulse that underlies any dynamic effect, but with that impulse alone, music cannot be made at all.[1]

Up to now, the common view that the first sixteen measures constitute an "introduction" has stood in the way of understanding the Prelude's formal structure. How can anyone think that a composer proposing to set up the main theme of a four-hour work would do it in some preliminary measures, and then put the main emphasis of his thought on a theme with which the "flow" seemingly begins, but which has only secondary significance in comparison to the opening theme? These commentators were led astray by the rests, which they had probably always heard irresponsible conductors curtail aphoristically. No, the "*Tristan* Introduction" begins immediately with the statement

---

1. Cf. Hans Pfitzner: "In reality, the poetic idea produces every comma in its domain, but in music the poetic idea is incapable of putting even two notes together to create an artistic organism," from his essay "Die neue Ästhetik der musikalischen Impotenz," reprinted in his *Gesammelte Schriften* (Augsburg, 1926), Vol. 2, p. 145.

of the main theme in a self-contained exposition.[2] Has anyone ever regarded the themes of Beethoven's *Appassionata*, Op. 57, and the slow movement of the Sonata in E♭ major, Op. 7, as "introductions" because they are divided into separate successions of notes articulated by rests? Beethoven's rests are not as long as those of the *Tristan* Prelude, but the principle is nevertheless the same. Those rests must not be curtailed in performance, for they are alive in the silence,[3] and the rhythmic line of the whole has natural centers of gravity which should not be damaged by shoddy performance. We perceive the thematic centers of gravity only when the rests are extended to their full value, and then what seems aphoristic and ineffective disappears.

We can best explain the structure of the main theme if we combine every two measures into a larger unit, simultaneously reduce the resulting 12/8 meter of the whole passage to a framework in 4/4,[4] and

2. Only Heinrich Porges [*Tristan und Isolde, Nebst einem Briefe Richard Wagners*, ed. Hans von Wolzogen, serialized in the *Bayreuther Blätter* 25–26 (1902–3); separate issue, Leipzig, 1906.—*Editor*] perceives it correctly when he says, "In the very first measures the fundamental tragic mood of the whole drama is articulated with clarity and precision." The feeling of precision would never emerge in an introduction deliberately set apart.

3. On this point, see the excellent discussion of the difference between impressive and expressive silence in Ernst Kurth, *Romantische Harmonik und ihre Krise in Wagners "Tristan"*, 2nd ed. (Berlin, 1923), pp. 440 *ff*. It is clear that these rests in the Prelude should be considered expressive ones, for in my view they manifest a rhythmically advancing "emotional struggle toward musical expression."

4. I later became aware that Johannes Schreyer does the same thing in his harmonic analysis of the Prelude in his *Harmonielehre* (Dresden, 1905), but he places the barlines differently so that the dynamic accents of the main motives fall in the middle of the measures. Anyone who studied prosody with Riemann, who purged all trochaic sentiments with fire and sword [because of his theory that all music begins with an upbeat—*Editor*] must inevitably agree with Schreyer and place the barlines before the final chords in the phrases. In that case, the cadential chord (deceptive cadence $F = \mathbf{\mathcal{F}}$) then correctly falls on 1. But I myself feel something in the nature of a gliding rhyme [referring to words whose antepenultimate syllables are rhymed—*Editor*] after the *sforzando* ninth chord, in spite of the $f \longequal{} ff \longequal{}$.

Points in favor of my placement of the barlines are: *first*, explanation of the third group of chords as a uniform seventh chord on *b* with four neighbor note alterations (not, as Schreyer has it, A–B[7]), which now fills out an entire double measure and is not dissected by the barline. *Second*, Siegfried Anheisser's observation, in his "Das Vorspiel zu Tristan und Isolde und seine Motivik," in *Zeitschrift für Musikwissenschaft* 3/5 (February, 1921): 257 *ff*., that the Grief motive concludes not on *d*, but on the tone *d♯*, whereas this point of culmination is left hanging in the air in Schreyer's study. *Third*, the apparent dynamics of the ascending Desire motive, which has its rhythmic center of gravity on the first rather than the third note. This can be proven by the passages where the motive fills out a single measure in the course of the opera, and there the first note is almost always placed on the downbeat * * *. Schreyer is also obliged to insert a 2/4 measure for the F-major chord in order to establish the larger metrical scheme once again. In addition, it should be noted in passing that the correct structural divisions of the entire Prelude do

take away all appoggiaturas and inessential tones from the chords, thus reducing the passage to its rough harmonic outline. The following picture then emerges:[5]

Example 1

Here in each double measure we see a strong beat with a feminine half-cadence. After the sixth measure an actual fermata occurs, right at the place where a pause is made in thousands upon thousands of older melodies. Riemann calls this time-honored phenomenon "cessation on the penultimate."[6] An echo effect not noted in the outline is inserted in this pause, and double-measure 6 is repeated an octave higher, enclosed by two fermatas.[7] The authentic cadence of the metrical period follows naturally after this standstill, and thus the period quite properly has eight measures. With the addition of the lower third, the full cadence is transformed into a deceptive one, which Kurth quite rightly calls characteristic. The full structure of the main theme is thus of remarkable simplicity.

Melodically, it is put together from three main motives: Grief (through m. 1), Desire (mm. 2–3), and Destiny (mm. 16–17).

For the sake of quick understanding, we are compelled to use names for the motives, but they have only the significance of "identification tags," as Wolzogen appropriately called them.[8] It is best not to change the names from those of this distinguished pathfinder in the

---

not emerge in Schreyer's analysis, because he repeatedly makes slurs across formal caesuras, as in mm. 13, 19, 20, and 21 of his diagram.

5. On the reasons for this style of notation, see the Appendix below, p. 220.

6. Hugo Riemann, *System der musikalischen Rhythmik und Metrik* (Leipzig, 1903), § 27.

7. In his doctoral dissertation, *Alessandro Scarlattis Kammerkantaten* (Munich, 1923), Paul Strüver notes the regularity with which the A sections of arias in Scarlatti's late works have a complete silence at this point, and he also makes particular mention of an aria in which an additional echo effect is inserted in this silence—exactly as in the *Tristan* Prelude!!

8. See, for example, Hans von Wolzogen, *Wagneriana: Gesammelte Aufsätze über Richard Wagners Werke vom Ring bis zum Gral. Gedenkausgabe für Festspielgäste zum Jahre 1888.* [*Editor*]

subject of the *Leitmotiv*, and it would have been better if all writers of thematic guides had retained uniform names.[9] Only the designation of the third motive as "Tristan" is definitely misleading.[10] I shall follow Kurth's admirable description of this motive and label it "Destiny."

This motive is actually nothing more than the cadential gesture of the whole theme.[11] It does not inaugurate the more "flowing" section, but is the powerful conclusion of the first thematic section (with VI or $\digamma$ substituted for *T*). The internal construction of this main theme is the *Bar*-form, concerning which I pointed out in my *Ring* volume that the second *Stollen* is usually transposed to a higher pitch level. Here the first Stollen of mm. 1–3 is repeated note-for-note a third higher as the second *Stollen* (mm. 4–7). At this point, the *Abgesang* (mm. 8–17) varies the motivic combination and is thus "similar to the *Stollen*, but not the same."[12] Both motives are extended by one note, and the harmony is changed. After the echo effect mentioned above, the new cadential motive follows, with the *a* of the violins taking the whole melody back to the tonic of the cello opening, the tonic having meanwhile been alluded to only in passing.

Simultaneously with this *a*, the Prelude's second theme (Glance motive) begins with an upbeat. This theme actually has only seven measures, but it has the effect of an eight-measure conception because of the *ritardando* in the last two. The conductor must accordingly extend this *ritardando* quite markedly. The second theme has a first subject of four measures, consisting of the actual Glance motive (a three-note ascent, with downward leap of a seventh), a variant of the same (similar ascent, with descent of a second), and the continuation (in the middle of which the seventh is inverted). Thus we see that this antecedent phrase is a minute *Bar*-form, and after the second eighth note of m.

9. The method of labeling employed by Grunsky, using lines of text, is highly artistic but too involved, in his admirable article "Das Vorspiel und der erste Akt von *Tristan und Isolde*," in *Richard Wagner-Jahrbuch*, ed. Ludwig Frankenstein, 2 (1907): 207 ff.

10. Even Guido Adler, in his *Richard Wagner: Vorlesungen gehalten an der Universität zu Wien* (Munich, 1904), p. 261, falls into this error when he calls the transformation of this motive in Scene 5 the "Heroic Tristan motive."

11. With his profound knowledge of inner connections, Kurth has clearly perceived and brilliantly demonstrated the intimate connection of the two motives of Desire and Destiny, but it is remarkable that when discussing construction, he often separates mm. 1–14 from the following, thus creating the impression of a caesura between the two motives. [See above, p. 197.—*Editor*]

12. *den Stollen ähnlich, doch nicht gleich*—Wagner's explanation of the relation of the *Abgesang* to the *Stollen* in his poem for *Die Meistersinger von Nürnberg*, Act III, Scene 2. [*Editor*]

21, it constitutes a partial cadence in the subdominant of the main key.[13] In close connection and without a change in bowing, the cellos begin the second subsection with a new variation of the Glance motive (*S, D* of D minor), which the second violins continue in imitation (*S, D* of E minor). It then ascends chromatically in sixteenth notes to a feminine full cadence in the tonic major (with the Glance motive in its original form). This subsection can also be regarded as a small *Bar*. The end of the exposition of the whole Prelude is reached with the A-major triad in m. 24.[14]

Ideally then, it consists of a main theme of eight double measures and a second theme of eight regular measures, each theme ending with an appoggiatura-cadence. Anheisser[15] points out that the A-major cadence reaches its goal with an appoggiatura from below, and that it is related to the cadences in which the Destiny motive produces the appoggiatura from above, but he overlooks the cadential character of the passages.

Thus we have the clear structure of an exposition before us, and not an introduction, but we have nonetheless still not clarified the construction of the entire Prelude. Form results only from *repetition*. Searching for repetition, previous commentators have again been led astray by the superficial appearance of the rests and the instrumentation into considering that the *piano* repetition of the main motive following the Prelude's dynamic climax corresponds to the beginning. Even Grunsky[16] designates the section before this *piano* passage as the "middle part" of the Prelude. The Glance motive inserted in the rests might well

---

13. This caesura has often been overlooked because of the slur above it, but its existence is proven by the numerous recapitulations of the passage in the course of the drama * * *.

14. Kurth wants to regard this cadence as the subdominant of E major. In doing this, I believe he goes too far in endeavoring to prove that the tonic is not sounded in the whole Prelude [see above, p. 200.—*Editor*]. To assume a cadence in the major form of the tonic in m. 24 does no harm to his splendid and thoroughly correct observation that the actual appearance of the tonic in Romantic music is more and more suppressed in favor of mere suggestions of it, and that in the *Tristan* Prelude, it is reduced to a minimum—the real tonic, A minor, is still not alluded to. An E-major section in fact begins in m. 25. But it will not do to assume its appearance two measures earlier in the middle of the phrase before the *ritenuto*. Here the E major has the distinct character of an intermediary dominant. We shall find this confirmed if we hear the seven measures from 18 (with upbeat) to 24 without bias in their context, and we shall then recognize that they show the clear progression: upbeat $T \mid Tp$ *(D) S* $\parallel$ *S (D) D* $T^+\parallel$.

15. Op. cit.

16. Karl Grunsky, "Wagner als Sinfoniker," in *Richard Wagner-Jahrbuch*, ed. Ludwig Frankenstein, 1 (1906): 242.

pass for variation, but this is overlooking the fact that the motive continues quite differently the third time (m. 89), and that it is subsumed into scattered fragments from all sections of the Prelude. The return of an exposition, however, does not depend on the repetition of isolated measures from it, however literal, but on the repetition of the entire motivic progression, even with variations. Now this motivic progression does not begin after the climax, but is actually that climax itself, and formally is thus simply a *forte* repetition of the exposition.

After the tonic is reached again in m. 63 with an extensive peroration of its dominant-seventh chord, the oboe family begins the recapitulation of the Desire motive with the $g\sharp$ in m. 66. In its original form, the Desire motive never appears in the course of the middle section, even though all the melodic elements in that section can be derived from this motive, as Anheisser ingeniously demonstrates. The silence that follows the first motive at the beginning of the Prelude is now filled in with a repetition of the first motive at the same pitch level. Then the clarinets enter with the motive in m. 70 (corresponding to m. 6 at the beginning) on *b*, again powerfully reinforced, and two measures later comes the third statement on the tone *d* (corresponding to m. 10). In the drive to the climax, the rests, fermatas, and echo repetition are omitted, and the cadential Destiny motive is linked to the third repetition of the Desire motive in m. 73, and thus forms a continuous line with it. Even the second theme (Glance motive) in m. 74 does not begin on the fourth eighth note of the measure as it did before, but on the first. Everything is pushed together, but nothing is left out. The entire exposition is there. Even the upward-surging sixteenths which prepared the A-major cadence at the beginning now begin *before* the conclusion of the antecedent phrase of the second theme, and carry the entire music to an enormous cadence, while the Glance motive, which once appeared in counterpoint against it, is now forcefully reiterated.

These sixteenths drive upward much more than in the cadence of mm. 23–24 and seem about to flow into the tonic *a* at the first eighth note of m. 81. To imagine this, we must naturally abstract from the harmonies of m. 80 and imagine $g\sharp^{7\circ}$ and E^{7} underneath, perhaps in the following manner:

Example 2

The *a* marked x does not sound in m. 81, however, but the line is restricted for three measures to the leading tone *g♯* (written *a♭*), from which it does not escape in spite of the two renewed assaults of runs. After the remarkable descent, the line finds its expiring but unresolved conclusion in the last note of the Glance motive (m. 85). The Glance motive, in counterpoint against these sixteenth-note figures, is completely in the tonality of A minor, if one imagines it harmonized approximately as follows:

Example 3

Even here, the resolution to the tonic should follow in m. 81. But this line does not escape the appoggiatura note (*b*) in spite of two new rhythmically varied ascents. The ingenious thing is that while these voices move straightforwardly in A minor, Wagner prevents the resolution of either of them by the addition of a completely contrasting harmony which simulates the tonality a tritone away. It projects the image of tormented inability to escape from this sea of sorrowful love.

In conformity with the *Tristan* style, there is naturally no full cadence, but rather a half-cadence on V. But even that is artificially protracted by two deceptive phrases which are unheard of before a half-cadence. Wagner creates by analogy with the former cadences: V, VI, V, VI, V, I, or in Riemann's notation: *D, Sp,*[17] *D, Sp, D, T*—something similar, quasi-intensified, before the dominant, which, if we designate the "*Tristan* chord" as a seventh chord on the second scale degree, looks in Riemann's notation as follows: *D̸ S̸ D̸ S̸ D̸ D*   and in outline

as follows: Example 4

17. I have indicated the sixth scale degree by *Sp* [i.e., the relative major of the subdominant—*Editor*] to show the parallel with what follows, in spite of the fact that in a deceptive cadence, it is actually the tonic *Leittonwechselklang* and therefore correctly indicated by *T̸*

This conception does not eliminate the originality with which Wagner twice reinterprets the *Tristan* chord as II of E♭ minor/major.[18] Perceived from the larger point of view of the unifying A-minor tonality, the whole modulation to E♭ shrinks to a mere illusion in face of the realization that these ninth chords on B♭ are simply Neapolitan-sixth chords which belong to the tonic and are forcibly surrounded by nonharmonic tones.[19]

In the passage from mm. 63–84, we see the entire exposition of the Prelude in the correct order, expanded by the final colossal half-cadence, but with everything condensed and newly formed into a powerful *forte* with harmonies stated by the trombones. A musician like Wagner is not content with the mere dynamic reinforcement of the woodwind theme, however. To this dynamic variation he adds another string figure.

But for him this does not consist of ornamental figuration or filler, but is the development of a new motive, Deliverance-by-Death, introduced by powerful runs as a variation of the Grief motive that occurs at this point in the exposition. The leap of an ascending sixth is enlarged into the run of thirty-seconds, and the chromatic descent of three notes is enlarged into the downward leap of a third.

This imposing "accompaniment figure" begins three measures before the entry of the main theme—in a quite subtle and beautiful fashion—with the reappearance of the dominant chord of the main tonality—a very old practice, but one frequently used by Wagner.

Now this is actually a variation not heard before—a "varied reprise," in the terminology of Carl Philipp Emanuel Bach. The accompaniment figure attracts the listener's attention in such a way that he often ignores the main theme underneath. If we compare these two passages—the exposition at the beginning (mm. 1–24), and this so-called climax (mm. 63–84)—we shall perceive that the same love-longing is in fact depicted in both, but that in the recapitulation everything is tremendously intensified. The delicate dissonances impart a quivering iridescence to the main theme, but here in the recapitulation, they are concentrated into a compact harmonization which starts in the same tonality, but moves in another direction and becomes condensed into an impenetrable barrier through which there is no other outlet than collapse.

---

18. It cannot be pure E♭ minor because of the major form of the ninth chord.

19. The appoggiatura *g*♯ is sustained as a common tone through all these harmonies up to the penultimate chord (m. 83), where it resolves normally to *a*.

If we regard mm. 63–84 as the recapitulation of the main section, it emerges that everything between that recapitulation and the cadence in m. 24 functions as a middle section in the dominant, E major. It is also clear that even this passage is ternary, since the initial contrasting section of mm. 25–36 is almost literally repeated in mm. 45–63. Between those two sections which correspond completely to each other— i.e., at the midpoint of the middle section—there are eight developmental measures (37–44) with a full cadence turning toward the tonality of the mediant (C♯ minor), which brings about the reappearance of the A-major triad by means of the familiar deceptive cadence. This time, of course, it should unquestionably be perceived as the subdominant of E major.[20]

The internal structure of these three parts of the middle section can be described as follows: *Part I*: two pairs of small units of two measures each. The first pair of units is composed of a turning around of the Glance motive: first the downward leap of a seventh, then the ascent of the Desire motive (not named by Wolzogen). The second pair of units is composed of the Renunciation-of-Love motive introduced each time by the Death motive in the bass. These pairs of units are followed by the antecedent phrase of the Glance theme from the exposition, varied by chromatic counterpoints.

Part II: Small *Bar* made from a new variant of the Glance motive, designated by Wolzogen only as number 7. The descent of the last two tones is transformed into an ascent. Each *Stollen* consists of this variant with its echo (every two measures), the four-measure *Abgesang* of the Glance motive with echo and a variant of the Destiny motive, which also constitutes a cadence here.

Part III is, as we have said, almost exactly like Part I. Only the instrumentation is varied (as though a four-foot stop were added). Further, the second pair of units continues differently, so that the Glance motive begins a third higher and does not appear in the original tonality until after this extra repetition. The cadence is finally formed in the dominant by a prolongation of one measure, while Part I of the middle section had closed in the subdominant in m. 36.

If then, we have recognized the middle section as being in a clear arch form (*Bogenform*) (m–n–m), we still have the last measures of the Prelude to consider, in which coda-like fragments return from all parts of the Prelude after the large half-cadence at the climax. These separate

20. On this passage, cf. Kurth, op. cit., p. 257.

fragments enter convulsively as if mortally wounded, and do not merge into a homogeneous presentation. In mm. 92–94 they lead to a complete cadence combining elements from the cadential formations of the middle section (mm. 42–43) in the first six eighth notes of its ascent, from the second theme (m. 24) in the chromatic sixteenths, and from the main theme (m. 17) in the suspension and the voice leading of the bass. With the resolution of the suspension in the violas (*b–a*), the Prelude is actually at an end.

But even here, the ear is cheated out of the expected A-minor chord by the addition of the lower third. A transition to the tonality of C minor is appended, and this tonality ominously controls the first act by means of the motive introduced with the words "Todgeweihtes Haupt! Todgeweihtes Herz!" This transition is the very reason Wagner did not call the composition a "prelude"—that designation would have necessitated a conclusion!—but thought of it as an introduction to the first act. In our discussion of the end of the first act, moreover, we shall see that the last period of the act corresponds to the Prelude, so that the two units frame the entire act in the manner of an arch form. For this reason also, the Prelude can really be regarded as an introduction only to the first act and not as a prelude to the whole work.

For greater clarity, * * * the design of this introduction according to its formal structure [is diagramed on the facing page].[21] Thus we recognize the form which in my *Ring* volume I called a "complete arch form" (*vollkommene Bogenform*) (m–n–o–n–m), with coda.

Anyone who discovers the marvelous brevity and terseness of these sections will be reminded of Goethe's phrase "the Master reveals himself first of all in restraint!" There is no trace here of "extravagant indulgence in dissonances and passion," but only the greatest concentration!

If we regard the beautiful echo section of mm. 37–44 as the eight-measure midpoint, then a total of 36 (24 + 12) measures, two fermatas plus a long *ritenuto* occur before the midpoint, and a total of 40 measures (18 + 22) occur after it. The two halves are thus absolutely the same! The enormously exciting effect of this work of art can only be explained

---

21. The A-minor tonality of this composition is as clear as anything would be that was clarified by the particular cadences appended here. Adler's remark (op. cit., p. 274) that "the tonal formula of the Prelude cannot be related to one tonic but fluctuates . . . between A minor and C major/C minor" can only be explained by the fact that Adler has obviously not separated the essential core of the Prelude sharply enough from the Transition to C minor at the end. What sounds like C major or C major/minor within that essential core—I do not see C minor anywhere!—is clear *Tp*.

Example 5

A minor

		no. of measures	Cadence	
Desire theme (amplified by Grief motive). Cadence: Destiny	[Main theme] a	17	*T*	MAIN SECTION 24 mm.
Glance theme, antecedent and consequent phrases	[2nd theme] C–A	7	*T⁺*	
2 pairs of motives; antecedent phrase of Glance theme	E–d	11½	*S*	MIDDLE SECTION 38 mm.
Variant of Glance motive. Cadence: Destiny motive	F–c♯	8	*⁺S*	
2 pairs of motives; antecedent phrase of Glance theme twice	E–Aᵛ	18½	*D*	
Desire theme (Deliverance-by-Death var.). Destiny	A–a	11½	*T*	MAIN SECTION 22 mm.
Glance theme, antecedent and consequent phrases linked together } overlapped	C–(e♭	7	*Tᵛ*	
Deceptive half-cadences, large half-cadence	E♭)–a 4			
Coda	a	10	*T*	10 mm.
Transition to c minor	c	17	*Tᵛ* of c	17 mm.
				111 mm.

by its marvellous *symmetry*, which contrasts with the totally different dynamic plan for the Prelude and thus translates a dramatic conflict into the realm of pure music. "Intensification" alone will not do it!

I cannot conclude these remarks without showing how the construction of the Prelude has been treated in the literature.

Guido Adler:[22] "The Prelude to the opera is constructed dynamically just like that to *Lohengrin*: a *crescendo* and a *decrescendo* characterize the contours of the proportions. Secondary motives compatible with the main thought are interwoven alongside the main motive, which is the characteristic and fundamental one for the whole opera."

Eugen Schmitz:[23] ". . . the Prelude, which like that to *Lohengrin* is sustained as a powerfully swelling *crescendo* that then sinks back again."

The gentlemen are mistaken. The *Tristan* Prelude does not bear the slightest resemblance to the *Lohengrin* Prelude, which is a theme with three variations (in the dominant, tonic, and subdominant), enclosed by two very short framing sections.

Hugo Leichtentritt[24] comes much closer to an actual understanding of the Prelude's formal construction. When I first published my analysis, I unfortunately did not know Leichtentritt's explanation, since it is not in the first edition of his book. I now take pleasure in mentioning Leichtentritt in the reissue of my analysis in book form. He has divided the Prelude in almost exactly the same way I did. He has simply not distinguished the Coda from the Transition (whereby he destroys the tonal unity), and his division C combines two subdivisions of my arrangement (mm. 26–37 and 38–45) into one single section. In doing so, the centermost part of the Prelude's middle section is not clearly delineated, and this hinders him from discovering the "complete arch form" himself. On the other hand, it is extraordinarily meritorious that he recognizes the intensification section as corresponding to the beginning. Of course, he does not venture to define this section clearly as the actual recapitulation, but speaks only of an "at least suggested recapitulation." At another moment, he seems vaguely inclined to regard the coda as a recapitulation of the beginning. Unfortunately he finally decides in favor of this incorrect view. He is also under the general delusion that the opening measures are an "introduction." All in all,

22. Ibid., p. 274.
23. *Richard Wagner* (Leipzig, 1909), p. 132.
24. Reprinted above, pp. 183—85.

however, Leichtentritt's explanation of the form is the best I have found up to now. Even his graphic presentation of the dynamic effect is very clear.

In addition, there is a very large essay on the subject by Siegfried Anheisser.[25] With the most subtle accuracy, he has discovered a great deal of interest about motivic aspects, as he perceptively discerns the efficacy of individual motives according to the "doctrine of the affections" which he upholds. I cannot discuss the question of how far the revival of this theory is justified. In any case, the fact that the Prelude is controlled by *one* mood agrees with it. Anheisser's study is meritorious in any case, because he points out that Wagner's *Leitmotivs* belong partly to objective music (motives which work like the old "reminiscence motive") and partly to subjective music (motives understandable by themselves through their affective content), and that particularly in *Tristan* they make an important step toward the second category and thereby approach more and more the fundamental basis of musical perception.

Anheisser's elucidation of the Prelude's various motives and his understanding of the character of intervals are excellent. Some musical points, however, strike me as not so well handled by him as by Kurth, who decidedly shows the more correct feeling when, for example, he hears something like an appoggiatura in the long solitary cello note *f'* of m. 1. Anheisser's statement that this measure actually belongs to D minor[26] and the following one to D♯ minor speaks as little for sensitivity to harmony as his division of the whole Prelude speaks for understanding of form. He divides the whole piece into

an Introduction	mm. 1–15
a Main Part	mm. 16–83
and a Conclusion	mm. 83–111

According to him, the Main Part is divided into three parts, of which the *first* is 26½ measures long and further breaks down into four segments (which end [27] at mm. 23,3 ‖ 31 ‖ 36,3 ‖ and 42,3). The *second* numbers 31 measures and breaks down into two segments (concluding at 63,3 and 73,3), and the *third* numbers 10½ measures. What kind of

25. Op. cit.
26. Even worse, certainly, is the remark of G. Capellen, in his "Harmonik und Melodik bei Richard Wagner," in *Bayreuther Blätter* 25 (1902): 11, who hears F major here and explains the *e* as dissonant!
27. By "24,3" etc., Anheisser means "m. 24, 3rd eighth note."

proportions are those? And how can one assume caesuras at m. 15 (when mm. 14 and 15 clearly prepare for 16), at m. 23,3 (in the middle of the phrase), at m. 31 (likewise in the middle of the motive), and at m. 73,3 (in the middle of the Destiny motive)—and then ignore the obvious caesuras in mm. 24, 44, and 94,4? He admits that the Destiny motive (his "motive 4"), which he calls a connecting prop and which opens several of his segments, could be understood as the cadence of the preceding segment, and he would thereby be in agreement with my interpretation of these passages. But since he decides in favor of the alternate organization, feeling for form must certainly have abandoned him.

His division is wrong because his principle of division—diatonicism or chromaticism—is not logically appropriate for the building of a form. Structural forces are harmony, melody, and rhythm. There can be no clarity, since he places the same melody (Glance motive) sometimes among the diatonic segments [I, 1 ‖ I, 2)b)] and sometimes among the chromatic ones [II, 1 ‖ III]. Anheisser's article contains no response to the fundamental truth that the architecture of a musical composition is nothing but a large-scale rhythm, so that after his discussion of beautiful forms in the Prelude, there is nothing more to say.

I should like to exclaim with Hans Sachs, "I tell you, gentlemen, the song is beautiful," and if I continue "I must endure, therefore let me single out my witnesses!"[28] Wagner himself steps into the circle. For the composer has left his poetic explanation in a document enclosed with his birthday letter to Mathilde Wesendonk in 1859.[29] Although this "programmatic explanation" is concentrated almost exclusively on the poetic meaning and scrupulously avoids any hint of musical technique, we can nevertheless extract from it several important conclusions about the purely musical plan.

In it we read: " . . . the musician who chose this theme for the introduction to his love drama could have but one care: how to impose restraint on himself . . . So just once, in one long-articulated impulse, he let that insatiable longing swell up from the timidest avowal of the most delicate attraction, through anxious sighs, hopes and fears, laments and wishes, raptures and torments, to the mightiest onset and to the

---

28. *Ich sag euch Herrn, das Lied ist schön* and *Ich . . . muss besteh'n, drum lasst mich meinen Zeugen ausseh'n*— quotations from the final scene of *Die Meistersinger von Nürnberg*. [*Editor*]

29. Reproduced in facsimile in Wolfgang Golther, ed., *Richard Wagner an Mathilde Wesendonk: Tagebuchblätter und Briefe 1853–1871* (Leipzig, 1904). [See above, pp. 47–48.— *Editor*]

most powerful effort to find the breach that will reveal to the infinitely craving heart the path into the sea of love's endless rapture. In vain! Its power spent, the heart sinks back to languish in longing . . ."

If we know how to read between the lines, it will strike us as significant that Wagner does not just mention the swelling up of insatiable longing, but that he also emphasizes the words "in one long-articulated impulse." What can that mean except in beautifully proportioned forms?

Wagner characterizes the Prelude's opening as "the timidest avowal of the most delicate attraction" and the *fortissimo* passage as "the most powerful effort to find the breach," and he connects these two phrases with the words "from" and "to." It is therefore clear that without any introductory thoughts, he sets out immediately toward his goal, which is the description of insatiable longing—first in budlike tenderness and finally in the mightiest rush. From the initial upbeat on, we consequently have the exposition, whose recapitulation is a magnificent variation of the same material. A middle section is clearly described with the words "through laments and wishes, raptures and torments." The unlimited material is actually controlled in "one long-articulated impulse." Then comes Wagner's thunderous phrase "in vain! Its power spent, the heart sinks back." Even here, the part I call the Coda, with its fragments sighing of mortal wounds, is represented as something separate. In Wagner's thoughts, there is not a trace of any psychological connection between this section and the beginning of the composition. My description is thus confirmed by Wagner passage for passage.

My assertion that the Prelude actually reached its end in m. 94, and that what follows is a modulatory transition to the first act, might be assailed. But for this also, I shall present evidence from the composer's own creative workshop. When Wagner set about composing a concert ending for his Prelude, it would have been the most natural thing simply to append it to the whole piece. It is psychologically impossible, however, that a good composer could attach an ending to his own work and leave something that in his view did not belong. And it would be just as impossible for him to cut off something that was an organic part of the work. If Wagner suppressed several of the final measures when adding the ending, then we have the psychological proof that he did not consider them an actual part of the Prelude, but regarded them as a transition to the first act. Now he attached this cadential supplement in precisely the measure I designated as the last dominant harmony of the final cadence (m. 93,4), extended this harmony for an extra measure, and in place of the F-major deceptive cadence attached a newly composed A-major tonic (*S* as appoggiatura to *T*). Melodically, the following passage is a soothing extension of the motive of Love's Happiness and the cadence of Act III transposed down a whole tone, while harmonically it is nothing but a tremendously expanded cadential gesture in A major. [First two units of 3½ measures *S T (D) D (D) D*, then three statements of the plagal cadence *S T* (the third statement as *S °S T* greatly extended), then three statements of the dominant cadence (over a tonic pedal point), and finally one more ornamented and greatly extended plagal cadence.] Thus the whole is really just an extremely long A-major chord, set exactly at the point I regard as the conclusion of the Prelude—at the violas' *a* in m. 94—a psychological proof that Wagner perceived the tonic of the piece at that point.

If the reader has followed my description of what a wonderful Apollonian construction the Prelude assumed in the composer's hands, he will also have seen that it is not a manufactured form, but a form developed from within. We can apply to this form Arthur Seidl's statement about Wagner's formally proportioned *melody*: "It is the melody of *natura naturans* (as we can differentiate here with Lotzean sensitivity), which overhears the inner life and weaving of natural moods; but not that of *natura naturata*, which only gapes at the symmetrical forms and rhythms of external sculpture and then faithfully reproduces them."

APPENDIX. [The "*Tristan* Chord"]

In the musical outline, I reduced the first two chords to their absolute simplest form and did not indicate the "characteristic dissonances"[30] (the added sixth in the first chord, and the seventh in the second chord), so as not to add to the conflict of opinions. Attempts to explain the "*Tristan* chord" constitute an actual historical development whose main stages are the following:

30. The "characteristic dissonances," according to Riemann, are dissonant chords built on the dominant and subdominant triads. The four basic characteristic dissonances can be defined in modern terminology as the major and minor forms of the triad with an added 6th, and the major and minor forms of the triad with an added 7th (the major triad with added 7th being, of course, the dominant 7th chord). Riemann regarded it as particularly significant that in each case, the added 6th or 7th is actually a member of the other triad under consideration. According to his derivation, the dominant 7th chord, for example, consists of the major form of the *dominant* triad plus the root of the *subdominant* triad. The other characteristic dissonances are similarly derived. For a complete exposition of this point, see Hugo Riemann, *Harmony Simplified, or The Theory of the Tonal Functions of Chords*, trans. H. Bewerunge (London, n.d. [c.1895]), p. 55. [*Editor*]

Salomon Jadassohn,[31] with no theory of chordal roots, declares each of the initial chords to be in a different tonality, and he accordingly assigns the first chord to the seventh scale degree of *f♯* (!). (According to Jadassohn, the first eleven measures go through fourteen tonalities: A minor, D minor, F♯, A minor, B, A minor, F♯ minor, C minor, B minor, C minor, C minor, F minor, E♭ minor, and E minor!)

Cyrill Kistler[32] regards the chord as "a diminished-seventh harmony with a minor triad on the seventh scale degree of A minor."

Carl Mayrberger[33] follows Sechter and characterizes the chord as a hybrid chord between A minor and E minor, and for the first time explains the appoggiatura character of the *g♯* by introducing the concept of "melodic chromaticism." This was the biggest step forward in understanding the chord.

C. Hynais[34] travels a similar path.

Max Arend[35] stands on Riemann's ground and correctly represents the chord as the subdominant with an added sixth (*b*) and a raised *d* (tending toward *e*). "What we have in these four measures," he continues, "is the cadence *T S D*. That is the kernel of these wonderful measures! *Simplex sigillum veri.*"

G. Capellen[36] was unsatisfied by all attempts at explanation and published quite new harmonic theories. Then a development set in which oriented the chord more and more firmly to the root *b*, so that eventually the character of the secondary dominant emerged, rather than that of the subdominant. The chord is now called B[7] and is regarded as the dominant of the dominant, E.

This is also true in the works of Schreyer,[37] Ergo,[38] and finally Kurth,[39] who in his profound book says directly: "The fifth, *f♯*, of the

31. *Melodik und Harmonik bei Richard Wagner* (Berlin, 1899).

32. *Harmonielehre* (Munich, 1879), p. 33.

33. "Die Harmonik Richard Wagners an den Leitmotiven des Vorspieles zu Tristan und Isolde," in *Bayreuther Blätter* 4 (1881): 169.

34. In the *Neue musikalische Presse* (Vienna, 1901), Nos. 4–7.

35. "Harmonische Analyse des Tristanvorspiels," in *Bayreuther Blätter* 24 (1901): 160 *ff*.

36. Op. cit.

37. Op. cit.

38. "Über Wagner's Melodik und Harmonik: Ein Beitrag zur Wagnerschen Harmonik," serialized in the *Bayreuther Blätter* 30–35 (1907–12), and later issued as a monograph.

39. Op. cit., p. 46 [See above, p. 187.— *Editor*]. Cf. also the note on p. 48 [p. 189 above—*Editor*] in which he likewise calls attention to the various explanations of the chord and concludes with a statement contradicting me: "Its chief emphasis derives from its dominant character in relation to its resolving chord."

chord undergoes an intensification of tension (directed toward the ensuing *e*), and appears in the chord lowered to *f*." This is one of the few points on which I am not able to follow Kurth. If we play the Desire motive first with the initial harmony altered to *f–b–d–g♯*, and then to *f♯–b–d♯–g♯*, we hear immediately that the first version (which actually appears in the Prelude at m. 66, for example, and in Act I at m. 242) is much closer to the actual sound than the second version.[40] From this it follows that the *f* is the more essential tone than the *d♯*, and further that the *d* is altered to *d♯*, not the *f♯* to *f*, and finally that the sound of the subdominant with an added sixth is much more closely related to our chord than the dominant-seventh chord is.

Kurth himself seems to have felt an additional misgiving about this interpretation, since in a paragraph expressly added in the second edition of his book, he felt obliged to prove the additional salient point that the chord does not resolve its seventh downward.[41] If one conceives the chord as a subdominant, then the *a* does not in itself have this pronounced seventh tendency, though in earlier periods it always moves up in one voice as in its familiar role in the augmented-sixth chord. The fact that such a justification as that on p. 49 of his book[42] was necessary is the best proof against interpreting the chord as a dominant.

I therefore stand firm in my view of the first chord as a subdominant "augmented 6-4-3 chord," and in the outline I reduced it from there to the simplest form of augmented-sixth chord, omitting for greater clarity only the "characteristic dissonance" (*b*) in the first chord and (*d*) in the following chord. The difference of views is certainly not very great, however, since the relationship of the subdominant and the secondary dominant is universally acknowledged.

It is even more difficult to get an agreement of opinion about the chords in mm. 10 and 11, of which Arend notes that the harmony is extremely hard to understand. Mayrberger and Schreyer explain the chord in m. 10 as the A-minor triad, Arend as the "C-major triad: *f* and *d–d♯* are appoggiaturas to *e*, and *g♯* is a *g* striving toward *a*." Capellen, on the the other hand, explains it as an E_6^9 with the root *e* lacking, and Kurth as E^7 with two neighbor-note adjustments: *f* to *e*,

40. The second version (a *major* triad with added 6th) also appears in the course of Act I, at the climax of the short love duet toward the end, for example, where it is a semitone higher than the pitch level cited here by Lorenz. [*Editor*]

41. Op. cit., p. 49. [See above, p. 190.—*Editor*]

42. See above, p. 190. [*Editor*]

and *c* to *b*. I think I hear four neighbor-note adjustments before B⁷: *c* to *b*, *d* (*c*ˣ) to *d*♯, *f* (*e*♯) to *f*♯, and *g*♯ to *a*. This solution has an analogy in *Götterdämmerung*, where the same chord progression, with *c* in the upper voice, presents simultaneously with the root *b* the most intensified form of the Servitude motive:[43]

Example 6

---

43. I have appended the example cited by Lorenz, from the final scene of the first act of *Götterdämmerung*. [*Editor*]

PAUL HINDEMITH

~~~~~~~~~

[*From* The Craft of Musical Composition]†

Schoenberg's presentation was formally theoretical, even though his ultimate purpose was pedagogical. By contrast, *The Craft of Musical Composition* has a distinct pedagogical cast and format, even though Hindemith was actually attempting to construct a systematic theoretical basis for his own composition. At the end of the first volume, he applied his principles to five pieces of music from the past, both distant and recent, in which he maintained an abiding and active interest.

Central to Hindemith's theory is a *two-voice framework* consisting of the bass voice plus the most important upper voice—"a skeleton which gives the chords the necessary contour" and traces "the spatial boundaries of the harmony." He also insisted that the "progression of the two-voice framework is wholly independent of the other tones of the chords."

Like Schoenberg before him, Hindemith rejected the idea that chords must necessarily be constructed in thirds. He devised a hierarchical arrangement of chords, dividing them first of all into two central groups and subdividing each group into three subgroups (see top of facing page).

Harmonic fluctuation for Hindemith meant the juxtaposition of chords from different groups with a consequent "up-and-down change of values and tensions," and he cautioned that harmonic fluctuation was "not to be confused with the scale of harmonic values which results from relationships within a key."

Hindemith defined a *guide-tone* as one of the two notes of a tritone, "the one which stands in best relationship to the root of the chord or, in doubtful cases, that tone which leads best to the root of the next chord if from group A, or to the guide-tone of the next chord if from group B." However, if one tone of the tritone is the actual root of the chord, then the other tone is the guide-tone.

Hindemith referred to roots which "support the burdens of larger harmonic groupings" as degrees, and to a succession of degrees as the *degree-progression*. Finally, *step-progression* involves seconds which "achieve a really dominant position when they become the guide-posts of the melody. As such they regulate its horizontal and vertical extension, and are thus the complement of the degree-progression, which is the guiding-line for its chordal coherence."

† *The Craft of Musical Composition*, Book 1: Theoretical Part, trans. Arthur Mendel (New York, 1942 revised ed., 1945), pp. 202–3 and 210–15. Copyright 1942 by Schott & Co. Ltd., London. Copyright renewed 1970 by B. Schott's Soehne, Mainz. All rights reserved. Used by permission of European American Distributor's Corp., sole U.S. agent for B. Schott's Soehne.

Table of Chord-Groups

A Chords without Tritone	**B** Chords containing Tritone
I Without seconds or sevenths	**II** Without minor seconds or major sevenths The tritone subordinate
	a With minor seventh only (no major second) Root and bass tone are identical
1. Root and bass tone are identical	
	b Containing major seconds or minor sevenths or both
	1. Root and bass tone are identical
2. Root lies above the bass tone	**2.** Root lies above the bass tone
	3. Containing more than one tritone*
III Containing seconds or sevenths or both	**IV** Containing minor seconds or major sevenths or both One or more tritones subordinate
1. Root and bass tone are identical	**1.** Root and bass tone are identical
2. Root lies above the bass tone	**2.** Root lies above the bass tone
V Indeterminate	**VI** Indeterminate. Tritone predominating
[Superimposed intervals of the same size]	*[Superimposed intervals of the same size]*

* * *

In the musical examples, the harmonic relations are indicated by the addition of the symbols for the non-chord tones.[1] By eliminating the

1. On the subject of non-chord tones, Hindemith offers the following:
   There exists no convenient and space-saving set of symbols for the clear indication of the various kinds of non-chord tones in analysis. For this purpose we may use symbols consisting of letters to which slight additions are made to indicate their varying functions:

latter, the harmonic fluctuation and the degree-progression are calculated. In the degree-progressions, the guide-tones are included in such
manner that the step from the root of a tritone-free chord to the guide-
tone, and vice versa, is indicated with a line leading from one to the
other. If for reasons of voice-leading the guide-tone has to approach
or leave the octave of the root of a tritone-free chord, instead of the
root itself, the octave is included in parentheses.

* * *

The Prelude to *Tristan* is one of the finest examples of the elaboration of a two-voice framework. The observer of the intervals formed
by the outside lines of the harmony will be astonished to see how
intervals of varying tension are juxtaposed. The procedure is illustrated
beginning with the very first chord: the interval of a minor third (written
as an augmented second) is followed by a major third, which represents
a decrease of tension; the tension is then sharply increased again in the
tritone on the first eighth of the third measure, only to be resolved
completely in the fifth which follows. In this admirable way the tensional

---

W   Changing tone (returning tone) [*Wechselton*]

D   Passing tone [*Durchgang*]

ⱽ   Suspension [*Vorhalt*]

ᴎ   Unprepared suspension (neighboring tone) [*Nebenton*]

N˙   Neighboring tone left by leap

ᴎ   Neighboring tone approached by leap

Ⅴ   Anticipation [*Vorausnahme*]

F   Unaccented free tone

Ḟ   Accented free tone

(Note: The symbols of the original German text have been used in the translation.
    Where the letters used are different from those which would naturally be
    used in English, the German words from which they are derived are given
    in brackets.—*Translator*.)

Our discussion of the non-chord tones is based on the assumption of normal
metric rhythm, in which the "strong beats" are stressed. When the opposite is true,
in syncopation, the relations of the non-chord tones are correspondingly inverted.
An unresolved suspension will then, since it normally occurs on the "strong" part
of the beat, occur on the "weak" (but now stressed) part, and the neighboring tones
approached and left by leap will occur at the ends of "strong" beats.

(*Craft*, Book 1, pp. 173–74.) [*Editor*]

Harmonic and Melodic Analysis

1 Fluctuation
2 Two-Voice Framework
3 Degree-Progression
4 Tonality

Melodic Analysis {
5 Degree-Progression
6 Step-Progression

development of the framework is calculated from beginning to end, as the section here notated illustrates.

No less remarkable is the handling of the *harmonic fluctuation* and of the *degree-progression*. The distribution of the harmonic tension produces a beautifully varied succession of sharp and mild chords— chords of Group A and chords of Group B. Yet this ebb and flow dispenses almost entirely with chords of the highest tension—those of group IV. In the degree-progression, both the roots and the guide-tones are admirably treated. The first measure with its upbeat is treated as a broken chord, because the ear relates the two tones; likewise the fifth, eighth, and ninth measures. In measure 9, the d^1 of measure 8 has to be taken into account, and thus beneath the a^1 of measure 9 there is a root, d^1. The six-four chord in measure 18 is so passing in character that one is justified in taking its bass tone as its root, just as in a six-four chord preceding the dominant in a cadence. The same is true in measure 32.

In the analysis of the *tonality* it should be noticed that those roots upon which tritone chords are built must be regarded as dominants of tonics lying a fifth below. Thus the tonal center of the first three measures is a, and of measures 5–7, c. If we set out the centers of the various tonalities in succession, we obtain the following series:

187.

from which it appears, in view of the repetitions of A and its support by its most closely related tones, that A is indisputably the tonal center of the whole; and this is still further confirmed in the later development of the piece.

One cannot expect, in so wonderfully constructed a harmonic organism, to find an equal perfection of melody. It is impossible to balance the two elements exactly; one of them must always predominate. Here melody yields first place to harmony. It confines itself for the most part to steps of a second and broken-chord formations. Thus nothing remarkable in the way of either melody degree-progression or step-progression can arise. The continual stepwise motion yields too little harmonic result for the degree-progression, and this stepwise motion is itself the step-progression, which is not built on large lines. But in the place where melody assumes somewhat greater importance (measures 25–32) I have added the melodic analysis.

WERNER KARSTEN

~~~~~~~~~~~

Harmonic Analysis of the "Tristan *Chord*"†

Hugo Riemann did not write at length about the *Tristan* Prelude, but his theories provided the harmonic and tonal foundation for Lorenz's otherwise more purely formal analysis. Karsten's study adduces some of Riemann's principles in relation to the Prelude in direct comparison and contrast to those of Ernst Kurth.

When we analyze the "*Tristan* chord"—that chord which as the first sonority not only opens but fatefully determines the music-drama *Tristan and Isolde*—we are no longer encountering new harmonic territory, but a chord that has already evoked an entire literature. There is hardly a textbook on harmony that does not cite precisely this chord as a model for an altered chord, and on the whole the authors have not been cautious in their harmonic interpretations. Ernst Kurth undertook a more serious attempt when he devoted an entire chapter in his fine book, *Romantische Harmonik*, to the "*Tristan* chord," not only on account of the great significance this chord has for the entire opera, but also on account of the uniqueness which makes it appropriate as the embodiment of Romantic harmony and its difficulties. Although for Kurth this chord wavers ambiguously from the musical and intellectual points of view, its harmonic structure for him is clearly and unequivocally fixed. He defines the chord as an alteration of the secondary dominant-seventh chord of A minor (i.e., the dominant-seventh chord of the dominant), that is, as B^7 (*b–d♯–f♯–a*) with *f♯* altered to *f*. It is surely significant, however, that another great music theorist, Hugo Riemann, interprets this chord with exactly the same certainty as an alteration of the seventh chord of the minor subdominant (in Riemann's terminology, VII of A

† "Harmonische Analyse des Tristan-Akkordes," in *Schweizerische Musikzeitung* 91 (1951): 291–96. Translated by the Editor and reprinted by permission of the publisher.

minor = a–f–d–B in descending order),[1] in which the note d is raised to $d\sharp$. The derivations thus develop from diametrically opposed directions: for Riemann, from below out of the minor subdominant region, and for Kurth, from above out of the major dominant region. This divergence is not just structural; that is to say, it is not just a result of the two theorists' well-known fundamentally different attitudes on the question of the dual structure of the tonal system of harmony. If that were the case, there would be no real problem but simply a terminological difference that could be resolved with the chord symbol from the one particular harmonic theory or the other. But the opposite is the case. Even aside from theoretical fundamentals, a real difference of opinion persists about the nature of the chord. If our conceptions of music theory are to make sense, then we cannot be indifferent about knowing whether a chord derives from the dominant region or the subdominant one. It is therefore justifiable to subject the chord once again to harmonic analysis.

The chord belongs to the class of so-called altered chords, which is to say that it is not purely triadic in character. But harmonic theory does not recognize any chords other than triads and their modifications or combinations with dissonant tones. Hence even with the "*Tristan* chord," we must ask from which triad it is derived, and what its tonal function is. If we compare the two explanatory chords of Riemann and Kurth, it is striking that even with a great difference in function, they enjoy a close acoustical affinity distinguished only by the chromatic shading of the two inner tones. Wagner's chord has three tones in common with each of the explanatory chords and deviates from each one in the fourth, thus standing halfway between:

Example 1

Riemann Wagner Kurth

---

1. Like many other theorists before and since, Riemann generated the major triad from the overtone series. In addition, however, he postulated a corresponding "undertone series" as the exact inversion of the overtone series. From that undertone series, he generated the minor triad in such a way that the fundamental note (root) is the uppermost one, or what we would ordinarily regard as the fifth. Seventh chords are then formed by adding an extra third at the bottom. Thus minor triads, plus the seventh and ninth chords based on them, are to be read from top to bottom. [*Editor*]

From the tonal point of view, the two parent chords are nearly equivalent in their relationship to the tonic. Riemann represents the harmonic progression as follows:

Example 2

Kurth as follows:

Example 3

Riemann's chord progression is perhaps somewhat more comprehensive, because it defines the tonality very clearly through references to dominant and subdominant, while Kurth's progression inclines only toward the dominant side. But that is not unusual, not even at the beginning of a composition. From a melodic point of view, the altered chord can be inserted at will into both chord progressions. For Riemann, then, *e* would lead very beautifully through *d♯* to *d*, the line the cello part actually follows in the score.[2] For Kurth, *f♯* would move through *f* to *e*, but only the last part of this progression (*f–e*) appears in the score, since *f♯* enters immediately in intensified form as *f*.

For the moment, no decision can be made between these two analyses of the chord. Each one taken by itself is correct and affords a contribution to the explanation, but neither one contains the whole truth. Even combining them does not decipher the essence of the chord. Rather we must question whether the full range of meanings is already exhausted with these two approaches, or whether latent in this sonority are still other forces not encompassed in the two explanations. Both analyses proceed from the self-evident supposition that the freely inserted tone *g♯* is not an actual chord tone but an appoggiatura to *a*. While there is strong evidence for this view, it cannot be denied that

2. Actually, the cellos terminate with the *d♯*, simultaneously picked up by the English horn, which supplies the continuation to *d*. In terms of the voice leading, however, Karsten's observation is nonetheless correct. [*Editor*]

the unusual character of the chord lies in its characteristic dissonant form, which works so powerfully that the subsequent resolution of the g♯ to a—only a partial resolution, of course, since no decision is made between d♯ and f—eschews any relaxing effect and has a character much more melodic than harmonic. It is therefore easy to regard the dissonant chord as just that. This is all the more justified as the chord plays a substantial thematic role throughout the entire opera as a characteristic sonority, though frequently in enharmonic reinterpretation. Kurth also emphasizes the chord's fluctuating roles as a flexible collection of linear tendencies and as a fixed characteristic sonority. He points out that after three *fortissimo* impulses which build up to the three *forte* statements of the opening motive, the Prelude itself culminates and collapses with this chord. He also points out that the identity of the enharmonically fixed sonority with the striving altered chord is so vast and interwoven that at the arpeggio descent from the Prelude's climax, Wagner's score has both types of notation intermingled in the various instruments.

It is a completely open question requiring preliminary investigation whether it is valid to convert this chord by inversion to "normal position" with the tones spaced by thirds the way we customarily do in analyzing a chord, or whether this chord is not uniquely determined by its position and particularly by the contraction of the octave to f–d♯'. The latter seems to me to be the case, since the two fourths at the top and bottom of the chord produce the peculiarly hollow sonorous effect which suggests emptiness and hopelessness as well as longing and fulfillment. Despite the noninvertibility of the chord, however, one cannot speak of an actual root in the sense of a fundamental, since none of the notes has preeminence. But a chordal support or chordal nucleus can certainly be determined and perceived as a supporting framework. This is indeed evident if the chord is regarded as a functional part of the three-measure phrase. In the first measure the underlying harmony is A minor. The manner in which the tonic is quite weakly suggested only on the last eighth note of the measure is extraordinarily typical of the ephemeral character of Romanticism. Even in Classicism, of course, there are beginnings in which the tonic is not clearly established at the outset but emerges only gradually as from a distant fog. But that veiling occurs only so that the tonic can afterwards be set forth all the more radiantly, while in the *Tristan* Prelude it is never sounded clearly at all, but only underlies the composition intellectually. Although the tonic is outlined in m. 1 only in weak contours and its essential determining element, the third, is lacking, this is still the clearest manifestation of the tonic in the whole Prelude. The tension chord under consideration follows in m. 2, and the resolution to the dominant-seventh chord of A minor ensues in m. 3. The fact that the tension chord moves to a dissonance is not such an unprecedented case as Kurth assumed. It is unusual, however, that the octave forms an appoggiatura to the seventh. How much more justified it is that the extraordinarily strong tension with which m. 2 is charged should come to rest in the mildest form of dissonance we know. In m. 3 we again have firm ground underfoot, so to speak, so that we can determine the beginning and concluding points of the phrase as the chord progression

Example 4

But what happens in between?

A contraction of the octave *e–e'* to *f–d♯'* ensues in m. 2, and this breathing space substitutes for tonal progression. It is quite wrong to search primarily for tonal significance in the form of a progression by fifths within a chordal formation which, as we shall see, contains an abundance of melodic tendencies. Tonal relationships no doubt play an almost hidden role, yet they are not the driving force. Here it is less a question of a succession of functionally different chords than of the revolving individual life of a single chord. The painful contraction of the octave is the fundamental on which the tonally undefined chord rests, and with the retraction to the octave it finds its resolution. Hence one can imagine the altered chord produced as follows:

Example 5

The second chord is produced by the contraction of the octave. In the third chord the contraction remains constant while the tones *a* and *c* anticipate the dominant progression to *g♯* and *b*, by means of which the "*Tristan* chord" is produced. And in the fourth chord the contraction relaxes back to the octave, by which means the dominant is reached. This description naturally has only diagrammatic value, and we must not overlook the fact that the position of the "*Tristan* chord," to which we granted structural significance, has not been considered. But another much more important objection arises, for a look at the score shows that in m. 3 the contraction *f–d♯'* does not return to the octave at all, but rather *d♯* progresses to *d*. To understand that this fact does not signify a refutation of previous considerations, we must examine the role of melodic forces in achieving the harmonic structure.

M. 1 is already of enormous melodic intensity. The listener remains in doubt up to the sixth eighth note what will happen, indeed what *has* happened, for he still has no support at all and does not know what the key is. *f* would be conceivable as a chord tone, perhaps in F major or D minor, but the resolution of the crescendo—the score prescribes *"langsam und schmachtend"*—makes the listener suspect that this tone will not rest by itself, but that it is striving to discharge itself in the manner of a leading tone. The melodic energy of m. 1 determines the entire course of the phrase. The tension accumulated in it is responsible for the generation of the altered chord in question and prescribes the course of all voices. Mm. 2 and 3 derive their character from m. 1. The *f–e* of m. 1 finds its echo in the bottom voice of mm. 2 and 3:

Example 6

but the continuation of the alto voice is nothing other than a repetition of m. 1:

Example 7

The tone *d♯*, which harmonically strives toward *e* because of the contraction, is forced by the melodic line flowing from the overwhelming intensity of m. 1 out of its upward-striving course into compliance with the law of m. 1. The bottom voice does this in exactly the same way. One can even wonder whether in the course of m. 2 the tone *d♯* undergoes enharmonic reinterpretation as *e♭* after having to relinquish the tension of its leading-tone relation to *f*. The fact that this is not notated means nothing, since in the Protean nature of these chords, it is impossible for all changes of meaning to be expressed in musical notation. If we search through the opera, we often enough encounter the altered chord in the version f–b–e^b–$g\sharp$. One additional circumstance allows the tone $d\sharp$ to relinquish its tendency to revert to upward movement, and to continue descending instead, according to the law of m. 1. Upward movement is removed from the tone $d\sharp$ by means of the freely entering upper voice, which is the true retrograde of the alto voice:

Example 8

The tone $d\sharp$ transfers its upward energy to the upper voice, which in turn realizes the initial melodic motive in the reverse direction. Super-imposed on the tone $d\sharp$, the upper voice simultaneously weakens the tension in the contraction f–$d\sharp'$, whose elastic striving toward the octave is by this time broken in two ways. Nevertheless the melodic progression does not force a complete abandonment of the harmonic progression from the minor tonic to the major dominant. The melodically induced reversal concerns not the original basic relationship, but only the octave tension.

The complex and multipolar nature of this ambiguous chord will be demonstrated more clearly if we pursue its further role first in the three-part cadence of the beginning, then in the later course of the Prelude. The first motivic phrase already discussed comprises mm. 1–4. The continuation occurs in the form of a sequence, as the first motive is repeated at another pitch level. The second phrase is defined by mm. 5–8. Apart from pitch level, it differs only in the upbeat. The first phrase begins with a minor sixth, whereas the second begins with a major sixth. Obviously the upbeat of the second phrase b–$g\sharp$ grows out of the final chord of the first phrase, E^7, but the harmonic sense of m. 5 is not nearly exhausted with E^7. The tones b–$g\sharp$ are certainly related to the preceding E^7 chord, but $g\sharp$ is immediately converted enharmon-ically to a^b in order to form an appoggiatura tension to the following g. If this were not the case, $g\sharp$ would remain a chord tone and could not accumulate the concentrated tension necessary for the appearance of the altered chord in m. 6, which corresponds completely to that of m. 2. With the unwritten transformation in function of $g\sharp$ to a^b, the harmonic sense of m. 5 turns out to be C minor, which then leads quite analogously from the problematic tension chord to the dominant-seventh chord, G^7, and needs no further comment.

The third phrase in the sequence shows modifications. While the actual core of the phrase comprises only three measures (9–11), the attached continuation must be regarded as an extension of the third unit of the sequence and belonging to it, so that we must discuss mm. 9–16 as a whole. The construction of a three-part sequence with an extension of the third unit conforms completely to the Classical tradition typified by Mozart and Beethoven. It is very interesting to compare the slow introduction of Beethoven's *Sonata pathétique*, Op. 13, to the *Tristan* Prelude, for it offers astounding structural as well as thematic parallels. It is also instructive in terms of its difference—thorough grounding in Classical tonality. Unfortunately, I must forego an exact comparative analysis.

The fact that the third unit of the sequence involves something greater derives from the larger space allotted to the upbeat, which enters earlier and is thereby lenthened by half a measure. The phrase is not concluded according to expectation when the resolving dominant-seventh chord is reached, but is spun out with a gradual thinning of the musical texture by application of the principle of subdivision often used in the Classical period. First follows a repetition of the last two measures an octave higher, then a repetition of the upper voice from the last measure, and finally a second echo of this voice in the higher register. But what is lost by these repetitions in density of texture is gained in motivic concentration and melodic intensity. The dynamic reversal of the ascending semitone is noteworthy: while in mm. 11 and 13 it is a dissolving termination, in mm. 14 and 15 it becomes the support for a powerful fusion of forces. The crescendo has an energy-loading effect and with the accumulation of fermatas, it produces an uncanny tension that finally explodes in the *sforzando* of m. 16, harmonically based on E^7. With it comes a release from the sultry languishing mood of the first fifteen measures. The released energy can now flow freely, and the way is prepared for that intensification—rich in melody, nourished by ever new sources, and never satisfied—which increases up to the three *forte* statements of the opening cello motive, in order to collapse hopelessly into the chords of that motive's continuation.

Let us return to harmonic analysis. Mm. 9–11 can now be compared to the corresponding measures of the first two phrases. Like the second phrase, the third also grows out of the final chord of the preceding one: the tones *d–b* derive from the G^7 chord. The continuation is different, however. The upper tone of the sixth descends two semitones instead of one. There are good reasons for this. If the third phrase were constructed as an exact analogy to the second, it would lead to Bb^7 in m. 11. But that would not correspond to the tonal line of the sequence whose cadential chords traverse the dominant of the main key (E^7–G^7–B^7). Thus, the third phrase must be a major third higher than the second. First a change in function from G major to A minor takes place on the tone *b*, producing the tonic foundation for the dominant in m. 11. But that does not suffice, for *b* as a chord tone is not capable of accumulating the energy necessary for continuation. A special effort is required from within the register of the chord tone, and that effort manifests itself in the double chromatic descent. But the extended descending line simultaneously determines the extended ascending line in retrograde, with which the dominant goal is reached.

If we disregard the interpolated tension chords, the harmonic framework of the sequence can be presented as the following simple chord progression:

Example 9

The nature of the chord in m. 10 is still not clarified, however. If one regards it in retrospect from the resolving chord, it corresponds in the bass line to the tension sonorities of the first and second phrases, and that bass line moves like a leading tone with a semitone step to the root of the dominant. However, the leading tone from above is lacking, which would constitute the parallel to the octave contraction of the first two units of the sequence. In any event, we could regard *c*–*g♯* as a contraction of the seventh *b*–*a*. Even if we wanted to consider the chord on the last eighth note of the measure with *f* and *d* resolved to *e*, we should be opposing harmonic explanation. The tension chord can sooner be compared to the corresponding chords of the first two phrases in chordal value. Superficially, certain parallels are noticeable. The first two tension chords consist of a perfect fourth in the upper voices and an augmented fourth in the lower ones, and these two intervals are placed a major third apart. The third chord differs in that the perfect fourth is in the lower voices and that in place of an augmented fourth, a diminished fifth appears, which is enharmonically identical to be sure and approximately the same in chordal value. Very close melodic correspondences are also present. The line from the first measure recurs in the tenor, and the upper voice of the second measure returns in the alto, while the initial alto voice is taken over in retrograde inversion by the oboe. With some appropriate transpositions, this chord's structural similarity to the two corresponding ones could be demonstrated. Although such a description would have in its favor this chord's approximate acoustical equivalence to the two others, it cannot be denied that the chord's harmonic reinterpretation would seem forced. I therefore prefer to say that this chord does not fit into the usual scheme of chordal structure. It cannot be explained independently as a harmony, but must be explained as a result of melodic voice leading and as a contraction from the point of view of the ensuing resolving chord:

Example 10

To a certain extent this also applies to the first two tension chords, except that those preserved even more reminiscences of ordinary harmony than the third chord, which certainly agrees with them in degree of dissonance, but in other respects presents a fusion of melodically striving voices. If we include the tension chords in our diagram of the sequence, they will be seen to develop naturally from the requirements of the voice leading:

Example 11

WILLIAM J. MITCHELL

The Tristan *Prelude: Techniques and Structure*†

The first attempt to apply the voice-leading principles and graphing techniques of Heinrich Schenker to the *Tristan* Prelude was that of Adele Katz in her *Challenge to Musical Tradition: A New Concept of Tonality* (1945). A considerably more refined, rigorous, and comprehensive attempt is that of Mitchell, the first American theorist to abolish the "traditional" view of G♯ in the first phrase of the Prelude, put forward in this volume by Roger Sessions, and to present a convincing argument for regarding it as the actual chord tone. Mitchell was also the first analyst to give serious consideration to Wagner's concert ending, regarding it as an integral part of the Prelude. In so doing, he treated the Prelude as a separate and self-contained piece rather than as an introduction to the first act of the opera. The first theorist to take serious issue with this and other aspects of Mitchell's study was Benjamin Boretz (in *Perspectives of New Music*, Fall–Winter 1972: 159 *ff*.).

* * *

THE INCLUSIVE PLAN

* * *

Example 1a presents the essential features of the outer parts in a linear-harmonic sketch. The upper part is notated in its proper register, but the bass has been assigned a register of convenience. Its proper octave registers will be indicated in the analysis of detail. Major-minor mixtures, so characteristic of the chromatic bent of the Prelude, intrude into the first sketches. Of interest in this respect is the predominance of the major mode brought about by the long ascent to $c\sharp^3$. Following the neighbor d^3, $c\natural^3$ replaces the major third momentarily, but the concert ending clearly affirms A major, as do most of the details, despite the minor color of the opening bars. The bass also participates in mixed colors, asserting f^1 and $b\flat$ (as a lowered or Phrygian second step) before the closing cadential bars.

† From *The Music Forum*, Vol. 1, ed. William J. Mitchell and Felix Salzer (New York, 1967), pp. 163–203. © 1967, Columbia University Press. Reprinted by permission.

Example 1

Example 1b presents some of the detail of a higher order. Up to bar 45, the A-chord, with the help of two harmonically oriented prolongations in the bass (bars 1–24, 24–45), works toward the structurally significant c♯³. It is through a change of octave registers that this goal is achieved. Note that, after the opening a, a¹, a² have been established, an ascent to c♯² occurs (bars 1–24). Only after this (bars 24–45) is the dominating upper-voice register attained. Bars 53–62 unroll an extended subdominant harmony as consonant support for the neighbor d³. The entry and extension of the dominant harmony (bars 63–73) presents d³ as a seventh which ultimately (bars 74–77) resolves to c³ supported by f. It is here that the delirious abandon of the music makes the case for A major momentarily dubious (bars 79–83), until in bar 84 the dominant harmony is asserted. It rules until the arrival in bar 95 of the concluding A-major—chord, plagally suspended. As suggested by the total shape of the bass and the Roman numerals, the Prelude expresses the functions, nonmodulatory, of A, albeit with a high degree of chromaticism.

THE ANALYSIS OF SECTIONS

Although the Prelude is essentially a continuous structure, the layout of Example 1b suggests a convenient subdivision into seven sections. These will be bars 1–17, 17–24, 24–45 (not 44), 45–63, 63–74, 74–84, 84–96, and further. * * *

Example 2

To facilitate references to motives used by Wagner in the course of the Prelude, the principal ones and the "Tristan chord" have been quoted in Example 2 and identified by means of a letter or, in the case of the Tristan chord, by a convenient abbreviation. It is by these tags that they shall be cited in the detailed analysis. Note that motives A^2, B, C, E, F, and G have in common a terminating rhythm of an eighth note followed by a quarter note, a feature that adds to their interrelationship. Similarly, all but the first of these contain a dotted eighth note followed by a sixteenth.

Bars 1–17. Although the opening bars, particularly the sonority *Tr* of bar 2, present a continuing challenge, the inclusive structure of the bass is clear. Its broad context is formed by the initial a making its way to F in bar 17. Between these, a prolonged arpeggiation of the E-chord takes place, consisting of e (bar 3), g (bar 7), b (bar 11), and E (bar 16). Each of these is preceded by the half step above as indicated in Examples 3a

and 3b. Above this bass, the upper voice moves from the opening a to
a^2 of bar 17. The connection between these two points is formed by the
$g\sharp^1$ of bar 3 making an ascent in a stepwise motion consisting of four
groups of three notes each until the terminal a^2 is reached (Example
3b). Observe, in Examples 3a and 3b, how this complete motion opens
up three octave registers and, in the octave exchanges of bars 12–15,
suggests hesitantly a higher register before settling on a^2 in bar 17. The
underlying sense of these seventeen bars is represented in Example 3c.

The details of the section are highly interesting. As Wagner
arpeggiates the tones of the E-chord, he uses the minor third, g, with
its major chord in bar 8, rather than g♯ and a thankless diminished
chord. The basis of such a technique is the chordal mixture wherein
the major third, g♯, replaced by the minor third, g, is reasserted in bar
16. The process of extending an overall a to F by means of an arpeggiated
E-chord is unusual * * *.

Example 3

a. Bars 1–17

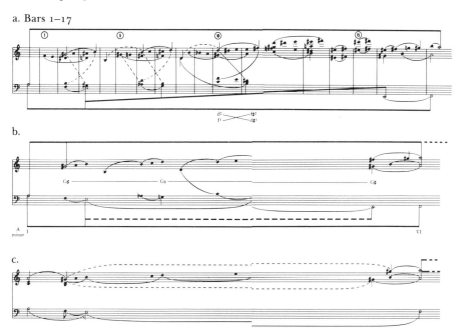

b.

c.

* * *

Let us examine the chord *Tr* in bar 2 of the Prelude. While the augmented sixth chord in bar 24 of Chopin's Mazurka, Op. 30, No. 2, derives readily from a diatonic $\substack{6 \\ 4+ \\ 3}$ (d, g♯, b, f♯^{1}), by simply sharping the sixth, b, *Tr* does not submit so readily, for its immediate derivation is $\substack{6 \\ 4+ \\ 2+}$ (f, b, d^1, g♯^{1}), a form of diminished seventh chord. This, in fact is the historic derivation of the sonority.[1] In order to derive *Tr* from the

Example 4

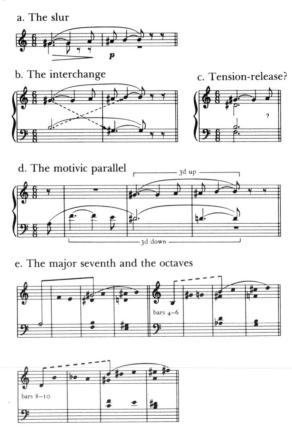

a. The slur

b. The interchange

c. Tension-release?

d. The motivic parallel

e. The major seventh and the octaves

1. A brief survey of the career of *Tr* in the hands of analysts appears in Alfred Lorenz, *Das Geheimnis der Form bei Richard Wagner* (Berlin, Max Hesses Verlag, 1926), II, 194 ff. [See above, p. 220 ff.—*Editor*]

source that provides Chopin with his chord (transposed to f, b, d^1, a^1), $g\sharp^1$ must be regarded as a long appoggiatura, moving on the sixth beat of the bar to a^1, the 3 of $^6_4+$. This is the prevailing contemporary analysis, represented by the Roman numeral II, and standing in the so-called second inversion.

Such a reading must be reassessed. Nothing that Wagner does with the chord suggests such a harmonic "functional" analysis. Note that the phrasing slur for the oboe in bars 2–3 begins on the $g\sharp^1$ under examination and carries through to b^1 (Example 4a). But this is not characteristic of the usual two-tone slur ($g\sharp^1$ to a^1) for the indication and execution of an appoggiatura. It should also be observed that the oboe's $g\sharp^1$ to b^1 is accompanied by a very frequent kind of chordal interchange as the bassoon leaps from b to g$\sharp$ (Example 4b). Furthermore, the oboe's $g\sharp^1$, the alleged appoggiatura, rests in a much more comfortable sonority than the release, a^1, which forms part of the chord of the so-called double dissonance. Something is wrong here, for appoggiaturas, at least traditionally, move from relative stress to relative quiet (Example 4c). Closely related to the oboe's music in bars 2–3 is the initial passage of the cellos, which is transferred in bar 2 to the English horn in such a manner that, after the initial a, the cellos play f^1–e^1–$d\sharp^1$, whereupon the English horn takes over to complete the motion from $d\sharp^1$ to d^1. Thus, a descending third, f^1–e^1–$d\sharp^1$–d^1, is answered by an ascending third, $g\sharp^1$–a^1–$a\sharp^1$–d^1 (Example 4d). Finally, the inclusive significance of $g\sharp^1$ is stressed by the fact that it stems from the opening a. This striking major seventh establishes a binding melodic connection which, considered with all of the preceding factors, must override any attempt to classify $g\sharp^1$ as an appoggiatura. Note that once the major seventh has been established, it is paralleled in bars 4–6 and 8–10 by the octaves b to b^1, d^1 to d^2 (Example 4e).

The reasons cited above seem persuasive, at least to this analyst, for regarding $g\sharp^1$ as a principal tone and a^1 as a dependent passing tone. Why is the prevailing analysis just the opposite? Probably, first, because the elevation of a^1 to the rank of a chord tone presents the analyst with a harmonic stereotype, a recurrent kind of augmented sixth chord. Probably, also because by a process of reverse harmonic expectancy, it would seem that the unmistakable dominant of bar 3 must have before it some recognizable kind of subdominant or supertonic chord. But such a mothering of the theory of harmonic functions seems excessive in the face of so many opposed textural and linear factors. Because $d\sharp^1$ of bar 2 is so clearly on the way to d^1 of bar 3, the underlying sonority of bar 2 has been represented in Example 3c as a form of diminished seventh chord * * *.

The sonority of bar 6 has the same derivation as *Tr*, but bar 10 presents a different case. If Wagner had followed the line of least resistance and continued with the pattern established in bars 1–4 and 5–8, bar 11 would have produced a B♭-major chord, as indicated in Example 5a. The basis of the manipulation employed to arrive at the B-major chord, so essential an element in the broad arpeggiation of the E-chord (bars 3, 7, 11, 16), is shown in Example 5b. If additional justification of the present reading of an arpeggiated E-chord were needed, this particular summoning by Wagner of a B- rather than a B♭-chord would provide it.

A parting word must be addressed to the harmonic meaning of the opening upbeat and bar 1. The present tendency, with which I am in agreement, is to consider it 1. In the past, the shape of the cellos' solo has been misinterpreted when the passage has been understood as an outlining of vi or iv. * * *

Example 5

* * *

Example 6

a. Bars 17–24

b.

A minor VI   IV   (II♯)   V   I

c.

Bars 17–24. Bars 1–17 have, in the structural activity of the upper parts, opened up three octave registers, from a to g♯^{1} and, in bar 17, a^1 and a^2. Bars 17–24 carry out a first ascent from a^1 to c♯^{2} by way of b^1, as indicated in Examples 6a, 6b, and 6c. The bass of these bars brings to completion the first harmonic expression of A minor-major by picking up with F (bar 17), moving on to D (bar 21), and, after an intervening B (bar 23), concluding with E–A of bar 24. An important prolonging element is the middle-voice descent of a sixth from a^1 (bar 17) to c♯^{1} (bar 24), as indicated in Example 6c. The tone a^2 and its register remain out of play until the following section.

The featured motive, motive *B*, is formed of concatenate thirds which carry out a broader connection between a–g^1–f^1 in bars 17–20–21 (Example 6a). The transitory nature of the supporting C-chord of bar 20 is explained in 6c. In bar 21, the apparent Neapolitan sixth is nothing more than a detail of the upper-voice motion from f^1 to d^1. Its accented position is characteristic of the prevailing texture of the Prelude, as has already been noted in discussing the rhythmic similarities of motives A^2, B, C, E, F, and G in connection with Example 2.

Bars 23–24 are complex. The descending sixth has, in bar 23, reached d♯^{1}, which stands over an inner voice b. This vertical third is inverted to become a sixth, d^1–b^1 (bar 24), in an arresting manner. The first violins, hitherto quiet, enter to span chromatically the distance from d♯^{1} up to b^1, while the cellos initiate a motion from b up to d^1. After they have reached the intermediate c♯^{1}, the second violins intercept and complete the motion to d^1. The bass, meanwhile, breaks from B through G♯ to E before cadencing on A. These techniques and their relation to broad structure are shown in the illustrations of example 6.

In summary, bars 1–24 form a unit, but for reasons of expository convenience they have been discussed as two subsections, 1–17 and 17–24. Over the bass, a, e, f, d, (b), e, a, three octave registers have been explored and, in the middle register, the first joining of a^1 to c♯^{2} has occurred.

Example 7

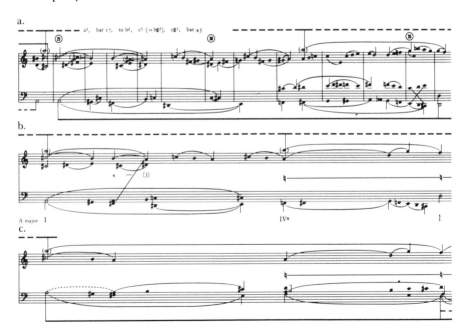

a.

b.

A major I   IV⁶

c.

Bars 24–45. These bars are closely related to bars 1–24. Over the broad spread of supporting harmonies, the true register and upper voice, $c\sharp^3$, are reached, as indicated in the three graphs of Example 7.

As usual in structural analysis, the bass and harmonic frame require attention initially. Bars 24–31 are property of the A-chord, Its first expression is as a triad, but in bar 31 it acquires a minor seventh, g^1, which gives to it the color of an applied dominant to the approaching D-chord. The intervening activity is a matter of chromatic inflection rather than a modulation to E major. This becomes apparent as soon as analysis disengages itself from the chords of detail and focuses on inclusive activity, as illustrated in Examples 7a, 7b, and 7c, which should be compared with the equivalent bars in Example 1b. The D-chord prevails in bars 32–40. It is expressed first in the position of the sixth (bar 32), but eventually connects with the root (bar 37). From this point on, the minor third, f, is exchanged for the major third, f$\sharp$. The chord on B (bars 41–43) is passing by nature, for it takes its departure from the preceding D-chord and moves on to the cadential G$\sharp$- and A-chords of bars 43–44. The succession of A–D–B–G$\sharp$–A (Examples 7c and 1) offers conclusive evidence that the tonal properties of A alone are expressed in this section. Modulation plays no role.

In bars 24–31, motives C, D, and E are featured. In essence, motive C moves in parallel tenths with the bass as it courses from $c\sharp^2$, through b^1, to a^1. This three-tone succession is extended by suspending b^1 over $F\sharp$. As a fourth, its normal resolution should be to a third. However, before the appearance of a^1, the bass has moved on toward $c\sharp$ as shown in Example 7b, which should be compared with 7c, where the generic relationship is presented. Note in these bars, as represented in 7c, how each principal participating voice moves surely from one to another tone of the A-chord. Of particular interest is the fine parallelism to the upper voice of bars 24–28, provided by the top part as motive E in bars 29–32 moves from c^2 to a^1 and then from $c\sharp^2$ to a^1. Intertwined in the manner of a cambiata are ascending secondary thirds, $f\sharp^1$–a^1, and e^1–g^1 (Example 7a).

From bars 32 to 40, over the support of the D-chord, an arresting change of register occurs that prepares the way for the arrival of $c\sharp^3$ in bar 45. At first motive B is employed, much in the manner of its earlier use (bars 17–21), but an octave higher. By means of the third a^1–g^2–f^2 the upper register, last sounded in bar 17, is reopened. In bar 36 and further, motive F continues this play of registers by transferring f^1–g^1 and g^1–a^1 (bars 36–37 and 38–39) successively to f^2–g^2 and g^2–a^2 (Examples 7a and 7b).

As a result, the situation presented in bar 40 is a D-major chord with a^2 in the top voice. The derivation of the linear-chordal relationships of bars 40 to 45 is sketched in Example 8. Under the pressure of increasing intensity and the shape of the motive, the top voice anticipates its normal accompaniment in such a way that a minor ninth, c^2, appears over the B-chord of bars 41–42. This is not a true chordal ninth, but an enharmonically written anticipation of the major third, $b\sharp^1$, of the G$\sharp$-chord of bar 43. It is this chord that presses on to the A-chord of bar 44 in an aroused transposition of the cadence of bars 16–17. Wagner's desired parallelism accounts for the chromatic color of the chord on G$\sharp$, rather than any putative flirtation with the key of C$\sharp$ minor.

The upper voice of the cadence of bar 44 is literally $b\sharp^1$–$c\sharp^2$. But it is the $c\sharp^3$ in bar 45, following the cadence, that is the tone sought after and prepared for by the transposition devices of the preceding bars. Note that it, too, is reached by an octave transposition of $c\sharp^2$. It is characteristic of the continuous nature of the music of the Prelude that $c\sharp^3$ should arrive one bar after the cadence. In fact, it should be noted that secondary factors add to the forward impulse of the cadence bar:

Example 8

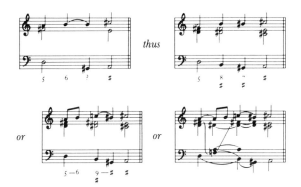

thus

or

or

the double basses and third bassoon retain A^1 and A^2 into bar 45; $d\sharp^2$ in the violas delays for three beats the arrival of $c\sharp^2$; the cellos press on by means of an $e\sharp$ to the $f\sharp$ of bar 45.

In summary of bars 1–24, 24–45: over two similar successions in the bass, the structural top voice connects a^1 with $c\sharp^2$ (bars 1–24) and then a^2 with $c\sharp^3$ (bars 24–45). A different kind of action ensues.

Bars 45–63. The A-chord, well established in the earlier sections, continues through bar 52, where it gives way to the subdominant harmony that prevails through bar 63. The dominant harmony of bar 64 is then prolonged in a manner that will be described in the following section. Above these harmonies, $c\sharp^3$ gives way in bar 53 to d^3, a structural neighboring tone. From each of these tones, downward motions are generated, $c\sharp^3$ to a^2 (bars 45–48, repeated in parallel fashion in 49–50, and twice in 51–52), and d^3 to a^2 to $f\sharp^2$ (filled in, in bars 53–62). These harmonic and linear prolongations are indicated in the illustrations of Example 9.

The motive employed in bars 45–52 is motive *C*, now an octave higher than its first statement in bars 25–32. However, the different continuations in bars 32 and 53 make an important difference in identifying the retained structural tone. While in bar 32 the action, carried out by motive *B*, emphasizes a motion picked up from a^1, the entrance in bar 53 of d^3 and its subsequent prolongation indicate that $c\sharp^3$ is its linear point of departure. For the rest, the reading of details for motive *C* is virtually the same as in its first statement (cf. Example 7).

Example 9

a. Bars 45–61

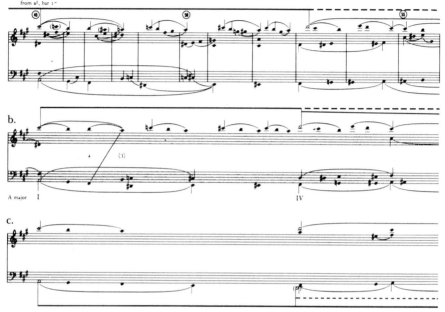

A critical point is reached in bar 55 which can be settled only by study of the orchestral score. What is the structural meaning of $c\sharp^3$ in bars 54–55? Is it the completion of a neighboring motion, $c\sharp^3$ (bar 45), d^3 (bar 53), $c\sharp^3$ (bar 54)? Or is it to be regarded as a passing tone within the D-chord, as d^3 moves through this $c\sharp^3$ and b^2 (bar 57) to a a^2 (bar 58)? The bass supports the latter reading, for the entire passage occurs within the D-chord, as indicated in Example 9. Furthermore, Wagner, by placing his accompanying voices above motive *B*, insures a retention of the proper register until motive *B* crosses over in bar 56 (Examples 9a and 9b). As noted earlier, most keyboard transcriptions create a false misleading hiatus in these bars by abandoning the register so resourcefully retained by the composer. The same important crossing of motive *B* and its accompaniment occurs in bars 59–62 and for the same reason. The underlying sense of the entire passage is shown in Example 9c. Observe that the position of the sixth struck in bar 58 is not a "deceptive cadence," but a necessary reaffirmation of the D-chord which continues,

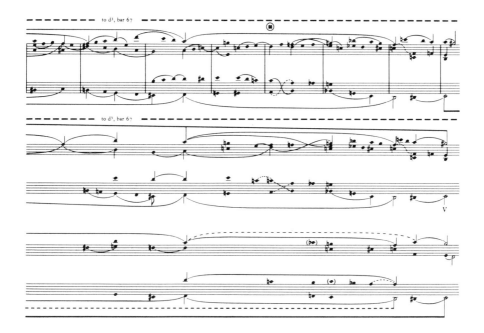

as indicated, through bar 62, before giving way to the dominant harmony. It is instructive to compare the reductions of motive *B* in Examples 9b and 9c with the earlier reductions in Examples 6b and 6c, for the increased chromaticism and complexity of voice leading are reflected in the voice exchanges of Example 9b (bass clef) and in the four-part reduction of Example 9c.

Bars 63–74. Except for bar 74, these bars are property of the dominant harmony. From bars 63–70, it is asserted by a retention of E in the bass. In bars 70–73, however, Wagner uses the same arpeggiation technique that appears in the opening bars of the Prelude.

Above this prolonged harmony, new events occur. As indicated in Example 10a, 10b, and 10c, a stepwise ascent in bars 63–67 connects $g\sharp^2$ with d^3, already asserted in bar 53. The technique whereby Wagner achieves this connection is executed by motive *G*, a motive that lives its life in two registers (a^2–b^1, b^2–$c\sharp^2$, etc.). Its origin lies in 5–6–5 relation-

Example 10

a. Bars 63–74

ships as indicated in Example 10b. Motive *G* continues as an accompaniment through bar 72 of the section under examination, and in bars 73–74 it is brought down from its exploration of upper registers by a series of descending transfers, as indicated by slurs in Example 10a.

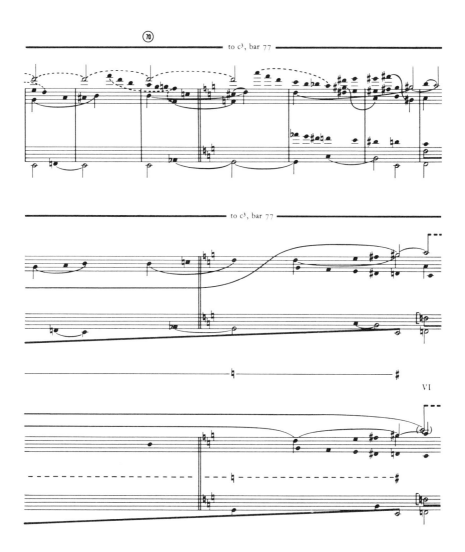

Once d³ has been reaffirmed in bar 67, it is retained by the flutes and reiterated by the first and second violins as each of these sweeps upward. Below this, woodwinds and horns in increasing numbers sound motive A^2, carrying it upward, much in the manner of bars 1–17, but

Example 11

a. Bars 74–84

less protracted, from g♯^{1} (bar 66) to a^2 in bar 74. Note that *Tr* has been modified in bars 66 and 68 by the necessity of retaining the structurally important d^3, as against the characteristic d♯. However in its following transpositions (bars 70 and 72), there is no need to modify the sonority, hence its original color remains intact. Specialists in the harmonic

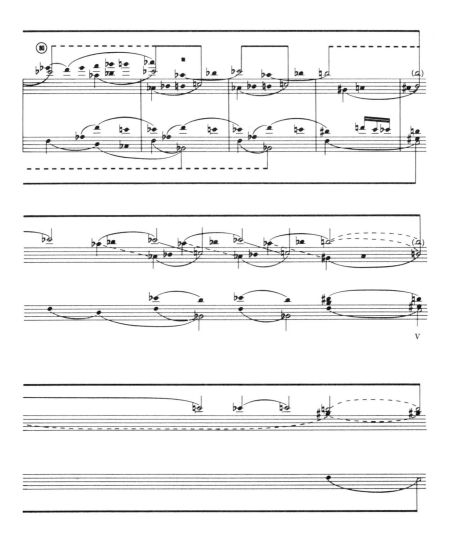

analysis of *Tr* would do well to observe and reflect on this modification brought about for structural reasons. However, beware of the run of piano transcriptions which modify the phrasing slurs.[2] Motive A^1 does

2. As in the transcription by Richard Kleinmichel.

not enter, except as aspects of it are incorporated into extensions of motive *G* in bars 70 and 72.

Bars 74–84. These bars, the dynamic and emotional climax of the Prelude, are organized around three prolonged harmonies, represented by the following bass tones: (1) f (bars 74–78) arpeggiated in the form of f (bars 74–76), c–A (bar 77), and F (bar 78); (2) B♭ (bars 79–82), the goal of descents from f (bars 80, 81, and 82); (3) e in bar 84, reached immediately from the neighbor f, and the basis of organization in most of the following section. These bass tones, f, B♭, e, representing the vi, ii (Phrygian), v of a minor, shoulder a feverish surge of the music. As noted earlier, the bass of bars 79–82, participating in this delirium, seems about to abandon all pretense of a relationship with the guiding tonality in favor of an excursion into other realms. The arrival of e, and the E-chord in bar 84, however, settles the issue in favor of a. Attention in these bars should be given to *Tr*, for its relation to the B♭-chord (bars 80–82), and its relation to the E-chord (bars 83–84), provide clear evidence that a♭ and the enharmonic g♯ are chordal elements rather than appoggiaturas,[3] as indicated in Example 11.

The prevailing motive in bars 74–78 is motive *B* in its most elaborate setting. Here again the orchestral score must be the analytic referent, for Wagner, as in the preceding instances, places his accompaniment above the motive initially to retain the proper register, as d³ of bar 67 resolves ultimately to c³ in bar 77. In essence c³ is fetched from a² of bar 74 as indicated in Examples 11a and 11b. By comparing the present setting of motive *B* with earlier ones (bars 32–36), it can be seen that a new element is needed to carry the motion from a² through b♭² (bar 76) to the desired c³ of bar 77. Note that in the earlier settings the motion from a² has descended by step to f². Actually this earlier motion is still present, but above it Wagner places the new motion. The derivation of this complex passage is shown in Example 12. In 12a the bass moves upward in tenths with the top voice. However, 12b, with its downward motion, opens up new avenues of voice leading which create several additional chromatically inflected chords of detail.

Having reached c³ in bar 77, the orchestra now spreads out to encompass an imposing range from B♭¹ to a♭³. Within this vast tonal

3. Dr. Lorenz, who regards g♯¹ as an appoggiatura, writes (p. 20)[See above, p. 212, fn. 19.-*Editor*]: "The appoggiatura, g♯, is present as a held tone up to the antepenultimate chord (bar 84) [83 according to the usual count] where it finds its normal resolution to a." Quite a feat!

edifice, woodwinds, brass, and cellos secure the registers pertinent to the overall structure. The complexity of interwoven motives in bars 80 to 84 requires an additional illustration in short score. Example 13 indicates motive derivations and the distribution of registers. Note that motives A^1, A^2, Tr, and B participate in the action, that motive A^1 is the agency by which the high point, ab^3, is brought downward to its proper register. The tones of motive A^1, ab up to f^1, etc. (bars 79–84), become ab^3 (bars 81–83) down to f^3 to f^1, e^1, eb^1, d^1 (bars 83 and 84).

Example 12

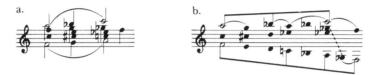

Example 13

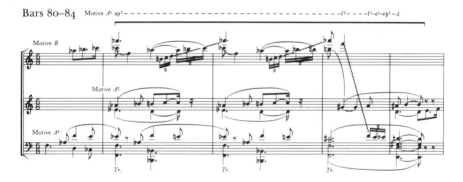

Example 11a incorporates most of the total activity of these bars. In 11b the coupling of ab^2 and ab^1, cb^3 and $c\natural^2$, are stressed. Finally Example 11c indicates the structural frame with the coupling brought into a single register above the broad march of the bass from f to Bb to e.

Bars 84–96, etc. As noted earlier, the present analysis will end with the beginning of Wagner's concert ending rather than with the transition to Act I, Scene 1. Hence we have been examining a Prelude, that is, a self-enclosed piece, rather than an Introduction leading to other actions. Wagner seems to have used both terms, Vorspiel and Einleitung interchangeably.

The structure of these closing bars is identical with a recurrent

Example 14

a. Bars 84–96

closing technique, represented in its generic form at the end of Example 1b. Specifically, b^2 of bars 83–84 connects with a^2 in bar 95, but with the help of a circling extension whereby b^2 moves first through a^2 (bar 92) to $g\sharp^2$ (bar 94) before its termination on the a^2 of bar 95, etc. Below this action, the prevailing structural bass, e, representing the dominant harmony, provides escort for the circling extension in the form of a

(bar 90), d^1 (bar 92) and B, e (bars 93–94), before giving way in bar 95 to the terminal A. All of these relationships are shown in Example 14.

The motives employed in the section are B, A^1, A^2, and the sonority Tr. Although these bars recall the opening bars of the Prelude as well as bars 36—40, the orientation is quite different. Each bass tone, e, a, and d^1, has its own extension. In bars 84 to 89, e is arpeggiated through the tones e (bar 84), g (bar 87), and b–$b^{\flat 1}$ (bar 89). Next, a is similarly extended by way of a (bar 90), c and $e^{\flat 1}$ (bar 91). The bass d in bar 92, however, drops down a third to B (bar 93) before moving on to the concluding and reaffirming e of bars 93–94. Note the quickening harmonic rhythms of these bars as e (six bars) passes on to a (two bars) to d^1 (one and a half bars) and to e (one and a half bars). Above these bass tones, the upper parts engage in an intermediate extension whereby b^1 (bar 84) moves to e^2 (bar 90) to connect with $g\sharp^2$ (bar 92), as pointed out in Example 14b. Note the fine parallelism to the changes of register and the connection between $g\sharp^2$ and a^2 in the concluding ascent ($g\sharp^1$ up to a^2) of bars 92–94.

The beginning of the concert ending is included in the sketches of Example 14. Although its motivic content is related to the concluding bars of Act III, it nevertheless joins with the preceding music of the Prelude in an arresting manner. As indicated in Example 14a, the upper appoggiatura, b^2, has been featured throughout. However the suspension of $f\sharp^2$ from the preceding music forms a strong transitional link. This tone has appeared earlier, in bars 10 to 16, and bar 73, as a prominent feature in the lengthening of $g\sharp^2$–a^2 into a motivically needed third, $f\sharp^2$–$g\sharp^2$–a^2. Its retention in bar 95 is heightened by the plagal support given to it by the bass.

THE FORM

Viewed as a linear-harmonic entity, the form of the Tristan Prelude is a continuous, uninterrupted whole, subserved by a series of prolonged harmonies and an inclusive, descending melodic structure. The derivation of the broad harmonies and the extension of the prime melodic structure are sketched in the illustrations of Example 15. The purely harmonic elements are, as indicated, I–II–V–I. The sketches of Example 15a and 15b, portray such a structure in A major, then in A minor, and finally in A minor with a lowered or Phrygian second step. Example 15c unites these modal variants in the manner of the Prelude and indicates the origin of the F-chord of bar 74 in an age-old 5–6–5

Example 15

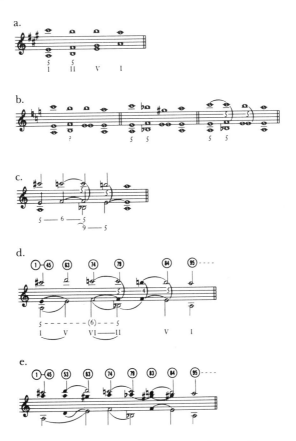

technique. It also shows the origin of the ninth over b♭ as a suspension. Example 15d illustrates the horizontalizing of 1 and 11 as first depicted in Example 15a. Out of this technique grow the v of bar 63 and the vi of bar 74. As a feature of this succession, the prime melodic structure acquires the neighbor d³. Note also the first suggestion of *Tr* between bars 79 and 84 in the working out of the linear technique 5–4–5. Finally, in Example 15e, a significant accompanying voice makes its appearance. It is the intervallic space created by this voice against the prime outer voice that is filled in by so many of the motivic elements, as already shown in Example 1b.

CONCLUSION

Three points remain to be mentioned as we bring this linear-harmonic analysis to an end. The first is the linking of the Prelude or, better, the Introduction, with the beginning of Act I, which hovers between C minor and E♭ major. The seeds of the modulatory transition are sown in bar 17, for the F-chord, which appears at this point and again in bar 74, becomes eventually the agent for the shift from A to C. Following its final appearance in bar 94 of the piece as usually performed, the music shifts its weight to the dominant of C, employing the F-chord, this time, as a subdominant. Note, in bar 107 and further, the imaginative way in which preparation is made for the ensuing solo of the young sailor. The ascending sixth is, of course, closely related to the similar interval of motive A^1.

The second point is concerned with the extraordinary difficulties that harmonic theorists have had in analyzing the chordal details of the Prelude in terms of one or another system of harmony. At best, chordal analysis provides only a one-dimensional view of a composition. Thus, even when some kind of agreement can be reached about chord names and functions, the resultant values are bound to be limited. However, in the case of the Tristan Prelude, even this kind of agreement over labels has not been reached, as can be discovered by a random sampling of available chord and key analyses.

The reason is not hard to find. There has been a preoccupation with each of the striking sonorities as individual sounds, or at most these have been related only to an immediate environment. This is, of course, not the only chromatic piece that has refused to reveal its harmonic meanings when its techniques are assessed on a chord by chord basis. It is axiomatic that the more intense the chromaticism, the greater the need to relate individual sonorities to a broad context. A simple case in point can be found in bars 32–40, where only a summoning of the inclusive frame provided by the D-chord can illuminate the meaning of the details. Without such a reference the analyst cannot help but record a confusing welter of chord labels and modulatory activities. With it, his problem shifts to one of assessing chords as elements of motion within a clearly marked area. Hence, the possibility of finding an insightful reading of detail becomes real and immediate.

The third and final point, to which the preceding considerations lead, relates to the attempt to find an embracing structure by means of linear-harmonic analytic procedures. Such an aim carries us well beyond the meaning of detail, for its ultimate problem is the relating to each other of the several pervasive frames with their contents. This can be a challenging and sometimes a despairing assignment. In the case of the Tristan Prelude, it has proven to be less formidable than in many another piece. For one thing, the harmonic pilings are strongly marked; for another, the broad contexts are easily found; and for a third, the controlling outer parts are always reasonably in evidence.

This does not mean, however, that there can be only one exemplary linear-harmonic analysis of a work such as this. Clearly, when so many diverse, often competing, factors await evaluation, when a desired objectivity is constantly menaced by the limiting slants of personal musical experience, a resolute effort must be made to reduce arbitrary readings to the zero point, to eliminate purely capricious judgments. When these hampering conditions are overcome, the success of an analysis can be measured by the degree of musical insight that it provides. Some will fall short of the mark; others will approach the heart of the work. It remains idle, however, to speculate on the most viable of all viable analyses, for in the end the analytic conclusions reached are individual judgments, however rarefied, rather than mechanical derivatives. This is a source of strength for linear-harmonic analysis, for it suggests a constant matching of the musical maturity of the analyst with the elusive essence of the work analyzed.

ROLAND JACKSON

Leitmotive and Form in the *Tristan* Prelude†

Like Ernest Newman and other *Leitmotiv* analysts, Jackson is principally concerned with thematic processes. But where others have been content with mere *description* of the placement of "motives" in relation to the drama, Jackson deals with motivic elements in a more purely musical way and thus achieves a particular type of *analysis*. In addition, he offers a critique of some of William Mitchell's points, particularly the latter's view of the concert ending.

† From *The Music Review* 36 (1975): 42–53. Reprinted by permission.

Analyses of the *Tristan* Prelude have reflected widely differing approaches. To late nineteenth-century writers such as Krehbiel or Lavignac it consisted of little more than a succession of *Leitmotive* anticipatory
to the opera itself, whose main function was to provide a psychological
preparation for the musical drama that follows. Other, more recent,
analyses, such as those of Lorenz or Mitchell, have treated the Prelude
more abstractly, in terms of an overall formal or tonal scheme, in
relation to which the *Leitmotive* were thought to play a generally
subordinate role.

In the present essay another, somewhat different point of view will
be developed, in which the *Leitmotiv* will be taken as central, but will be
considered from a purely musical rather than from a literary or dramatic
standpoint. For it is felt that in his treatment of the *Leitmotiv* Wagner
reveals himself as a musician as fully as he does as a tone-poet. Here
indeed he shows himself to be a master of musical detail (one might
even say a miniaturist), at times skillfully combining several ideas into
one, or subtly connecting and interrelating one motivic idea with
another. In this regard his process of composition might be called
inductive, in that it seems to proceed from details to the whole, rather
than, as is sometimes assumed, from a preconceived plan of the entire
work. His formal design is made up essentially of an ever-changing
succession of musical ideas, each flowing directly into the next, yet each
pointed up (often by the harmony) as an individual and even separate
entity within the musical continuity. And it is mostly through a process
of skilful juxtaposition, or through a meaningful accumulation of
individual *Motive*, that the total form comes into being.

I

Ever since Edgar Istel pointed out some time ago that Wagner
undoubtedly derived his opening from a strikingly similar passage in
Spohr's earlier opera *Der Alchymist*,[1] musical scholars have occasionally
cited the relationship, but principally for its interesting historical implications. They have generally neglected to consider the fascinating
musical and artistic differences that a comparison of the two passages
might reveal. Here one is, of course, struck immediately by Wagner's
greater musicality. But, aside from this, a comparison points up the
richness and complexity of Wagner's opening in contrast to Spohr's

---

1. *Die Blütezeit der musikalischen Romantik in Deutschland* (Leipzig, 1909), p. 112.

Example 1

Spohr: *Der Alchymist* (1830)

much simpler formulation and thereby tells us something important concerning Wagner's treatment of the *Leitmotiv* (*vide* Ex. 1). Spohr's passage is in essence little more than a colourful harmonic succession touching upon two keys, while Wagner's represents an ingenious blending of elements that are distinctively melodic as well as harmonic. Wagner, to be sure, adopts the principal details of Spohr's harmony: the augmented sixth to dominant chords, the expressive colouring with non-chord notes, and the abrupt sequential repetition of the first phrase in a key a third higher. But he also introduces several significant alterations that are genuinely his own. Thus, Spohr's Italian sixth chord is turned into a more intense French sixth, and the resolution is taken directly—*via* parallel sevenths—to a dominant seventh chord (which Spohr had indeed used in his second phrase, but only after a leading-note sixth chord). Spohr's final long *appoggiatura* on A♯ is shortened, most likely to allow the dissonant dominant seventh chord to sound through more fully. And Spohr's brief auxiliary note G♯ is, contrariwise, turned into a long *appoggiatura* falling emphatically on the first beat of the measure. This latter change has the effect of making the dissonant, and as yet unresolved, initial sonority be heard as a chord in its own right. This, the so-called "Tristan chord," has called forth innumerable interpretations—rather surprisingly, it might be added, in view of its obvious derivation from Spohr's augmented sixth (here might be mentioned, for example, William Mitchell's proposal of a diminished seventh chord on G♯ with a raised fifth, D♯,[2] or Ernst Kurth's of a dominant seventh chord on B with a lowered fifth, F♮).[3]

2. "The Tristan Prelude: Techniques and Structure" in *The Music Forum*, I (1967), p. 174. [See above, p. 242—*Editor*.] Mitchell feels that the root is G♯ on the basis of the linear importance attaching to it in respect to the opening note A. Historical reasons aside, it is difficult to accept musically an interpretation whereby the "Tristan chord" would have the same harmonic function as its resolution (A: VII$_9^0$–V$_7$). Moreover, Mitchell's rejection of the augmented sixth on the grounds that this chord could not resolve directly to a dominant seventh chord overlooks the fact that Haydn had already resolved it in this way in his Sonata No. 49 in E♭ (1790), mm. 23–24.

3. *Romantische Harmonik und ihre Krise in Wagners Tristan* (Berlin, 1920), p. 44. [See above, p. 187. *Editor*]

Perhaps the most significant, and imaginative, of Wagner's changes, however, is the insertion of an entirely new melodic line at the beginning. This (for the most part) descending chromatic idea in the cellos effectively counterbalances the ascending chromatic idea in the oboe. Moreover, it makes the entrance of the woodwind chords, beginning in measure two, far more striking, by leading into them with the markedly contrasting tone-colour of the upper cello register. More important still, the new opening lends the passage harmonic depth taking it quite beyond Spohr's rather flat and one-dimensional succession of chords. By suggesting a Neapolitan sixth chord on F prior to the entry of the first chord, the cello opening gives this chord a double implication; for not only is it heard as an augmented sixth chord in respect to its own resolution, but as a dominant on B (as Kurth had indeed proposed) in respect to the preceding Neapolitan sixth. This pivotal, or two-dimensional, aspect of the chord, falling as it does between two quite different and highly colourful harmonic progressions, probably accounts for a great deal of the fascination it has held for musical analysts.[4]

It is intriguing to speculate on whether Wagner may have drawn upon still other musical sources in these opening three measures. Kurth pointed out that the "Tristan chord" (spelled F–C♭–E♭–A♭) had already appeared in Beethoven's Sonata in E♭ (*op.* 31 No. 3).[5] And to this it might be added that the opening line in the cellos bears a curious resemblance to the beginning of Berlioz' "Roméo seul" (the second movement of *Roméo et Juliette*), wherein a single string section, in this case the first violins, also leaps upwards to an elongated note F, and then descends by half steps to E♭ (*vide* Ex. 2).

Example 2

(a) Berlioz: *Roméo et Juliette,* II

ppp

(b) Beethoven: *Opus 31, No. 3*

m.35

---

4. See Roland Jackson, "The Neapolitan Progression in the Nineteenth Century" in *The Music Review*, XXXI (1969): 41–42.

5. Kurth, *op. cit.*, p. 74.

What is so very remarkable about these various possible borrowings is the evidence they provide of Wagner's skill in bringing together several diverse ideas into one thematic statement. No longer are the ideas heard separately, but rather as parts of a single, and powerful, musical gesture. Wagner's great combinative skill, and his use of this skill elsewhere in the Prelude, aside from the opening, will now occupy our attention in the second part of this essay.

II

Thomas Mann spoke of the *Leitmotiv* as "a magical formula, casting meaning on what had come before as well as on that was to follow."[6] His remark is typical of many concerning the *Leitmotiv*, in that it pertains primarily to the dramatic rather than to the musical uses of the device, to its power to convey tangible meanings or subtly to connect situations that on the surface appear to be unrelated. In other words, such references are of value more for what they tell us about the characters, or about hidden psychological implications, than for any illumination they may cast upon the musical continuity.

Wagner's *Leitmotive* in particular are musically employed in a far more complex manner than has usually been assumed, or than the mere labelling of melodic patterns has implied. The opening three measures of the Prelude, for example, consist of a number of different musical ideas, as we have seen, all of which Wagner fuses together into what in effect is a single theme. And the ideas, or sub-ideas, that make up this theme return later in the Prelude in other combinations—that is, as new composite themes. Indeed, from this initial, predominantly chromatic theme, and from the clearly contrasting diatonic theme first introduced at measure 17, Wagner fashions most, if not all, of the other thematic material used in the Prelude. The first, chromatic, theme may

Example 3

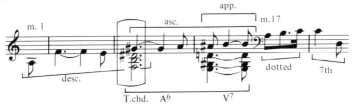

6. Cited by Reinhold Brinkmann in *Riemanns Musiklexikon* III (Mainz, 1967), p. 513.

be subdivided into at least five *Motive*, or *Leitmotive*, all of which assume musical importance later: (i) the (mostly) descending chromatic line in the cellos; (ii) the ascending chromatic line in the oboe; (iii) the "Tristan chord"; (iv) the eighth note *appoggiatura* figure (A♯–B), which almost invariably returns in a dissonant connotation; (v) the underlying chord progression itself, the augmented sixth to dominant. The second, diatonic, theme may be subdivided into two melodic patterns, a falling seventh and a rising three-note dotted figure (*vide* Ex. 3). Wagner's compositional technique may be seen, then, as primarily one of transforming and rearranging the internal components or *Motive* in such a way as to arrive at ever-differing thematic shapes or complexes. The components may appear singly (e.g., the *appoggiatura Motiv* in mm. 14–15) or in new combinations. It is this latter, the combinative aspect of Wagner's art, that is especially fascinating, and a number of examples drawn from the Prelude will serve to illustrate it.

It is significant that Wagner, after presenting the chromatic and then the diatonic theme in several restatements, begins in measure 22 to bring together elements drawn from both. Thus, in a thematic statement commencing in this measure, the diatonic theme (here, as well as earlier [m. 20], presented in a retrograde form) has set against it in counterpoint a three-note descending chromatic *Motiv*, which by its identical rhythmic placement suggests a connection with the cello line of the opening. And in measure 23 a new thematic complex beginning with the entrance of the Tristan sonority (here in second inversion), and continuing with an extended version of the ascending chromatic *Motiv*, culminates in an unusually emphatic form of the *appoggiatura Motiv*, set against a cadential A major chord (*vide* Ex. 4).

Example 4

The new theme in measure 25 is again begun with a reference to the Tristan sonority. The diatonic theme, placed in the upper voice, shows a redistribution of its five notes, whereby notes 4–5 (the falling seventh) are placed prior to 1–2–3 (the dotted figure). And to conclude, Wagner overlaps and last two notes of the dotted figure (G♯–A) with the first two of the ascending chromatic *Motiv* from the opening. This theme (Ex. 5) in many ways points to the twentieth century.

Example 5

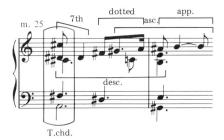

In measure 36 Wagner fashions what seems to be an entirely new melodic idea simply by joining together the dotted figure and the two-note rising *appoggiatura* pattern. And for an accompanying harmony he returns to the initial chord progression, *i.e.* the French sixth to dominant seventh chord (*vide* Ex. 6).

Example 6

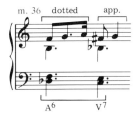

In measure 69 we may observe a thematic idea (whose first statement had occurred in m. 64) in which the dotted figure now assumes an entirely different melodic shape, although its rhythmic distinctiveness clearly marks it as being related to the earlier forms taken by this *Motiv*. The melodic succession here may in fact be associated with that of measure 36 in that the dotted figure is, as it was there, followed immediately by the *appoggiatura* (this is more apparent in m. 64). And finally, in m. 70 (*vide* Ex. 7), the "Tristan chord" signals the return of the opening thematic material (cf. mm. 5–6), although now the *Motive*

are rearranged into a different texture, with the four-note rising chromatic pattern somewhat hidden within the harmonic progression (the augmented sixth to dominant).

Example 7

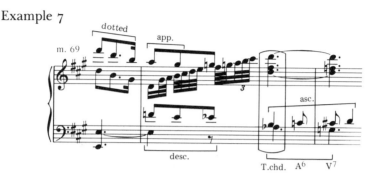

These examples, then, provide ample testimony to Wagner's ingenuity in rearranging his *Motive*. And often, in fact, he does so in such a way as to suggest entirely new thematic material. Thus his newly formed themes at measures 25, 36 and 64 have been almost universally accepted by musical analysts as distinctive—that is, as in no way related to the two main themes, even though, as we have seen, they are wrought from the same basic motivic components. Analyses of the Prelude have often failed to recognize this internal motivic structure or to take into account its possible importance in the form as a whole. We will now consider some of the explanations that have been advanced in regard to the total form of the Prelude.

III

From Wagner's own voluminous writings on music we learn relatively little concerning his approach to musical form. He seems generally, in fact, to have preferred to describe his own music in poetical, rather than in technical or analytical terms. Ernest Newman quotes Wagner's own description of the *Tristan* Prelude, for example, as a piece which progresses from "the first timidest lament of inappeasable longing, the tenderest shudder, to the most terrible outpouring of an avowal of hopeless love . . . traversing all phases of the vain struggle against the inner ardour, until this, sinking back powerless upon itself, seems to be extinguished in death."[7] Although this affords a profound insight into

---

7. Ernest Newman. *The Wagner Operas* (New York, 1963), p. 205.

the emotional content of the piece, as Wagner had perceived it, it does not really aid us in an understanding of the musical structure of the Prelude, although one might plausibly associate the words "terrible outpouring" with the final *fortissimo* surge up to the sustained "Tristan chord" in measures 80–83, or "sinking back . . ." with the quiet return of the opening theme in measure 83 *et seq.*

Albert Lavignac was among a number of writers who, shortly after Wagner's death, published résumés of his *Leitmotive*.[8] He labelled the main themes of the *Tristan* Prelude, for instance, on the basis of their reappearance in the first act. His designations of themes have, with some modification, been generally accepted ever since: Confession of Love (m. 1); Desire (m. 2); The Glance (m. 17); The Love Philtre (m. 25); Death (m. 28); The Magic Casket (m. 36); and Deliverance by Death (m. 63). Although many of these themes are, as we have seen, motivically derived from previous themes, they are quite distinctive musically; moreover, their recurrences provide a basis for laying out the form of the Prelude as a whole.

Ex. 8 would seem to support the idea that Wagner constructed his form gradually from a number of relatively short segments, rather than from a large-scale or pre-existent scheme. As Ernest Newman wrote: "The Prelude is . . . not a schematic mould imposed upon the "thematic material" from the outside but a form that has come into being simply as the outcome of the ideas."[9] That is, Wagner's attention seems to have been directed more to the internal structure of the individual sections than to their external arrangement according to some traditional scheme. These individual sections were built up primarily by restating a particular theme, either in entirety or in part, several times in immediate succession, usually in the form of a melodic or a harmonic sequence (*e.g.*, the three statements of the opening theme, followed by partial reiterations).

There do exist, to be sure, certain elements in the Prelude that give evidence of Wagner's consideration of the larger aspects of the form. The climactic return of the "Tristan chord" (mm. 80–83) has already been mentioned. Then, too, the four recurrences of the deceptive cadence (asterisked on the chart), three to the chord of F and one to A, each marked by the same expressive *appoggiatura* of an augmented 4th to a major 3rd, were very likely intended to serve as a means of

---

8. *Le voyage artistique à Bayreuth* (Paris, 1897), translated as *The Music Dramas of Richard Wagner* by Esther Singleton (New York, 1914), p. 283 *ff.*
9. *Op. cit.*, p. 211. [See above, p. 157. *Editor*]

Example 8

Grief and Desire		Glance		Love Philtre		Death		Magic Casket		Deliverance-by-Death	
1	17	17	24	25	28	28	32				
		32	36					36	44 *A		
				45	48	48	54				
		55	63							63	74 (& Desire)*F
		74	83 (T chd.)								
83	89 (& Glance)							89	94 *F		
		94	100								
101	106										

delineating (as well as of pointing up) the more important sectional divisions in the form.

Another interesting aspect of the larger design brought out by the chart is Wagner's tendency in some of the later thematic statements to work in references to other themes, thereby making these statements somewhat more complex than they had been earlier. Thus the Desire *Motiv* appears in the background during the Deliverance-by-Death theme (m. 63 *ff.*); the section devoted to the Glance theme (m. 74 *ff.*) concludes with a lengthy, and powerful, presentation of the "Tristan chord"; and in the return to the theme of Grief and Desire (m. 83 *ff.*) the lengthy silences that appeared at the beginning of the Prelude are now filled in with references to the Glance theme.

At the same time, a connection with earlier types of form is not altogether lacking. The diatonic theme at measure 17 tends to be heard as a contrasting or "second" theme—and its beginning (mm. 17–20) suggests the key of C major, *i.e..* the relative of the "first" theme, which begins in A minor. Further, both of these themes return later (and on the same pitches), only in reverse order: theme two (m. 74 *ff.*) followed by theme one (m. 83 *ff.*). This would correspond with the "reversed" recapitulations occasionally used by Berlioz (*e.g., Symphonie fantastique,* first movement) and, to some extent, with Liszt's arch forms (*e.g., Les Préludes*). Typically Lisztian, too, is the *fortissimo* restatement of the second theme, which changes its character in relation to the initially quiet presentation. And, as is so often true of Liszt, each of the thematic returns outdoes in intensity the previous one: the second theme is led up to by a lengthy *crescendo* on the dominant (m. 63*ff.*); while the first theme is preceded by the climactic sustaining of the "Tristan chord" (m. 80*ff.*).

Example 9

PRINCIPAL SECTION

(Barform)		(Barform)	
1 –	17	17 –	24

MIDDLE SECTION IN THE DOMINANT, E (SMALL ARCH FORM)

(A)		(B)		(A)	
25 –	36	36 –	44	45 –	63

RETURN

63 –	74	74 –	83

CODA

83 –	106

How does such an analysis differ from the one (*vide* Ex. 9) proposed by Alfred Lorenz, who conceived the Prelude as a large arch form (*i.e.* ABA) with coda?[10] The main point of divergence concerns the positioning of the return, which, in Lorenz' view, should be at measure 64 (rather than at 74, as I have suggested). Lorenz was led to this conclusion by his recognition that the Desire *Motiv* appears against the Deliverance-by-Death theme, twice on G♯ (mm. 66, 68) and once on B (m. 70)—that is, on the very same pitches as in the opening—and that the deceptive cadence (m. 74) corresponds exactly with the one that had been used

---

10. *Der musikalische Aufbau von Richard Wagners Tristan und Isolde* (Berlin, 1926), p. 12*ff.* ("Das Vorspiel"). [See above, p. 204 *ff.—Editor*]

in measure 17. A major difficulty with Lorenz' interpretation, however, is that the underlying harmony, except in measures 71 and 72, is essentially different from that of the opening, being based on an E major (dominant) chord, one of the few sustained harmonies in the piece, whose main purpose, it would seem, is to emphasize (by means of the deceptive cadence to F) the entrance of the second theme at measure 74. And aside from this, the Desire *Motiv* is introduced rather subtly in an inner voice part (two oboes and an English horn, then two added clarinets), as contrasted with the principal, Deliverance-by-Death, theme in the upper voice part (violins, violas, cellos). Wagner's intention would seem to have been to provide a mere hint of the *Motiv* here, as compared with its actual return at measure 83.

Lorenz' more detailed analysis of individual sections as either representing bar forms (theme one or theme two) or as an arch form (the middle section) seems procrustean, in that it attempts to force Wagner's freely unfolding repetitions of themes and parts of themes into regular and simple schemes, *i.e.* into AAB (the bar) or ABA (the arch).

William Mitchell's recent Schenkerian analysis of the Prelude [11] raises some basic questions concerning the nature of Wagner's harmony, or of his tonality and its significance in respect to the total form. Mitchell feels that Wagner "heard the Prelude in A major-minor", and that "the concert ending, placed by him in A, adds a substantial confirmation."[12] He supports this idea mainly through a consideration of the high and low goals of the lines (and the connections between them) and of the harmonic cadences.

Example 10

measures:	17	24	44	63	74	84	94	106
cadences:	(E)–F	(E)–A	(G♯)–A	(d♯⁰₇)–E	(E)–F	(T.chd)–E	(E)–F	(A♭aug6)–G

The principal cadences (most of them incomplete) do for the most part point to the tonality of A, as may be seen in Ex. 10. Mitchell's principal formal divisions of the Prelude correspond generally with

11. *Op. cit.*, pp. 162–203. [See above, p. 242 *ff.*—*Editor.*]
12. *Ibid.*, p. 163.

these cadences, except that he prefers measure 45 to 44, since "it is the C♯³ in bar 45, following the cadence, that is the tone sought after and prepared for by the transposition devices of the preceding bars,"[13] and measure 96 to 94, since it forms a link to the substitute ending in A major. This ending, substantiating the main key of the Prelude, takes precedence for Mitchell over Wagner's final excursion to G, which, he feels, is done merely for the sake of leading into the first scene of the opera. Only a few temporary modulations, according to Mitchell, colour the principal key of A: two to the subdominant (mm. 32–40 and 52–63), one to the dominant (mm. 63–74), and one that makes use of "prolonged harmonies" on F, B♭ and E (mm. 74–84).

In comment, it might first be asked whether Wagner's concert ending is indeed more satisfactory artistically. For it may confirm the key of A, yet its thematic content (being borrowed from the end of the opera) differs totally from that of the rest of the Prelude, which, as we have seen, had up to this point been totally unified.

But the principal question is whether the details of Wagner's harmony support a single tonal conception, as Mitchell would have it, or whether in fact they imply a great many different keys, each of very brief duration. For the frequent shifting from one key to another is a principal means whereby Wagner makes distinctive the successive state-ments of his themes—that is, a statement is underscored and set apart by being placed in a key different from those of the surrounding statements. The individual keys are usually defined by a brief chordal progression, consisting often of two or three chords. The progressions themselves are for the most part incomplete or deceptive cadences; and one progression will occasionally follow another by means of a harmonic sequence. Consider, for example, measures 32–40, in which, Mitchell feels, "the D chord prevails" (on the basis of the cadences in mm. 32 and 36).[14] Here the Glance theme appears four times in succession (mm. 32, 33, 34, 35), each time being presented in a somewhat different melodic form and, more significantly, in a different tonality (defined by the harmonic progression). The following measures are occupied with statements of the Magic Casket theme (mm. 36, 38, 40, *etc.*), this being presented in a like manner:

---

13. *Ibid.*, p. 186. [See above p. 252. *Editor*]
14. *Ibid.*, p. 183. [See above, p. 251. *Editor*]

The Glance:	m. 32	e:	vii$^{\varnothing}_{7}$–VI
	33	a:	vii$^{\varnothing}_{7}$–IV$\sharp$6
	34	C:	V7–I7
	35	d:	iv6–vii$^{\varnothing}_{7}$-i
The Magic Casket:	36	F:	A6–V7
	38	G:	A6–V7
	40	E:	N7–V7 *etc.*

Most of the thematic statements in the Prelude could be similarly separated, that is, as being distinctively in their own key. The overall effect of the piece, heard in this way, is very different, then, from what Mitchell has proposed; rather than a single unified focus governed by tonality, the main impression it conveys is one of great diversity, born of a richly variegated succession of thematic ideas. In Wagner the "pure" light of Classic tonality is diffused or broken up (as through a prism) into a multitude of individual harmonic colours. And a significant part of his musical creativity resides in the way he brings out these individual colours through the themes.

IV

The *Tristan* Prelude (and the opera as a whole) is generally considered one of the decisive turning-points in musical history, leading eventually to the dissolution of tonality, presumably through the excessive use of chromaticism. In the present article the point of view has been set forth that Wagner's use of themes and *Motive* was equally revolutionary and equally important for future developments in music. He had, to be sure, inherited the technique of theme transformation from Liszt and Berlioz; but in his hands it became a far more subtle vehicle of expression, realized especially through the reassembling of motivic components in various ways so as to allow one theme to give rise to others, these new themes frequently appearing to be totally different from the original ones.

It is strange that Wagner tells us so little in his writings about this presumably intrinsic aspect of his musical composition. Some statements he made to Draeseke in 1859,[15] however, take on a special significance in this regard. After singing the opening theme of the *Eroica* Symphony

---

15. Quoted by Curt von Westernhagen in his *Richard Wagner* (Zürich, 1957).

he is reported to have remarked: "in this and in the beginning part of the development based on this *Urmelodie*, how one is able to discern the course of the entire symphony!"[16] And further, in regard to the *Egmont* Overture, he said "one must comprehend it from a single point outwards."[17]

If such statements are not truly appropriate in respect to Beethoven (*pace* Reti), they do, none the less, shed considerable light on Wagner's own approach to musical composition, in which (as we have seen) a single idea (or ideas), often in the form of a motivic complex, assumes a central importance for the work as a whole, radiating outwards, and permeating an entire musical fabric. Such a procedure, certainly, had the most profound implications for Wagner's immediate followers—for Strauss, Debussy, Wolf, Mahler and, in a very deep sense, for Schönberg. Many musical traits that attain prominence in the works of these composers are already latent in the *Tristan* Prelude: the concentration on a few succinct thematic ideas; the overlapping of *Motive*; the inverting of themes; the coalescing of *Motive* within the themes; the recurrence of a basic sonority (or *Leitharmonie*) in various musical contexts; and the "motivic" significance sometimes attaching to particular chordal progressions. These many attributes of Wagner's style attained their fullest, indeed their ultimate, realization in the music of the twelve-note composers.

EDWARD T. CONE

"Yet Once More, O Ye Laurels"†

If Roland Jackson's concluding point be granted, then it was surely inevitable that *Tristan* should eventually be examined from the perspective provided by nontonal theoretical conceptions. Such a perspective is that of Cone, who contributed the following study to the special issue of *Perspectives of New Music* commemorating the sixtieth birthday of Milton Babbitt, the American composer primarily responsible for the systematic formulation of twelve-tone theory. At the conclusion of his analysis, Cone reexamines the perennially vexing question of G♯ vs. A as the chord tone of the Prelude's first harmony.

Babbitt's reply, from his essay that serves as preface to the same issue of *Perspectives*, appears here as a postscript.

I

A number of years ago, in discussing the opening of *Tristan und Isolde*, I mentioned a hypothetical gloss on those measures that seemed to me to exemplify "the point at which analysis proper passes over into what I call prescription: the insistence upon the validity of relationships not supported by the text."[1] I was referring to the suggestion that the E of the 'celli (m. 1) could be linked with the G♯ of the oboes (m. 2) in

Example 1

† From *Perspectives of New Music* 14/2 and 15/1 (1976): 294–306. Reprinted by permission of the publisher.

1. "Analysis Today," in *Problems of Modern Music*, Paul Henry Lang, ed., W. W. Norton & Co., New York, 1960, pp. 35–36.

such a way as to initiate what, through octave-equivalence, could be construed in quasi-serial terms as a complete inversion of the opening motif. (See Ex. 1: the familiar motifs are labelled X and Y; the linked inversion of Y, Z.)

Because I was citing that reading only to rebuff it (I called it "wrong-headed"), I did not reveal its source. Now, however, since I intend to deal with it in a more friendly spirit, I must give credit for its invention (as I thought then) or its discovery (as I think now) to Milton Babbitt, who expounded it to me in conversation. Whether he was serious I am not sure; but I should like to take him seriously for a while, for further investigation of the score has revealed that motif Z, produced by the linkage he proposed, is often echoed by later developments.

I shall not need to rely on such melodic details as the one introduced in mm. 25–26 (Ex. 2), where the initial descent of a seventh is so striking as to obscure the possible derivation of what follows from the model in question (although their contours are similar and their chromatic rises

Example 2

identical). Instead, I shall call to witness passages predominantly characterized by a prominent ascending third succeeded by a conjunct rise, at least partially chromatic. Such, for example, is found in the lovers' first-act dialogue shortly after they have drunk the potion:

> *Tristan:* Du mir verloren?
> *Isolde:* Du mich verstossen?

Here a direct quotation is made from mm. 10–11 of the Vorspiel, but with the addition of an upbeat to the ascending Y—a rising third that transforms it into an overt statement of Z, although one modified by the substitution of a minor third (already adumbrated by the major

Example 3

sixths of the second and third statements of X in the Vorspiel). At the same time, this motivic form calls attention to the fact that the descending F-E-D♯ could be construed together with the preceding A as conspiring to suggest a similarly contoured version of X, a motive otherwise missing from this complex (Ex. 3).

Example 4

The melody that dominates the introduction to Act II unites an ascending major third with a rising scale in which diatonic motion yields to half-step successions (see Ex. 4). That this theme comprises an expansion of our model is confirmed by the striking development it undergoes at the hands of the clarinet shortly after the curtain rises (just before Isolde's "Sorgende Furcht beirrt dein Ohr"). There Z, literally transposed, is embedded in a series of rising thirds followed by a chromatic scale. Furthermore, the same passage conceals an augmentation of Z in its untransposed form, supported by a chord—V[7] of A—originally associated with that form (Ex. 5).

Example 5

Shortly before the end of the same scene, Isolde's eulogy of Frau Minne ("Des kühnsten Mutes Königin") is framed by two significant references. The first, which quotes the opening of the Vorspiel, essentially retains its voice-leading (Ex. 6). Like its source, it moves to a

Example 6

dominant of A. In the second, the opening combination is transposed, modified, and expanded in such a way as to produce a perfect cadence on A; its effect is that of a resolution of the previous version. And here the major third is clearly connected with the chromatic rise, as strings and voice alike overlap the woodwinds (Ex. 7).

Example 7

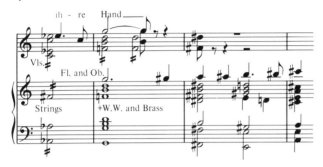

During the love-duet, as Tristan celebrates the power of the potion:

> Da erdämmerte mild erhab'ner Macht
> im Busen mir die Nacht,

an even franker vocal statement can be found (Ex. 8). This scene offers,

Example 8

in addition, evidence to support the contention that Wagner was consciously using the technique of octave-displacement in connection with our motivic linkage. It is found just before the orchestral transition to "O sink hernieder." Tristan brings the preceding section to a close:

> Das Sehnen hin zur heil'gen Nacht,
> wo urewig, einzig wahr,
> Liebeswonne ihm lacht!

The orchestra presents two variations on a progression leading through the "Tristan-chord" to a dominant seventh on E. During each of these the first violins, doubled by violas and clarinets, state a motif that connects a high F♯ with the F♮ an augmented octave below; the second time, the violas, joined by flute and oboe, continue in such a way as to reveal in an unusually clear form the linked melodic line that originally suggested Z (Ex. 9).

Octave-displacement also characterizes a theme prominently associated with Brangäne and later with King Mark: here what was originally a rising step has been converted into a descending seventh. The

Example 9

Example 10

connection with Z may not be obvious when the theme is first heard, in connection with Brangäne's flattering address to Isolde in Act I Scene 3, "Wo lebte der Mann," (Ex. 10). But its return to underline the king's final words in Act III, "Warum, Isolde, warum mir das?", makes the derivation more perceptible. This time the passage follows one (Brangäne's "Sie wacht, sie lebt!") that introduces yet another reprise of the opening of the Vorspiel by a brief statement of the Love-Death motif. Since the theme in question is now similarly introduced, its relation to the Vorspiel is underlined. The key, too—A major—strengthens the identification.

My last example is actually the first to be heard during the course of the work. I have saved it until now because it is the most complex, suggesting as it does a linkage that employs, not only the original form of X but also its retrograde. The passage is a famous one: the return of the "Tristan-chord" and its associated motifs at the climax of the Vorspiel. Here a normal statement of X by horns and 'celli is preceded by a measure containing an almost literal reversion of the same motif in the violins; it is this reversion (subjected to octave-displacement!) that gives shape to the violin line as it continues in counterpoint against the normal form. At the moment the violins arrive at their climactic A♭—the first note of the current version of X and hence the last of its retrograde—the trumpets appropriate that note (in a lower octave) to initiate their statement of Y. The connection between violins and trumpets completes the outline of Z (Ex. 11).

Example 11

II

If the principle of interlinear linkage is accepted as operating at the opening of the Vorspiel, it may throw some light on the still much-argued question of the harmonic basis of the passage. Is G♯ or A the chordal tone in the oboe line? Is the A a passing tone or is the G♯ an appoggiatura?

Answers have usually been based on principles of chord progression and four-part voice-leading. But suppose we look at the resultant unitary line produced by the splice in each of the three opening phrases (Ex. 12). A purely melodic analysis yields interesting results. In the first phrase, the oboe G♯, because of its strong contrast with the opening A, produces a dissonance against the 'cello line (regardless of whether the F or the E is taken as harmonically conjoined with the A). The A that succeeds the G♯ effects complete melodic consonance—an octave with the opening A, a major third with F, a fourth with E. From this point of view, then, the G♯ should be taken as an appoggiatura.

In the next phrase, however, the situation is reversed. The oboe-clarinet B is already generally consonant; this time it is the immediately subsequent C that is dissonant against the initial 'cello B. Were one to accept this evidence alone, one would conclude that here the B is the harmonic tone and the C passing. Yet the almost exact sequence effects such a powerful association with its model as to suggest that it should be heard in the same way. From the sequential point of view, the 'cello B is a "wrong note", elicited by the harmonic demands of the preceding chord. This phrase, then, is ambiguous: the oboe-clarinet B is melodically consonant, but it sounds dissonant by analogy with its model.

No such analogy is available for the third phrase, which departs widely from the original. This time the oboe-clarinet D is consonant with all four 'cello notes that have preceded it, whereas each of its two successors (D♯ and E) is dissonant with at least two of those notes. The

Example 12

transformation is complete: the initial accent of the chromatic rise, originally an appoggiatura, has become a full-fledged principal.

III

The examples just adduced, it is true, should not and cannot convince one of the necessity or even the advisability of trying to hear the opening measures of the Vorspiel in a manner contradicted by the instrumentation. But they do support the view that one can find there, in addition to the usually recognized motifs, what might be called a latent countermotif—latent because its melodic line has not yet been explicitly articulated, counter because that implied line runs in opposition to the actual voice-leading of the passage. Only later is the motif overtly articulated and supported by the texture.

* * *

* * * if there are some who find my development of Babbitt's surmise with regard to the opening of *Tristan* overly fanciful, they might consider that passage in the light of a neutral source given as generalized a formulation as possible—e.g., the conjunction of a third with a succession of chromatic steps. An abstract germ-pattern of this kind can be heard, not just as Babbitt suggested, but as permeating the texture of the entire sequence (Ex. 13). Broadly interpreted—e.g., the steps as possibly diatonic as well as chromatic—such a germ could be understood as embodying the motivic potential of much of the music-drama that follows. A thorough examination of its role might go far toward explaining why *Tristan* has sometimes been exaggeratedly described as developed from a single motif.[2]

Example 13

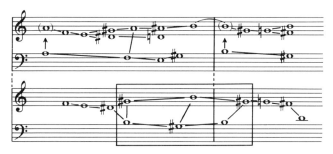

2. For an analysis of Schoenberg's Op. 16 No. 2 from a related point of view see Paul Lansky's "Pitch-Class Consciousness," *Perspectives of New Music* 13/2 (1975): 30–56. Lansky finds in the composition various "interpretations" of an originally "uninterpreted" source-motif.

MILTON BABBITT

〜〜〜〜〜〜

[Reply to Edward T. Cone]†

* * *

I gratefully respected Ed Cone's discretion in not exposing me as the source of a "wrong-headed" observation, but now that he has resurrected it to a status that I had neither proposed nor—perhaps because not—foreseen, I welcome the opportunity to revive the spirit in which it was offered. The question at issue was two-headed: (1) what need was there to formulate tonal explications of the opening of the *Tristan* prelude when there was so much satisfactory else to be heard there, enough even to satisfy a devout Brahmsian, and (2) why, particularly, invoke counterfactual tonal explanations, like the familiar one that if the "dominant sevenths" which end each of the first three "phrases" had resolved where normally, tonally they should, the successive roots of the hypothesized triads of resolution would spell out an "A" (major or minor) triad? But the "dominant sevenths" not only do not so resolve but are prolonged into the next "phrase" by repetitions, while a harmonic analysis—without reference to roots—could focus upon the inversional symmetry (with regard to the midpoint) within the two pairs of "chords" of the first and second statements, so that the "dominant seventh" is perhaps most coherently, contextually understood as an inversion of the first chord, the "Tristan chord", with both registrally deployed so that there is no intervallic repetition. And the upper line proceeds through G♯-B, B-D, D-F♯, that is, not through just a "Tristan chord," but through the pitch-classes of the central "Tristan chord," that of the second of the three statements, and there is still more. The canonic relation, the most widely relied upon mode of association among lines (or lynes) in highly contextual music (Op. 16, No. 3 is just the most gossiped about), was proffered as yet another instance of a perhaps suggestive hypothesis, whose acceptance or rejection at least would stimulate questions as to the criteria of confirmation or disconfirmation of explanatory or justificatory assertions. And apparently it has.

† From *Perspectives of New Music* 14/2 and 15/1 (1976): 21–22. Reprinted by permission of the publisher.

The Transfiguration

RUDOLPH RETI

~~~~~~~~~

[*From* The Thematic Process in Music]†

Reti's theoretical position concerned what he called "thematic or 'motivic' structure," and his principal concern was the interrelationship of thematic processes and the derivation of motives and themes, however disparate in character, from a common source—often a single idea. In the following extract, he demonstrates that certain motivic configurations from the opening of the Prelude have repercussions in the Transfiguration and other parts of the opera as well.

The striking feature of which everyone thinks first when Wagner's operatic technique is discussed is the *leitmotif*. It is well known that this refers to a technique whereby persons or ideas from the operatic plot are associated with certain shapes that emerge in the musical course whenever their programmatic correspondents appear on the stage or are alluded to, even indirectly, by the text. Of course the device as such—to correlate musical phrases with programmatic ideas—is of old usage, though Wagner developed it to a systematic technique, especially in his later operas.

However, it is perhaps significant that the term "leitmotif " was not invented by Wagner himself but by his friend Wolzogen.[1] For Wagner

---

† *The Thematic Process in Music* (New York, 1951), pp. 336–42. Reprinted with permission of Macmillan Publishing Company. Copyright 1951 by Rudolph Reti, renewed 1979 by W. Stanton Forbes.

1. It would be more accurate to say that Wolzogen *appropriated* it—from Friedrich Wilhelm Jähns, who first used the term in his catalogue of Weber's works, *Carl Maria von Weber in seinen Werken* . . . (Berlin, 1871). [*Editor*]

was well aware that, though the leitmotif idea created a more intimate and more specific connection between music and text than had ever been thought possible, it alone was not sufficient to produce a structural whole in opera. By filling the score with obvious motivic references, the higher structural postulate that the compositional course has to be formed in thematic consistency and thematic logic was by no means entirely fulfilled.

In this sense we see in Wagner's operas an almost double thematic picture not unlike that encountered in Berlioz's *Symphonie fantastique*: a surface picture formed by the frequent reiteration of the obvious thematic figures, the leitmotifs, and beneath it a second, less obvious picture brought about by the normal imitations, variations, and trans-formations of the basic material. And though the popular interest in Wagner's structural conceptions is mainly centered on the external leitmotif technique, his achievement of forging an opera into one architectural whole by inner thematic consistency is in an evolutional sense at least as important. Of course, in practice the two principles cannot always be clearly distinguished. For, naturally, the composer is not anxious to make the listener constantly aware whether a shape is a leitmotif or a regular thematic figure. On the contrary, by letting, on the one hand, leitmotifs whenever possible emerge as parts of the organic thematic design and, on the other, by endowing ordinary thematic phrases with leitmotivic effects, Wagner develops a convincing entity from two phenomena that are separate in principle: thematic structure and thematic symbolism.

We may try to demonstate the double effect of this structural endeavor by a description of some important thematic elements in Wagner's *Tristan und Isolde*. The opera opens with three famous bars, centered around an accented harmony known among musicians as the "Tristan chord." * * *

How many treatises have been written about this one chord, trying to "explain" its harmonic mystery! However, in accepted theoretical, that is, harmonic terms, this chord cannot be explained. Of course one can parse the chord, classifying it as a manifold suspension, the resolutions of which are resolved again. But does this bring us closer to an understanding of the meaning of this harmony as a compositional utterance?

However, the chord—or rather the reason that the composer chose it—is easily understood from a thematic angle. For, compressed into one chord, the musical story of the whole opera is latent in this initial harmony.

* * * The opening period of the Prelude to *Tristan* * * * is a series of three almost identical groups, in each of which the important chord forms the accented center. The chord itself is a summation of two fourths, one placed above the other. In each chord one fourth is augmented, the other perfect.

The chords of the three groups, the three "Tristan chords," show a particular relationship. The lower part of the first chord, F–B, appears as the upper part of the second chord (now with an altered accidental reading F♯–B). Analogously, the lower part of the second chord, A♭–D, becomes the upper part of the third chord, now notated as G♯–D.

In this way the whole opening period seems as though it were released, in a widening cycle, from the first chord. Adding to the atmosphere of mystic symbolism that emanates from this shaping is another feature: the melodic course of each of the three groups is formed by two lines (marked by braces) of which one mirrors the other in contrary motion. For instance, in the first group the two lines read F, E, D♯, D, and G♯, A, A♯, B.

If it was the composer's intention, through a shaping *based on two corresponding elements*—*two* fourths that form the harmonic utterance and *two* melodic lines that are a shape and its inversion—to express the programmatic symbolism of *Tristan und Isolde*, he certainly accomplished it in a construction of almost hypnotic power. And if these symbols were to be called leitmotifs, then we must admit that the leitmotif technique appears here carried to the very depths of the work's structure and content.

From the beginning we may turn to the end of the opera. Does the opera's musical and dramatic resolution, the so-called "Love-Death,"

bear any structural connection to its beginning? If we know how to read, we will detect that the "Love-Death" grows as a melodic radiation from these same opening chords. Comparing the series of three chords as they appear at the opening of the opera (example a) with the melodic rise of the "Love-Death" (b), we see (by means of the braces) that the picture of the "Love-Death" is an absolute image of the scheme expressed by the three chords. The reader is urged to check the validity of this statement, which is not an approximation but literally true. Only one accidental is omitted (in the phrase marked c); otherwise the succession and pitch are preserved to the last detail (although in an enharmonically changed notation). As the chords themselves grow, by their own magic mechanism, one out of another, the whole design is already determined by the opening chord.

The thematic symbol of these ceaselessly interlacing fourths—theme and symbol are indeed one in this work—reaches in the "Love-Death" its climax, but we find it throughout the whole work as the structural basis of the opera's most emphatic parts. In the fifth scene of the opening act, when Tristan appears before Isolde for the first time, the winds blare irresistible, endlessly sustained fortissimos, which no musical ear, having once heard them, will ever forget:

and this group is but another expression of that theme which later appears as the "Love-Death" and, therefore, of the fourths forming the opera's mysterious opening chord.

The union of the lovers, the central scene of the second act, is full of such thematic and symbolic pairs of fourths. The agitated theme in the second act's Prelude, picturing Isolde's impatience for the arrival of Tristan, displays the fourths forged into one melodic line. Compare:

Save for the accidentals, this theme reiterates the opening chord even in pitch, the second (upper) fourth mirroring the version in which the fourth appears in the preceding example (Tristan's entrance).

Tristan and Isolde's reunion, then, presaged by characteristic successions of rising fourths (example a), culminates in an outburst (**example b**) which, viewed as one line, forms a perfect and augmented fourth:

This symbolic shaping is continued in the following breathless outcries:

This is symbolism in utter intensity. For by linking (see braces) the detached exclamations of the lovers at the moment of their first union, the hidden theme of the "Love-Death" sounds through.

No doubt, again symbolically, Brangäne's warning voice is heard as a contrary motion of the same theme:

And when the opera reaches its very end, the mystic chord sounds once more, together with a melodic line mirroring the pattern of the work's opening, now at last resolving the tensions into final harmony. Compare the beginning (a) with the ending (b) of the work in these sketched excerpts:

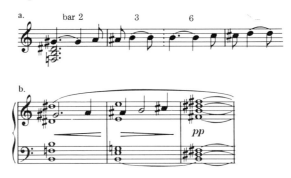

Thus we see as the core of Wagner's leitmotif symbolism a method of thematic forming which not only is of inexorable strictness, but, in addition, has the capacity of creating musical form. Indeed, it was neither the leitmotif as such, nor the "infinite melody," nor even the lack of "numbers" that made opera become an architectural unit. (The lack of closed "numbers" is merely a surface feature, since Wagner's seemingly continuous scores are often interrupted by musical entities complete in themselves, such as the "Prize Song," the "Fire Spell," funeral or wedding marches, and so forth.) But when the mind of a genius evolves a thematic plan like the one desribed above, through which the whole work, theme by theme and scene by scene, grows out of a few opening chords, so that the initial cry of longing is finally transfigured into an all-embracing manifestation such as the "Love-Death," then a historic course is completed: *opera has become a unified musical form.*

LEONARD B. MEYER

[*From* Emotion and Meaning in Music]†

Aesthetician and theorist, Meyer takes a different view of the vocal part in the Transfiguration than Tovey. The following passages are from his chapter called "Principles of Pattern Perception: The Law of Good Continuation," and he subjects the opening measures of the Transfiguration to melodic analysis on the one hand, and then to rhythmic analysis in accordance with principles taken from poetics.

Some aspects of a process may exhibit continuity while others do not. The sequential opening phrase of the "Liebestod" of Wagner's *Tristan und Isolde* (Example 1) establishes a process which leads us to expect a definite continuation. Up to measure 5 the clarinet and voice present essentially the same line. But at measure 5 the sequential process is broken in the vocal part while the instruments continue the sequence.

Example 1

For the sake of clarity, let us turn our attention first to the vocal part, then to the instrumental line, and, finally, to the relation between the two.

Although the sequential process is broken in the vocal line at measure 5, since we expect the line to begin on A and move to D as the horn part does, the over-all line (Example 2), which began with the A♭ in the first measure and moved upward through the B♭ to C♭ and

† *Emotion and Meaning in Music* (Chicago, 1956), pp. 97–101 and 112–15. Reprinted with permission of the author and The University of Chicago Press.

then C♯, is not broken. The tones which we expected are presented, but not in the order expected on the basis of the established sequential process. On the other hand, while the break in process represents no basic break in the line, it does herald a delay in the over-all line, which does not continue its upward surge until the final measure, when the motion to the upper A♭, a natural point of completion, is reached.

Example 2

Notice that this break in the melodic sequence is accompanied by discontinuity of rhythm, which is all the more striking because of the continuousness of the instrumental line. Actually the vocal part in measures 5 and 6 is syncopated against the instrumental line and, as we shall see presently * * *, involves important rhythmic changes. These changes and deviations from the instrumental rhythm should not be confused with the slightly delayed entrances in measures 2 and 3. For though the latter have an expressive effect by delaying and disturbing the process, they work within that process, while the rhythmic changes in measures 5 and 6 are both more striking and more important.

Example 3

The instrumental line presents a strong contrast to the vocal line. While the vocal line involves a break in process and rhythm at measure 5, the instrumental line persists with single-mindedness (Example 3) on its sequential way as the whole motion is accelerated. The second measure of the motive is now omitted so that the motion of an ascending fourth followed by descending half steps is heard in each successive measure. The interesting thing about the process is that, though part of the melody is omitted, the intervallic progression upward is not altered, for the new motive always begins on the same tone as the second half of the motive does (Example 4). As a consequence of this modification the process continues basically as before but at a more rapid rate.

Example 4

The acceleration is again increased in measure 7, where the entrances of the motive occur at the half measure. However, this increased rate of progression also marks the end of the sequence. For the interval A♭ to D♭ in measure 7 does not continue the sequence but instead serves to reunite the vocal and instrumental lines. Both the point at which the break takes place (the A♭) and the melodic motion of the union (measure 7) are foreshadowed in the previous measures. The important breaking point, the A♭, is implied by the motion from D (in measure 5) through the C and B♭ (in measure 6). The melodic motion is implicit in the vocal line of measure 6. That is, if the vocal line of measure 6 had moved upward in fourths, it would have had the same melodic contour as both the instrumental and vocal line have in measure 7. The unification of the instrumental and vocal lines is emphasized and articulated by a more decisive harmonic motion. And both melodic and instrumental lines move upward to the high A♭, toward which they have been tending from the beginning.

Here, then, we have the simultaneous occurrence of (1) a break in process (in the vocal line) from the point of view of sequential progression but only a delay from the point of view of over-all motion; (2) a continuous process (in the instrumental line) whose mode of progression is altered in detail but not in basic motion; and, finally, (3) the stabilization of both processes through their reunification and through their motion to a point of relative repose. The relationship between the progress of the vocal line and the instrumental line is particularly interesting. For the feeling of delay in the vocal line is intensified by the accelerated motion of the instrumental sequence and vice versa.

The melody under consideration presents an interesting example of alternative possibilities of melodic continuation * * *. The opening

of the two-measure motive creates a structural gap by skipping from
E♭ to A♭. The ensuing descending motion (A♭, G, G♭, F) begins to fill
this gap, establishing a continuity process which leads the listener to
expect a return to the opening E♭ (see Example 5). But the introduction
of a rising progression (G♭, A♭, B♭) during the course of the descent
gives rise to alternative expectations. The tendencies inherent in this
new process are supported by the rising melodic line from measure to
measure (see Example 2). Not only is the arrival of the low E♭ delayed
in favor of this rising progression, but from measure 5 to measure 8
the ascending motion is itself delayed. And the arrival of both low and
high E♭s (measures 7 and 8), thus makes a significant contribution to
the feeling of resolution which prevails at the end of the whole period.

Example 5

Notice that just as the point of process disjunction and the beginning
of delay in the large melodic shape were marked by an unexpected
tonal sequence and bolder temporal gaps, so in the smaller motive delay
is acompanied by a less regular sequence of tones and a slight rhythmic
disturbance. The parallelism between the motivic construction and the
over-all phrase organization is another instance of the architectonic
nature of musical processes.

Since the affective quality of the whole is conditioned by that of its
parts, the smaller delays in continuity must also be examined. These
take the form of those devices that are generally discussed under the
subject of ornamentation. In the example under consideration, these
take the form of appoggiaturas which act to delay the normal continuation of the quarter-note motion (Example 6). That is, we expect the
motion initiated by the skip of a fourth—for instance, from E♭ to A♭
in the first presentation of the motive—to continue on the next beat.
Various alternatives are possible within the style system. The motion
from the fourth might, for example, move as part of a triad on up to
the C; it might move stepwise after the fourth, as in the melody which
begins the slow movement of Beethoven's Symphony No. 2; or it might
begin to close the structural gap by descending at once, as in the "Faith"
motive from Wagner's *Parsifal* (see Prelude, measures 44f.) However,

what does happen is that the tendency toward further motion is delayed by the repetition of the A♭, and the effect of this delay is heightened because the repeated tone is a dissonance.

Example 6

* * *

Our conception of rhythmic process results not only from the immediate organization of melody, harmony, dynamics, texture, and so forth but also from their past organization within the particular piece being heard. The passage from *Tristan* already considered * * * furnishes an interesting illustration of the influence of prior melodic organization upon rhythmic processes. The melodic reversal discussed earlier is accompanied by a striking rhythmic reversal, which we can now examine in more detail (see Example 7). Each of the opening measures establishes a clear iambic rhythm with trochaic subgroups. This organization is supported by the phrasing in the clarinets, the harmonic motion, and

Example 7

by the rhythm of the text itself. Notice that the main rhythmic accent always occurs on the top note of the ascending melodic line, after or before a skip of a fourth. When this top tone appears, even though out of its expected order, it is given an important accent partly because of its kinship with earlier accented tones (see Example 8, measure 5). Since it is the first tone of a group, it becomes the accented portion of a trochaic group; and this change from an iambic rhythm to a trochaic

Example 8

one constitutes a rhythmic reversal which in conjunction with the melodic changes is a powerful affective force.

The analysis would be incomplete, however, if we failed to recognize that this change of process is not confined to the rhythmic organization. The placement of the main accent of the group on the second beat of the measure creates a syncopation in which the metric organization is also disturbed (see Example 9). While the instruments continue the

Example 9

original metric scheme, if anything enforcing it through the accelerated rate of sequential progress, the voice part places its primary accent on the second beat of the bar and its secondary accent on the fourth beat of the bar so that, in effect, the whole voice part is syncopated against the instrumental parts.

This cross rhythm is resolved in measure 7, but rhythmic stability is not achieved until measure 8. And here again we see the influence of prior rhythmic-melodic groupings; for the upward skip of a fourth maintains its original anacrustic effect, and the series of fourths in the seventh and eighth measures are without a strong downbeat (Example 10). Even in the instrumental parts where downbeats do appear, they

Example 10

are obscured by the over-all series of anacruses, which reach a real downbeat only at the final A♭. That the accented placement of the A♭ is no accident can be seen if the melodic motion of measure 8 is compared with that of measure 2. The comparison makes it clear that measure 7 is a variant of the first measure of the two-measure motive used at the beginning, but it is so arranged that it achieves no decisive downbeat within the bar. In other words, we again find an example of the welding together of parts which were formerly divided so that ⌣⌐⌐⌣⌐ becomes ⌐⌣⌣⌣⌐.

This unification of the final two measures has consequences in organizing the structure of the whole period of eight measures. Notice that the reversal in measure 5 not only changes the rhythm within the measure but also that between measures; i.e., that the accented measure in the opening phrase is the second of the group, while in bars 5 and 6 the first measure of the group is accented (Example 11). As a result

Example 11

of this the second phrase does not easily split itself into segments, for our attention is carried, so to speak, from the downbeat in measure 5 to the final downbeat in measure 8. In short, the total period might be schematized something like this:

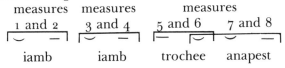

*   *   *

Bibliography

The best introductory studies of *Tristan and Isolde* are Ernest Newman's chapter in *The Wagner Operas* (New York, 1949) and the *English National Opera Guide 6*, Series ed. Nicholas John (London & New York, 1981).

The Wagner literature is virtually inexhaustible. Extensive bibliographies will be found in Newman's biography listed below, and in standard encyclopedias such as *Die Musik in Geschichte und Gegenwart* and *The New Grove Dictionary of Music and Musicians* . A nearly complete list of the writings about Wagner published during his lifetime is given in Nikolaus Oesterlein, *Katalog einer Richard Wagner-Bibliothek . . .*, 4 vols., Leipzig, 1882–95; repr. 1970. A useful bibliography of more recent literature will be found in Herbert Barth, ed., *Internationale Wagner-Bibliographie*, 3 vols., Bayreuth, 1956, 1961, 1968.

I. WAGNER'S WRITINGS

A. *Sämtliche Schriften und Dichtungen*, 6th edition, 16 vols., Leipzig, n.d. [1914]. The first 10 volumes, except for the poems of the operas, were translated by William Ashton Ellis as *Richard Wagner's Prose Works*, 8 vols., London, 1892–99; repr. New York, 1966.

Wagner's essay with the closest connection to *Tristan* is *"Zukunftsmusik"* (*"Music of the Future"*); best translation by Edward L. Burlingame, *Art, Life and Theories of Richard Wagner Selected From His Writings*, New York, 1875; 2nd ed., 1909.

Vols. 13–15 of the *Schriften* comprise a reprint of Wagner's autobiography, *Mein Leben*, as originally published in 1911. An anonymous English translation as *My Life* appeared at the same time and has been reprinted several times. A critique of the translation is given in David Irvine, *Wagner's Bad Luck: An Exposure of 800 Errors in the Authorised Translation of Wagner's Autobiography*, London, 1911. The passages suppressed in the original publications are translated in Ernest Newman, *Fact and Fiction About Wagner*, London, 1931, pp. 199–202. The definitive German text was finally published in Martin Gregor-Dellin [and Gertrud Strobel], ed., *Richard Wagner. Mein Leben: Erste authentische Veröffentlichung* (Munich, 1963); trans. Andrew Gray, ed. Mary Whithall, Cambridge, 1983.

Excellent new translations of Wagner's most important essays from the first Paris period appear in *Wagner Writes from Paris . . .: Stories, Essays and Articles by the Young Composer*, ed. & trans. Robert L. Jacobs and Geoffrey Skelton, New York, 1973.

B. *Wagner's Correspondence:* About 40 volumes of Wagner letters have appeared so far, and additional letters are scattered in at least as many more volumes as well as countless periodical articles. The following list contains only the most useful anthologies and those individual volumes of correspondence most relevant to *Tristan.*

Altmann, Wilhelm, ed. *Richard Wagners Briefwechsel mit seinen Verlegern.* Vol. 1: *Briefwechsel mit Breitkopf & Härtel.* Leipzig, 1911.

———, sel. and ed. *Letters of Richard Wagner.* Trans. M. M. Bozman. 2 vols. London, 1927.

Burk, John N., ed. *Letters of Richard Wagner: The Burrell Collection.* New York, 1951.

Ellis, William Ashton, trans. *Richard Wagner to Mathilde Wesendonck.* New York, 1905; 3rd ed., 1911. See also the article by Julius Kapp, "Unterdrückte Dokumente aus den Briefen Richard Wagners an Mathilde Wesendonk," in *Die Musik* 23 (1931): 877–83.

Hueffer, Francis, trans. *Correspondence of Richard Wagner and Franz Liszt.* 2 vols., London, 1897; repr. 1973.

Strobel, Gertrud, and Werner Wolf, ed. *Richard Wagner: Sämtliche Briefe.* Leipzig, 1967–. A projected complete edition of Wagner's letters, of which 4 vols. have appeared so far.

Richard Wagner: Briefe an Hans von Bülow. Jena, 1916.

II. BIOGRAPHICAL AND CRITICAL STUDIES

Barth, Herbert, Dietrich Mack, and Egon Voss. *Wagner: A Documentary Study.* New York, 1975. A handsome iconographical study.

Bekker, Paul. *Richard Wagner: His Life in His Work.* trans. M. M. Bozman. London, 1931.

Burbidge, Peter, and Richard Sutton, ed. *The Wagner Companion.* New York, 1979.

Ellis, William Ashton. *Life of Richard Wagner.* 6 vols. London, 1900–08. Vols. 1–3 are a translation of the first 2 vols. (3rd ed.) of Glasenapp's biography listed below. Ellis's 6th vol. takes the story up to the completion of *Tristan* and is an interesting, if rather oldfashioned, study of the artist's mind during the *Tristan* period.

Glasenapp, Carl Friedrich. *Das Leben Richard Wagners.* 6 vols.[Originally issued as the 3rd ed. of his *Richard Wagners Leben und Wirken,* 2 vols., Cassel and Leipzig, 1876–77; 2nd ed., 1882.] Leipzig, I: 1894; 4th ed., 1905. II: 1896; 5th ed., 1910. III: 1899; 4th ed., 1905. IV: 1904; 4th ed., 1908. V: 1907; 5th ed., 1912. VI: 1911.

As official biographer, Glasenapp had access to materials unavailable to anyone else for many years. His final volume has the additional value of an eyewitness account. In spite of the fact that much new material has come to light since Glasenapp's time, and that the biography has been maligned for what Guy de Pourtalès called "a partiality which is more comic than reprehensible," this monumental achievement remains a goldmine of information and an indispensible reference. All subsequent biographies are based on it to some extent, often unconsciously on the part of authors who frequently depart from Glasenapp in matters of interpretation.

Gregor-Dellin, Martin. *Richard Wagner: Sein Leben, Sein Werk, Sein Jahrhundert.* Munich, 1980; abridged trans. J. Maxwell Brownjohn, San Diego, 1983.

Lindner, Edwin. *Richard Wagner über Tristan und Isolde: Aussprüche des Meisters über sein Werk.* Leipzig, 1912. A valuable anthology of extracts from Wagner's essays and letters directly dealing with *Tristan.*

Newman, Ernest. *The Life of Richard Wagner.* 4 vols. New York, 1933–46; repr. Cambridge, 1976. The standard biography in English, unequaled since it was written.

————. *Wagner as Man and Artist.* London, 1914; 2nd ed., 1924; repr. 1963. The biographical section is out of date and contains many errors and misinterpretations, some of which Newman later modified in the foregoing biography. The remaining two-thirds of the book contain an excellent critical evaluation.

Strauss, Richard. *Treatise on Instrumentation by Hector Berlioz Revised and Enlarged.* Trans. Theodore Front. New York, 1948. Strauss's additions to Berlioz's text comprise a highly valuable study of Wagner's orchestration.

Strobel, Otto. "Richard Wagner," in *The International Cyclopedia of Music and Musicians.* 5th ed. Nicholas Slonimsky, ed. New York, 1949. By far the best "capsule summary."

————. *Richard Wagner. Leben und Schaffen: Eine Zeittafel.* Bayreuth, 1952. A biography in outline and a handy reference for authoritative and up-to-date factual information.

Taylor, Ronald. *Richard Wagner: His Life, Art and Thought.* New York, 1979.

Vogel, Martin. *Der Tristan-Akkord und die Krise der modernen Harmonie-Lehre.* Düsseldorf, 1962. A useful summary of theoretical and compositional interpretations of the "*Tristan* chord."

Westernhagen, Curt von. *Wagner.* Trans. Mary Whithall. 2 vols. Cambridge, 1978. The best biographical study since Newman's.